DATE DUE			

The United States and Central America
1944–1949

Thomas M. Leonard

The
United States
and
Central America
1944–1949

Perceptions of Political Dynamics

The University of Alabama Press

Library of Congress Cataloging in Publication Data

Leonard, Thomas M., 1937–
  The United States and Central America, 1944–1949.

  Bibliography: p.
  Includes index.
  1. Central America—Politics and government—1821–
1951. 2. United States—Foreign relations—1945–1953.
3. Central America—Foreign relations—United States.
4. United States—Foreign relations—Central America.
I. Title.
F1438.L58 1984   327.730728   83-5032
ISBN 0-8173-0190-9

For Yvonne

Contents

MAP

Foreword

The years 1944 to 1949 represent a crucial period for Central America. The strong-armed dictatorships that had taken control of most of the states in the 1930s began to crumble; and there were signs that more moderate forces, representing middle sector and working-class interests opposing the elitist oligarchies, were emerging to modernize Central America's political structures and to broaden the base of its economic development. Guatemala's Ubico and El Salvador's Hernández Martínez both fell in 1944. Carías's long rule in Honduras ended in 1948, and Anastasio Somoza stepped down from the Nicaraguan presidency in 1947, though he continued to run the country through his control of the *Guardia Nacional*. The 1948 civil war in Costa Rica, checking both the growth of leftist radicalism and continued rule by the populist National Republican party, brought to power the long-term social democratic influence of Pepé Figueres's National Liberation party. The hegemony of the United States in the political, economic, and military spheres, so thoroughly solidified during World War II, was suddenly being challenged by these new forces. The policy the United States pursued toward Central America during and after these years would have much to do with the quality and manner of development for the remainder of the twentieth century.

The perceptions of Central America by U.S. policymakers thus take on important dimensions for this period. A number of recent studies (Aybar, Millett, Bell, Immermann, and others) have focused on the events of this period and the ramifications of U.S. policy. What is unique about this new work by Thomas Leonard is its emphasis on the events and people in Central America in the late 1940s as perceived by

State Department observers and policy formulators. In careful country-by-country analyses, Leonard examines the reports of U.S. diplomats and the Central American desk officers in Washington, which indicated clear patterns of thought that emerged during this five-year period. It is noteworthy that the reporting in the field was often accurate and perceptive, yet interpretations of the data and policy enunciation did not always reflect the observations of the Foreign Service officers in Central America.

Leonard raises some important questions regarding the manner in which U.S. policy toward Central America was formulated. His work emphasizes the serious problem U.S. foreign policymakers faced in understanding the dynamics of development not only in Central America but also in the Third World. As such, this book offers fresh insight into understanding U.S. policy as Central America struggled to free itself from domination by archaic oligarchies and dependency upon U.S. capital and markets.

Ralph Lee Woodward, Jr.
Tulane University

Preface

Today, Central America is beleaguered by pressure for change. The established order is threatened and, in the case of Nicaragua, has fallen. The root causes of the current crisis are found in the region's disparity of wealth and the political stagnation of elitist governments. Present-day events, however, are not the first attempts to correct the status quo. From 1944 to 1949, demands to right economic, social, and political wrongs appeared across the isthmus. During these years, the region was ignored by U.S. policymakers, who were more concerned with the military containment of communism in Europe and Asia than with the social and political foment in Central America. Greater awareness of the pressures for change between 1944 and 1949 contributes to a better understanding of the contemporary crisis.

This study of Central American politics, as seen by U.S. policymakers, is based upon the diplomatic records and personal papers of those individuals. Each of the five countries—Costa Rica, El Salvador, Guatemala, Honduras, and Nicaragua—is presented separately because the situation varied in each nation. The conclusion draws together the similarities and differences among the reform movements in each of the five nations.

I am indebted to the University of North Florida's Quality Improvement Program, the Eleanor Roosevelt Institute, and the Harry S. Truman Library Institute for grants to support research. The hospitality of Marty and Teri Galvin, of Chevy Chase, Maryland, enabled me to spend numerous days in the National Archives. The contribution and patience of typist Mary Ellen Wofford are appreciated. Although space does not permit the acknowledgment of all librarians and archivists who

xi

gave of their time, some can be recognized: Patricia Dowling and Kathy NiCastro (National Archives); Erwin Muller (Harry S. Truman Library); John Jacob (George C. Marshall Research Foundation); and Peggy Pruett and Bruce Latimer (University of North Florida). The comments and suggestions made by Tom Campbell (Florida State University) and Bill Kamman (North Texas State University) were helpful in revising the initial drafts; and those made by the readers for The University of Alabama Press in completing the final manuscript. I remain responsible for any errors or misinterpretation of the diplomatic records.

Thomas M. Leonard
University of North Florida

The United States and Central America
1944-1949

Introduction

NEAR the end of World War II, U.S. foreign policy was not prepared to meet the challenge of Central American politics. The reasons are found in the history of United States-Central American relations and twentieth-century economic and social trends in the region. One was not compatible with the other.

U.S. interest in the Caribbean was not fully awakened until late in the nineteenth century. Until then, the primary policy objective had been to prevent European countries from expanding their possessions in the area. The Monroe Doctrine (1823) was evidence of this policy in general, and the Clayton-Bulwer Treaty (1850) its application in a particular instance. The Americans lacked any regional imperialistic ambitions worth taking into account. The periodic interest in the annexation of Cuba, William Walker's filibustering in the 1850s, and Secretary of State William H. Seward's desire to acquire islands during the 1860s verified the limited national concern with the Caribbean region.

In the late 1880s, however, several factors influenced a change in the U.S. attitude. Economic considerations came first. Investment in Cuban sugar production, the search for markets, and a concomitant need for coaling stations aroused the interests of the business and commercial communities. The Americans also joined the world's altruistic crusade to upgrade so-called inferior peoples, who included those of the Caribbean. Strategic interests intensified as a result of the Spanish-American War and the subsequent construction of the Panama Canal.[1]

Although presidential policies differed, by 1914 the Caribbean had become a U.S. sphere of influence. Theodore Roosevelt's "corrollary" to the Monroe Doctrine provided the United States with a "moral mandate," as an international police power, to interfere in the internal affairs of the Caribbean nations. William Howard Taft's secretary of state, Philander C. Knox, was a forceful figure who was sympathetic to big-business interests. Taft accepted his opinion that the United States should take its rightful place as a major commercial and financial power, just as it recently had in the political and military world. Dollar Diplomacy replaced Roosevelt's Big Stick.

Immediately after his inauguration in March 1913, Woodrow Wilson vehemently criticized Dollar Diplomacy and declared that his foreign policy would favor no particular interest group. This outspoken foe of imperialism, however, carried out more armed intervention in Latin America than any of his predecessors.[2] Thus, from 1900 to 1915, U.S. policies toward the Caribbean region ranged from keeping Europeans out to protecting and expanding investments. Although these policies served U.S. interests, Americans often failed to consider their impact upon the Caribbean nations.

Central America, as a Caribbean subregion, fell within these broad policy objectives of the United States. The need for regional tranquillity caused by the construction of the Panama Canal contributed to a U.S. intolerance of Central American political and financial instability. In an effort to achieve stability, the United States attempted to impose political order. The ideal of national order was predicated upon adherence to constitutionalism, which became one of the banners justifying American intervention in the internal affairs of Central America.

Applying the constitutional ideal to this region, however, proved to be a difficult task. Since 1821, the five republics—Costa Rica, El Salvador, Guatemala, Honduras, and Nicaragua—had been plagued by political jealousies and rivalries. Liberals and conservatives were in constant conflict. Crossing national boundaries, they not only received comfort but also aid in conducting revolutions that often resulted in international wars. Effort to establish a union among the five republics was often a tool by which those in power attempted to keep the opposition out. Only

Central America

Costa Rica's development was more peaceful, a factor that contributed to its reluctance to participate in regional politics. Thus, U.S. foreign policy objectives were at crosscurrents with Central American reality and suggested that American policymakers failed to grasp the nature of the region's political dynamics.

The United States first intervened under the constitutional banner in 1906, when it and the Mexican government negotiated an end to the Guatemalan-Honduran/Salvadoran conflict. The region was threatened by war in 1907, when Nicaraguan President José Santos Zelaya attempted to spread his influence over Honduras and Salvador. The United States and Mexico offered to mediate, resulting in the 1907 Washington Conference that determined to "settle all outstanding difficulties and to establish Central American relations on a permanently peaceful basis."

The conference produced several conventions. The two most important were a ten-year General Treaty of Peace and Amity and the establishment of a Central American Court of Justice. The General Treaty recognized the U.S. ideals of constitutionalism and respect for national integrity by providing for the nonrecognition of a government that came to power by a coup d'etat or revolution; nonintervention in the internal affairs of other states; and to work constitutionally for the nonreelection of presidents. The Court of Justice was envisioned as a nonpolitical tool to settle disputes among the five nations.[3]

For the next decade, U.S. policy toward Central America was based upon the principles established at the 1907 conference. Dana G. Munro, of the State Department's Division of Latin American Affairs, noted that the "energetic insistence by the government that these principles be observed practically put an end to the international wars" that frequently broke out in Central America.[4]

These same agreements, however, failed to limit U.S. intervention in the region. Zelaya's brutal and corrupt Nicaraguan regime resulted in revolution and subsequent American military intervention, justified as an aid to the Nicaraguans "in their just aspiration towards peace and prosperity under constitutional and orderly government." The United States served as arbitrator of the 1911 Honduran revolution, which resulted in the provisional presidency of Francisco Bertrand. Although the Court of Justice was often hampered by poorly trained judges whose decisions were influenced by nationalistic desires, the U.S.-inspired 1914 Bryan-Chamorro Treaty was its death knell. Certain of the treaty's provisions were viewed as an infringement of rights by Salvador in the Gulf of Fonseca and Costa Rica on the San Juan River. Both appealed to the court, which ruled in their favor in 1916 and 1917.[5] These rulings, however, were ignored by the United States and Nicaragua. When the convention establishing the court expired in 1918, no effort was made to renew it.

By the end of World War I, the "whole work of the [1907] conference" had been discredited, according to Munro.[6] Although State's Latin American Affairs Division placed blame upon the Central Americans, it failed to recognize the adverse impact of U.S. actions upon the region. What the Americans preached, they did not practice.

Central American political stability ended in 1919, when government changes occurred in Honduras, Salvador, Nicaragua, and Costa Rica, and in Guatemala a year later. Except in Costa Rica, which returned to its traditional aloofness from regional affairs, political intrigue and rivalries among the other four states brought the region to the brink of war in 1922. Finally, that summer, Secretary of State Charles Evans Hughes succumbed to pressure from Sumner Welles, Dana G. Munro, and Francis G. White of the Latin American Affairs Division and called for a conference of the five Central American states. It was held in Washington, D.C., from December 4, 1922, to February 7, 1923. The American objective was clear, as it had been since the start of the twentieth century: establish political stability through respect for constitutional government and an end to political change through revolution.[7]

One of the twelve agreements reached at the conference offered hope that the U.S. objective could be achieved. In the Treaty of Peace and Amity, the five Central American nations agreed not to grant recognition to governments that came to power through a coup d'etat or revolution, unless legitimized by free elections, except if those elections sanctioned a revolutionary regime, a revolutionary leader, a close relative, or a high-ranking civilian or military official who had been in power six months before or after the event. The pact also provided that governments could not assist exiles or contending parties anywhere in Central America nor interfere in each other's internal affairs and prevent revolutionary activities within their borders. To the Americans, this treaty was a distinct improvement over the one in 1907. Hughes and Welles were confident that the new agreements provided a "distinct advance in the prevention of

revolutionary and internal disturbances" and significantly contributed to
Central American political stability.[8]

The objective proved to be elusive. Between 1923 and 1932, Honduras,
Nicaragua, Guatemala, and El Salvador experienced political changes
that challenged the principles of the 1923 treaties. Only Costa Rica
remained free from political upheaval. In Honduras, Tiburcio Carías
won a plurality, but not a clear-cut majority, in the October 1923 elections. When congress failed to come to grips with the issue, fighting
erupted the following February. Subsequently, U.S. Marines were
landed, ostensibly to protect American lives and property, and Sumner
Welles was dispatched to work out a solution, which provided for the
December 1924 election of Miguel Paz Barahona. He was not in violation
of the 1923 treaties and therefore was accorded recognition. For the next
eight years, Honduras experienced political quietude. In 1932 Carías
captured the presidential election by a substantial margin and was quickly
granted U.S. recognition. The 1923 treaties had not been violated.[9]

Conservative Carlos Solorzano won the 1924 presidential election in
Nicaragua under questionable circumstances. Two years later, he was
forced from office and political chaos resulted. Again, U.S. Marines were
dispatched to protect lives and property. Henry L. Stimson was sent to
work out a solution. It included U.S. supervision of the 1928 and 1932
presidential elections, won respectively by José Maria Moncada and
Bautista Sacasa. The establishment of constitutional government, however, failed to end the resistance movement of Augusto P. Sandino, which
proved to be an embarrassment to the United States. Sacasa governed
until 1936, when he was overthrown by Anastasio Somoza. Because by
then the 1923 treaties had been voided and U.S. policy had changed,
Somoza was quickly granted recognition.[10]

In 1930 Guatemalan General Manuel Orellana engineered a coup
d'etat. The United States withheld recognition and persuaded the four
other Central American states to do the same because he came to power
through revolution, a violation of the 1923 treaties. On instructions from
the State Department, Minister Sheldon Whitehouse labored for free
elections, held in February 1931. Jorge Ubico ran unopposed, but, because the 1923 treaties were not violated, he was accorded recognition.[11]

In El Salvador in December 1931, Vice-President and Secretary of War
Maximiliano Hernández Martínez engineered a coup and headed a
government sanctioned by the congress. The United States withheld

recognition, but its influence over the other Central American nations soon waned. In 1933 Costa Rica announced its intention to withdraw from the 1923 treaty obligations. A year later, all four nations denounced the treaties and extended recognition to El Salvador. Isolated and under new policy direction, the United States also extended recognition.[12]

The United States was unable to achieve its goals as idealized at the 1923 Central American Conference. Twice—in Honduras and Nicaragua—direct intervention provided for political solutions. Diplomatic pressure provided for an end to the 1930–31 crisis in Guatemala, but it failed in El Salvador.

During the period 1923–33, U.S. policy regarding political turmoil also changed. The chief of the Latin American Affairs Division, Stokely W. Morgan, observed that the 1923 treaties failed to deal with Central America's political reality. Dana G. Munro, a division analyst, wished that the United States was not so committed to the treaties' principles. The 1924 Democratic party platform included a statement opposing direct intervention. In 1928 Franklin D. Roosevelt, writing in *Foreign Affairs,* criticized unilateral intervention. President-elect Herbert Hoover, in a 1928 goodwill tour of Latin America, which included stops in Honduras and Nicaragua, expressed the same idea. Successive heads of the Latin American Affairs Division, Francis G. White and Edwin C. Wilson, explained that it was no longer necessary to extend unwelcome protection or to meddle in the affairs of Central America. Under Secretary of State J. Reuben Clark's *Memorandum on the Monroe Doctrine* repudiated the interventionist twist given the doctrine by President Theodore Roosevelt. Enunciated as the Good Neighbor Policy by President Franklin Roosevelt in 1933, the new approach signaled an end to direct U.S. intervention in Central American politics. The principle of nonintervention in the internal affairs of other nations was affirmed at the Seventh International Conference on American States, at Montevideo, Uruguay in 1933, and the 1936 special Inter-American Conference, in Buenos Aires, Argentina.[13]

Application of the nonintervention policy to Central America was immediate. U.S. Marines were withdrawn from Nicaragua in 1933. Secretary of State Cordell Hull encouraged the Central Americans, convening in 1934 at Guatemala City, where they denounced the 1923 treaties, to devise methods for orderly constitutional governments and for the maintenance of friendly relations among themselves. U.S. recognition of the Hernández regime in Salvador soon followed. The self-imposed extensions in office by Hernández in 1935 and 1939, by Ubico in Guatemala in 1935 and 1941, and by Carías in Honduras in 1936 and 1943, as well as Somoza's seizure of power in Nicaragua in 1936, went unchallenged by the United States. The dictators were well entrenched. Costa Rica escaped political tyranny, and the presidential elections of 1936 and 1940 gave indications of effective constitutional government. Costa Rican politics, however, was enjoyed only by that nation's elite.

Although U.S. policy toward Central America in the twentieth century sought stability, it ignored social and political factors that were potentially explosive. The agricultural economies of the region contributed to a stagnant social structure, which in turn became the seedbed for political confrontation. Except in Honduras, the region's environment naturally supported the growing of coffee, first produced by Costa Rica in the 1830s. El Salvador, Guatemala, and Nicaragua soon followed. Increased demand for bananas in the United States and improved storage and transportation caused that industry to flourish by the end of the nineteenth century. Foreign companies, notably the Standard Fruit and Steamship Company and the United Fruit Company, came to dominate Central American lowland agriculture.[14]

Because of the lack of local capital, experience, and will to build the supporting infrastructure, foreigners constructed railroads, bridges, utilities, and communication systems. By the 1920s foreign capitalists owned and operated the most efficient plantations, which produced the bulk of the region's exports; controlled the banking systems; and dominated retail business. Foreigners came to exert powerful influences on governments to maintain domestic stability, assure cheap labor, and grant concessions that compensated them for the risks undertaken. For personal profit, ruling elites throughout Central America granted the exorbitant concessions and privileges to the foreign investors. In the process, national interests were sacrificed.

When world trade ran smoothly, the foreign investors and local elites complimented themselves for generating economic progress. From 1890 to 1914, however, Central America's financial structure was jarred by world economic conditions. During the 1890s, the panic in the world's financial markets brought on a tightening of credit sources and a decline in commodity prices, which in turn exposed the weaknesses of economies dependent upon foreign financing and one or two products. Inflation further aggravated the situation. Financial systems pegged to silver suffered from a drop in world prices of that ore; this increased indebtedness in terms of local currency. At the same time, decreases in banana and coffee prices lowered government revenues. This led governments to issue irredeemable paper money, further depreciating local currencies. Dislocations in world trade during World War I increased Central America's dependence upon the United States as a market and credit source. As long as prosperity prevailed in the United States, Central America's economic weaknesses were obscured, and local leaders were lulled into a sense of complacency. The Great Depression quickly stifled the Central American economies. Plummeting banana and coffee prices resulted in lost profits and higher unemployment.

World War II brought economic recovery to Central America, which contributed raw materials and foodstuffs to the Allied war effort. Infant industries as well as new agricultural commodities and minerals diversified the economies. Rising prices further stimulated them. As a result, labor and salaried workers demanded a bigger share of the national income.

The twentieth-century economic growth of Central America also planted the seeds for the "revolution of rising expectations," which had both political and social connotations. An urban white-collar middle class developed with the agriculture, banking, retail, and transportation industries. Liberal reforms in education expanded the number of professionals and skilled laborers. University professors and students also became more numerous. This amorphous group, labeled the "middle sector,"[15] shared several characteristics. Relatively affluent, it enjoyed the benefits of a modernizing society, but was denied the right of political participation. As a consequence, it clamored for constitutional government at the oligarchy's expense. When the dictators emerged during the 1930s, the middle sector bore the brunt of political repression. Newspapers were closed, political parties outlawed, and leaders jailed, exiled, or executed. During World War II, the middle sector was inspired by the Allied objective to crush tyranny as well as the idealistic goals of the Atlantic Charter and Four Freedoms. If dictatorships in Europe and Asia were to be destroyed, surely the tyrants of Central America were to be toppled.

The second component of the "revolution of rising expectations" consisted of the unskilled farm and laboring classes. As Central America's agricultural and related industries evolved during the twentieth century, the social and economic gaps among the laboring masses, the middle sector, and the elite dramatically widened. Its plight worsened by the depression, labor increased its demands for social and economic betterment. Capitalists labeled such demands "Communistic." Except in Costa Rica, the dreaded ideology was outlawed and alleged Marxists were brutally suppressed. When a degree of prosperity returned to the working class during World War II, its determination not to drift backward intensified.[16]

The significant changes in Central America's political and social makeup that occurred before World War II came to the forefront of the political arena before the war ended. Efforts to maintain or restore prewar dictatorships were challenged, and demands for social change were pressed. At this time, U.S. policy was pledged to nonintervention in Latin American domestic affairs, and the United States was meeting the communist challenge in Europe and Asia. The United States was content to apply its containment policy to all of South America. The Inter-American Treaty of Reciprocal Assistance in 1947, popularly known as the Rio Pact, and the establishment of the Organization of American States at Bogotá presumably secured Central and South America from a communist invasion.

Then Central American states followed the U.S. lead against global communism. Governments cracked down on local communists, severed diplomatic relations with Moscow, and generally supported the U.S. position at the United Nations.[17] Such actions only served to intensify the struggle between the Central American elites and those groups outside the political and social apparatus. Because the region was not a priority area to the United States at that time, U.S. officials became observers of its political dynamics.

This book examines the perceptions held by United States officials of Central American political dynamics from 1944 to 1949. Three tiers of officials were engaged in the observation process. First were the ambassadors and staff officers assigned to each of the five countries. The majority of them had begun their diplomatic careers from 1915 to 1925 and served in several positions throughout the world prior to their Central American appointments. Few were Latin or Central American specialists. The turnover of personnel assigned to each of the five republics from 1944 to 1949 was rapid. Only Ambassadors John Erwin (Honduras), Edwin Kyle (Guatemala), John Stewart (Nicaragua), and Walter Thurston (El Salvador) and Consuls Alex Cohen (Costa Rica), Overton Ellis (El Salvador), John Faust (Honduras), and Maurice Bernbaum (Nicaragua) remained in one country for three years or more. Only two served in more than one: George Shaw in Nicaragua and El Salvador and Ernest V. Siracusa in Honduras and Nicaragua. The average assignment lasted two years. As a result, the diplomatic reports from each nation were more factual than analytical and often lacked historical perspective.

Reports from the Central American posts, and other sources, were directed to the State Department's Division of Caribbean and Central American Affairs, reorganized in 1946 as the Central America and Panama Affairs Division. Four men analyzed the materials: Ellis O. Briggs, William P. Cochran, Robert Newbegin, and Murray A. Wise. All had gained considerable Latin American experience before joining the division. Briggs, Cochran, and Newbegin were stationed at several South American posts, and Wise taught in Colombia for seven years. Gordon Reid and William Tapley Bennett, who joined the division in 1948 and 1949, respectively, lacked regional field experience. The views of both field and division personnel followed similar patterns.

Above the division office were three assistant secretaries of state for Latin American affairs during the 1944–49 period: Nelson A. Rockefeller, Spruille Braden, and Edward Miller. Rockefeller, although sympathetic to the need for social and economic reform, exerted little policy influence before resigning in 1945. Braden expressed interest in encouraging democracy throughout the region, but the limitations of the U.S. nonintervention policy provided only the opportunity to express support for Central American constitutionalism. Miller, who took office in 1948, was sensitive to the need for regional economic growth, but, given the U.S. commitments to Europe and Asia, nothing was accomplished.[18]

These commitments elsewhere were evident in the activities of the three secretaries of state from 1944 to 1949: Edward R. Stettinius, Jr., James F. Byrnes, and George C. Marshall. They considered Latin America only within the context of halting the spread of global communism.[19]

Although perceptions of Central American political dynamics held by U.S. officials varied from country to country, several general trends in regional politics were apparent. The traditional oligarchical struggle of "outs" wanting "in" continued. In El Salvador and Guatemala, a split was growing within the military, where younger officers were of a more liberal mind. The middle sector group, pressing for constitutionalism, was not considered a significant political force. Until late 1947, communism was believed to be of local character only, dealing with the legitimate demands of the poor; thereafter, concern grew about Soviet penetration.

American officials determined that the elite, outside the power structure since the 1930s, was disorganized and in disarray except in Costa Rica, where it resisted reform efforts until 1947, though it did not defeat José Figueres's army in the 1948 civil war. In Guatemala, the elite opposed the policies of President Juan José Arévalo. After failing to gain control of congress in 1946, it was linked to several unsuccessful plots to overthrow him. Salvadoran landowners remained tied to conservative army elements that prevented President Salvador Castaneda from bringing about political or social change. In each nation, the elite was struggling to maintain the old order. Not so in Nicaragua and Honduras. The Nicaraguan elite was believed not to be antiauthoritarian, just anti-Somoza, illustrating the struggle of "outs" wanting "in." In Honduras, the Americans believed that the elite was satisfied with the rule of Tiburcio Carías.

During the 1930s, the military became the major prop of the Central American dictators, except in Costa Rica, where the small army was deliberately underfunded by congress. In El Salvador and Guatemala, the political role of the military was most evident. After the fall of Hernández and Ubico in 1944, U.S. officials detected a split between older and younger officers. The former group aligned itself with the landowning elites to resist political and social change. The younger officers were more interested in reform, and by 1949 they were the more influential element, particularly in Guatemala. Despite rumors of a similar split in the Honduran and Nicaraguan military, the Americans believed that it remained loyal to Carías and Anastasio Somoza, respectively.

Middle sector pressure for political reform erupted in 1944, first in El Salvador and then in Guatemala. In both countries, university students initiated demonstrations that gained support from other middle sector elements and resulted in the ouster of Hernández in El Salvador and Ubico in Guatemala. The quest for democracy, however, was short-lived in both countries. The military had regained its dominant influence by February 1945 in El Salvador. In Guatemala, Arévalo ignored the middle sector. According to U.S. officials, in Honduras and Nicaragua this sector was less successful because of a lack of leadership and organization. The Honduran middle sector only protested against the Carías dictatorship in 1944. Somoza temporarily bowed to pressure from this group when he rejected a proposed constitutional amendment preventing the extension of his presidential term beyond 1947. The gesture proved to be an empty promise, and the middle sector remained ineffective. U.S. officials failed to understand the goals and strength of the Costa Rican middle sector, particularly its leader, José Figueres, who was described as a political opportunist and potential revolutionary.

Throughout the 1930s, Central American governments played upon the sympathies of the lower class, but provided few practical benefits. The spokesmen and demands for economic and social improvements from 1944 to 1949 were branded as communist by the elites, an opinion not shared by the Americans. Through late 1947, U.S. officials believed that communism was local in nature and not linked to Moscow. The agitators and their demands were considered to be legitimate. After 1947, as the United States attitude toward the Soviet Union hardened, so did the perception of Central American communism. It was recognized that the deprivations of the lower classes provided a breeding ground for international communism and that the region was potentially important to Moscow for propaganda purposes and as a training center. This was particularly true in Costa Rica and Guatemala, where communists had gained influence in government and sponsored programs threatening the status quo.

The political dynamics of the five Central American nations changed in varying degrees from 1944 to 1949. The established order was challenged by demands for constitutional government as well as economic and social reform. For the most part, U.S. officials understood the changing conditions, but, because of cold war commitments elsewhere, remained observers only.

1

Costa Rica

By 1940, Costa Rica had gained the reputation of an almost ideal democracy. Several factors contributed to this perception. Constitutional government was practiced, the military was apolitical, middle sector pressure was nonexistent, and demands for economic and social reform received national attention only at election time. After 1940, this tranquil picture was greatly altered. The catalyst was Marxist labor leader Manuel Mora, who increased his political presence as well as demands for economic and social change. Although the landowning elite successfully resisted the implementation of his programs, it failed to understand or countervail the emerging middle sector, led by José Figueres. Vigorously anticommunist, this sector also opposed the elitism of Costa Rican politics. The struggle for power climaxed in the 1948 civil war. The landowners and Marxists became strange bedfellows in an unsuccessful military effort against Figueres's revolutionary forces.[1]

Evidence was ample to support the popular view that Costa Rica was a harmonious society. Described as an industrious people, small landowners permeated a society not marked by a rigid class structure or racial problems. A larger percentage of the national budget was expended on education than on defense. Twentieth-century politics were considered to be simple, usually involving the transfer of power from the incumbent executive to a chosen successor at regular four-year intervals.

This popular opinion was shared by the U.S. vice-consul in San José, Alex A. Cohen. A native of the Netherlands, he had later migrated to the United States. He was appointed as a clerk to the San José embassy in 1942 and promoted to vice-consul in 1946. He believed that politics were enjoyed by all Costa Ricans and that, once an election was over, campaign animosities were forgotten and everyone went back to work. When the political process failed to resolve the conflicting interests, "there was always a group of patriotic and highly respected citizens who somehow or the other managed to reconcile conflicting viewpoints." True, this system implied a government of the few, but Cohen concluded that it worked fairly well "despite the fact that such an oligarchical system . . . inevitably tended to preserve the advantageous position of the haves in relation to the have nots."[2] Because of this environment, U.S. Foreign Service officers anticipated a tranquil duty tour in San José.[3]

By 1940, however, the pressures for change were apparent in the dichotomy of three distinct social classes: the landowning elite, the middle sector, and the laboring poor. The upper class had originated during the nineteenth-century development of coffee and subsequently banana farming and cattle raising. By the 1920s, large-scale landowning dominated these three agricultural industries; for example, 5 percent of the coffee growers owned more than 50 percent of the coffee production. The upper class also included bankers; large commercial interests, often allied to or representing foreign capital; and a few successful professionals. This unorganized group worked to maintain the status quo, but in the process permitted the economy to stagnate. Economic development was left to other groups acceptable to the elite, such as foreign capitalists and immigrants who established large-scale farms, commercial enterprises, and manufacturing plants.

In the twentieth century, a distinct middle sector arose. In urban centers, it was composed of government and commercial white-collar groups, skilled workers, small businessmen, and professionals. It also included farmers who produced foodstuffs for domestic consumption. Not identified with the elite, the middle sector was denied an effective voice in Costa Rican politics. As a result, this group came to champion the election of honest men, adherence to constitutional order, and a discussion of national issues.

Throughout the twentieth century, the social gap widened among the upper, middle, and lower sectors. The last group included small farmers, farm laborers, and, in the urban areas, unskilled labor. Their poverty and social deprivation drew the attention first of former priest Jorge Volio and his Reform party in 1924. After the party's demise, their cause was championed by Manuel Mora, who, as a twenty-year-old law student in 1930, organized the Marxist-orientated Workers and Peasants Block.[4] A year later, he founded the Costa Rican Communist party, which was accepted as a member of the Communist International in August 1935 at the Seventh World Congress of that body meeting in Moscow. There remained "reasonable grounds," however, to believe that the Costa Rican communists were not fully indoctrinated in Marxism.[5]

Ideological questions were given scant public attention until the late 1930s, when pressure for economic and social reform entered the political arena. The chief protagonist for change was the Communist party, which announced that its primary aim was to transform the Costa Rican economic system so "that the practice of one group exploiting another would cease." The communists called for a government social security program for the unemployed, workmen's compensation, old-age benefits, standardized wages, and a labor law to legalize labor unions and permit workers to strike. The party also demanded government control of transportation, public utilities, and agrarian law to eliminate *latifundismo*. The Soviet Union was described as the only nation in the world in which workers and *campesinos* were not considered outcasts. Such exhortations were threatening to the Costa Rican socioeconomic elite, which appluaded President León Cortés's (1936–40) promises to save the nation from the "red hordes" of international communism.[6] In its desire to maintain the status quo, however, the elite failed to offer alternatives to Mora's proposals.

The years 1940–44 marked a turning point in political life. On the one hand, *personalismo* continued as a major factor in national politics. When the National Republican party candidate, Rafael Calderón Guardia, won the 1940 presidential sweepstakes, U.S. officials attributed his success, in large part, to an agreement struck with outgoing President Cortés whereby the latter was granted the opportunity to name certain administrative officials. Shortly after Calderón's inauguration, the two had a falling out and became political enemies. The feud was exacerbated by the alleged fraudulent 1942 congressional elections, in which the National Republicans won nineteen of the twenty-two seats available. Subsequently, the animosity intensified when President Calderón indicated he would remain in office beyond the four-year term. Although influenced by the example of his close friend Anastasio Somoza, in Nicaragua, and the third-term reelection of U.S. President Franklin D. Roosevelt, Calderón also wanted to avoid an investigation of corruption within his administration. When Cortés refused Calderón's suggestion in the summer of 1943 that central bank President Jorge Hine run unopposed as a compromise candidate, the rift proved to be irreparable. Calderón resolved to do everything he could to block Cortés's second presidency, and Cortés was equally determined to rid the government of *Calderonistas*. [7]

More significant than the personal confrontation was the increased public awareness of socioeconomic issues, particularly measured by the growth of the Communist party. Its political presence increased from 1932, when it polled 1,132 votes in the national election, to 1942, when its congressional candidates received 17,060. Although Manuel Mora was the only party member sent to congress, others were elected to several provincial councils during the ten-year span. In the 1940 presidential election, the Communist party received an estimated 15,000 of the 90,000 votes cast. Its power was enhanced by its ability to attract large crowds of demonstrators, sometimes estimated as high as 20,000. President Calderón was linked to the party in 1943 when he accepted a Labor Code, reportedly written by Mora and directed by him through congress before deputies had an opportunity to examine it. Of the five hundred vaguely written articles, three were considered important: 90 percent of the laborers working for any employer must be Costa Rican and this 90 percent should receive 80 percent of the payroll; a laborer who resigned or was dismissed was entitled to one month's pay for each year of his employment; and all laborers, including household servants, were to be covered by contracts. The code caused the National Republicans to lose favor with local capitalists.

The dissolution of the Communist International in May 1943 also brought an end to Costa Rica's Communist party, but it was replaced a month later by the Vanguard party. Its officers, organization, and stated goals repeated those of its predecessor, so any difference between the two was "far from apparent." The archbishop of San José, Monsignor Victor Sanabria, gave public approval for Catholics to join the new party if they wished. He was influenced by his own liberal views regarding the need to solve Costa Rica's social problems, and because of the party's divorce from Moscow, he concluded that Vanguard was local in character. Fay Allen Des Portes, who had served as minister to Bolivia and Colombia prior to his 1943 appointment as ambassador to Costa Rica, concluded that Sanabria's actions served to increase Vanguard's political popularity and influence.[8]

Both issues—*personalismo* and social reform—were evident in the 1944 presidential campaign. In his effort to recapture the presidency, León Cortés founded the Democratic party and was selected as its standard-bearer. His popularity was enhanced by the relatively good reputation of his administration during the years 1936– 40. Throughout the campaign, the *Cortesistas* charged that National Republican candidate Teodoro Picado would continue Calderón's policies, which had brought inflation, U.S. dominance in determining Costa Rican foreign policy, and governmental mismanagement and corruption. Cortés promised, if elected, to see that Calderón and his cabinet were impeached for embezzlement. Picado's followers made similar charges of corruption against Cortés's previous administration. Cortés also was accused of sedition for his pro-Nazi stance during World War II, which allegedly hindered the government's confiscation of German-owned property and the deportation of enemy aliens. Such accusations by the *Calderonistas* and *Picadistas* portrayed a Cortés victory as a triumph of the fifth column. On election eve, Democratic party campaign manager Ricardo Castro Beeche begged in vain for U.S. intervention to preserve Costa Rican democracy, a request interpreted by Des Portes, in San José, to be within the framework of traditional politics, the "outs wanting in."[9]

There was a more important campaign characteristic, according to U.S. Chargé d'affaires Edward G. Trueblood, who had arrived in Costa Rica in June 1943 and remained for eighteen months. He correctly noted that, for the first time in Costa Rican political history, the competing parties were sharply divided over ideological differences. This was due to the so-called communist problem associated with Picado's candidacy. Picado was considered to be Calderón's "stalking horse . . . without any brilliance" until September 22, 1943, when he reached an agreement with Vanguard leader Manuel Mora. For his part, Picado promised to carry out a program identical with Vanguard's August 1943 declaration: lower living costs; improvement of social conditions; support to labor and farm union movements; and political reform, beginning with the election to congress of persons possessing larger intellectual and moral stature. In return, Mora pledged to work for Picado's election victory without claim to any political position or economic privilege within the new administration. Mora also agreed to respect the church, its philosophy and property. Throughout the campaign, the Mora-Picado group emphasized the need to improve upon the social advances already made. It insisted that its social reform program conformed with Pope Leo XIII's pronouncements and the ideas of progressive world leaders, such as U.S. President Franklin D. Roosevelt, Britain's Prime Minister Winston Churchill, and the late Chilean leader Pedro Aguirre Cerda. The State Department's Division of American Republic Affairs concluded that Mora's views on labor-management relations were "sound and moderate" and could be achieved in a peaceful manner.[10]

The Democrats, or *Cortesistas*, opposed the liberal socioeconomic philosophy evident in the Mora-Picado pact. The party represented Costa Rican conservatives, upper-class businessmen, and professional people. They viewed the peon as an "extremely ignorant person, incapable of greater responsibility" and felt he "must be looked after by the landowners and employers." Fearful that the nation's patriarchal structure was being undermined by communism, the *Cortesistas* were not convinced that Mora had abandoned his revolutionary objective when the Communist party was transformed into the Vanguard. The Mora-Picado pact increased the Democrats' determination to obtain a Cortés victory. The pact also resulted in rumors that anticommunist dictators Jorge Ubico, in Guatemala, Maximiliano Hernández Martínez, in El Salvador, and Anastasio Somoza, in Nicaragua, would intervene on behalf of the Cortés faction.[11]

Campaign events throughout 1943 indicated to American officials that Picado would win in February. The large rallies in Alajuela, Cartago, Limón, Puntarenas, and San José illustrated the positive effect of the Mora-Picado agreement. The same forces dominated the electoral boards everywhere except in Alajuela and Heredia. An estimated 85,000 National Republicans were registered, compared to 45,000 Democrats. As expected, even by some *Cortesistas*, Picado won the February 13, 1944, elections with 78,341 votes to Cortés's 42,646. Charges of voter intimidation and fraudulent vote counting were rampant. Throughout the country, Picado's victory was received with apprehension. The feeling was widespread that Picado's high-handed methods would result in a Costa Rican "dictatorship along Central American lines." Also, there were rumors of a *Cortesista* revolution. To Chargé d'affaires Trueblood, the significance of the election was broader. The nation, he observed, was embarking on a new political path in which "traditional political battling over personalities [was] giving way . . . as elsewhere, to a struggle between two radically opposed social philosophies."[12]

From election day in February until his inauguration on May 8, 1944, President-elect Picado endeavored in vain to gain endorsements from the landowning and business segments. He appealed to the landowners by comparing the 1943 Labor Code to a "new suit which has to be altered in order to fit properly." To increase agricultural production, he advocated the use of technology, establishment of new foreign markets for exports, and protection of the domestic market from competition. To gain the confidence of the banking and business community, he promised an austere national budget, no longer to be "a national industry designed to protect people without employment." These promises failed to gain the elite's support, according to Ambassador Des Portes, because of Picado's continued identification with Mora. The president-elect's promise to build highways to the uninhabited interior for the development of state-protected farms was only one example of his association with Mora's alleged advocacy of social reform without financial restraint. The combination of alleged election fraud and association with elements antithetical to the elite's interest gave Picado's administration an inauspicious start on inauguration day, May 8, 1944. The U.S. embassy staff in San José did not share the opinion of Assistant Secretary of State for Latin American Affairs Spruille Braden that Picado would be successful in his efforts to restore the democracy which "that little country had formerly enjoyed."[13]

Until the 1946 midterm congressional elections, U.S. policymakers failed to reach a consensus of opinion regarding Picado's administration. Costa Rica was void of political turmoil, but remained beset by harbingers of conflict. For the two years following Picado's inauguration, several U.S. reports indicated political calm in the country. Importantly, former President Rafael Calderón Guardia withdrew from public life. Immediately after taking office, President Picado visited several rural towns to discuss problems with local officials and opposition leaders wishing to meet with him. His annual message to congress in May 1945 suggested no rapid steps toward social reform, but stressed the need for increased economic productivity.

Congress did nothing to inflame public opinion by limiting its activities to routine matters. Picado's promise not to interfere in the 1946 congressional elections and to appoint a commission to recommend changes in the Election Code allayed popular concern over election fraud. Vanguard leader Manuel Mora, preaching a policy of labor-management conciliation, professed that socialism and capitalism could coexist after the war. Finally, the embassy third secretary, Livingston D. Watrous, who had been in San José since 1940, explained that Picado governed a nation that was traditionally averse to bloodshed and revolution as well as a people "unable to discuss any subject for a period of more than three days."[14] These factors indicated that Picado would complete his term free from political turbulence.

Despite the appearance of political calm, Costa Rica was experiencing several problems. For this reason, embassy officials speculated that Picado would be cast adrift alone or be forced to draw support from the *Cortesistas*. Living costs continued to escalate, the federal budget remained unbalanced, and shortages of some basic foodstuffs persisted. Picado refused advice to initiate strong measures to solve these problems on the grounds that such actions were counter to the country's political history.[15]

Politically, the administration faced opposition from several sources. President Picado's relationship with the Calderóns remained strained by his continued association with Manuel Mora. Relations were further worsened by Picado's appointment of his brother René as interior minister. René Picado intensely disliked the Calderón family and vowed not to tolerate any interference by them in the current administration. The precarious Picado-Calderón relationship was evident in congress, where the twenty-eight National Republican delegates usually followed the dictates of the former president in their opposition to Picado's call for governmental assistance in agricultural and industrial development, budget and tax reform, and social and educational programs.

The split was also evident within the administration. A December 1944 agricultural law, directed through congress by Mora, provided for the importation of rice, sugar, beans, and corn to relieve shortages and dampen inflationary pressures. The law was favored by Finance Minister

Bonilla Lara and National Bank Director Julio Peña, both of whom believed that increased consumption would stimulate the economy. Opposed were Agricultural Minister Joaquín Peralta and Interior Minister René Picado, both of whom maintained that high food prices were necessary to protect and encourage domestic agricultural production. Although such divergent viewpoints might have been dismissed as normal political debate and the efforts of individuals to absolve themselves from responsibility for the nation's economic ills, U.S. Chargé d'affaires S. Walter Washington interpreted the disagreement as evidence "that the moderate sector of the opposition had not been won over" to Picado's camp.[16]

President Picado's relationship with Vanguard leader Manuel Mora remained a political liability. Picado's promise to absorb both Mora and his party into the government, rather than allow him any preponderant influence, failed to materialize. American officials were also wrong in their belief that Mora would need to move politically to the right or find himself confined to his previous position as leader of an opposition reform party. Despite Picado's efforts at rapprochement with the political right, Mora's Vanguard party remained the president's strongest pillar of support.

Mora continued to work for legislation that would benefit the lower classes: extension of social security benefits to all sectors of the population, low-cost housing, quality education, the secret ballot, women's suffrage, revision of electoral laws to suppress fraud and corruption, and establishment of a civil service code. The party's four-point proposal for Costa Rica's economic growth threatened the wealthy class. The plan called for state regulation of agricultural production to reduce the nation's dependency on coffee and bananas; state control and distribution of all privately owned agricultural lands above 500 hectares not used for cattle-raising; a national council of industrial production to develop essential industries; and fiscal reform, including an income tax, to reduce government spending and eliminate corruption. Vanguard's call for conciliation in September 1944 and Mora's February 1945 radio address advocating the substitution of class collaboration for class warfare failed to dampen the apprehension. Vanguard's plea that social legislation be based upon the policies of former President Calderón and papal encyclicals also fell on deaf ears.

Mora successfully bargained for wage increases for workers at the

U.S.-owned electric firm *Compañía de Fuerza y Luz* and the Northern Railway Company. He also negotiated the recovery of lost salaries for government public works employees, who had lost their jobs as a government economy measure. The large coffee growers, however, refused to discuss the application of the Labor Code to their industry, nor would local capitalists discuss labor issues with Mora.[17] Improvement of the workmen's plight remained an anathema to the upper class. Picado's continued association with Mora kept the elite from rallying to the president's side.

U.S. opinion regarding Mora lacked consensus. In December 1944 Hallet Johnson replaced Des Portes as ambassador. Prior to this assignment, Johnson had held posts in Europe and within the State Department. His initial impression was that Mora was a "moderate, and Vanguard an entirely national organization," whose relations with Moscow were at best tenuous. Vanguard's program, Johnson concluded, "would be defined in most countries as merely a liberal program." Manager of the national bank Julio Peña and Archbishop Sanabria shared this opinion. The archbishop pictured Mora as "truly devoted to the amelioration of the conditions of the lower classes," and contended that communism was not a threat to Costa Rica, but rather that it was a camouflage used by the landowning classes, which were opposed to labor and social legislation. The State Department's Legal Division, however, viewed Vanguard with a more jaundiced eye. It noted that the policy of conciliation also had been adopted by communist parties elsewhere, including the United States, and was convinced that the Communist International was operating clandestinely in Costa Rica.[18] The latter opinion was rejected, however, by Secretaries of State Edward R. Stettinius and James F. Byrnes. Both concluded that Mora was a Marxist of local character and that his relations with Moscow were not important.[19] Communism was not a threat in Costa Rica through 1946.

Outside government circles, several other groups opposed the Picado administration. U.S. embassy officials in San José believed that the strongest single faction consisted of the followers of former president León Cortés. His support came from the country's rural areas, particularly Alajuela and Heredia provinces. Because Cortés controlled approximately more than a quarter of the congressional membership, Ambassador Johnson considered him important to both the 1946 congressional and 1948 presidential elections. Cortés offered his support to the Picado administration provided it break with Vanguard. Rebuffed, Cortés was linked to revolutionary plots aimed at Picado's overthrow. Those alleged connections, like his "announced" retirement from politics in June 1945, were viewed as efforts to keep his name in the newspapers and thereby gain financial support.[20]

American officials in San José accorded even more significance to the emergence from private life of Otilio Ulate, who used his newspaper *Diario de Costa Rica* to criticize the Picado administration. In November 1944 Ulate joined a committee of opposition leaders—León Cortés, Peña Chavarria, Alfred Volio, Fernando Velverde, and Rafael Angel Chavarria—to present a common front against the administration. In February 1945 Ulate encouraged the opposition to unite forces and predicted it would gain control of congress in 1946, provided elections were free. Ambassador Johnson believed that Ulate could become the standard-bearer of many prominent citizens who otherwise might fail to rally behind any other individual.[21]

The third opposition group outside government to emerge during the first half of Picado's administration was the Social Democratic party, founded in March 1945 as a result of the merger between the *Centro para el estudio de problemas nacionales* and *Acción Democrática* groups. Established in 1940, *Centro* was an organization of young professionals, students, and white-collar workers who rejected communism as a means to solve Costa Rica's social and economic problems. *Democrática* was composed largely of younger *Cortesistas*, who broke from the former president following the 1944 election. This group disdained the personalism connected with all parties and the policies of the older leaders. Among the Social Democratic party notables were José Figueres, Rodrigo Facio, and Alberto Martén.[22]

Ambassador Johnson noted that the three opposition groups—*Cortesistas, Ulatistas,* and Social Democrats—had only one common bond: dislike of the Picado administration. Yet they could not submerge their differences in order to capitalize upon their collective strength. This opinion was shared by the commander of the Caribbean Defense Command, General Willis D. Crittenberger, who also maintained that the opposition was in such disarray that it posed no real threat to government stability.[23]

As the Picado administration approached its midpoint, the U.S. embassy staff was struck by the "feeling of instability which has permeated the political scene." Described as a "colorless . . . stolid unimaginative type," the unemotional Picado was able to withstand the steady stream of criticism and to ride "two horses which balk at running along side each other." His election had been marred by fraud and marked the first time in Costa Rican history that ideological differences made their way into the country's elections. His base of support remained fragile, as reflected in his Cabinet membership of both left and right—Vanguard and *Calderonista*. The latter group, in particular, showed little loyalty toward Picado. Mora, recognizing his minority position, insisted on only achieving the goals in Picado's campaign platform. Congressional failure to achieve those goals was attributed to the Vanguard-*Calderonista* feud. Outside government, the opposition, split by factional jealousies and devoid of capable leadership, offered no real threat to Picado beyond rumored violence.[24] The *Calderonistas* and the opposition groups outside government shared one common bond: dislike of social reform.

The 1946 congressional elections provided an opportunity for an additional measure of the nation's ideological thinking. Anxieties intensified as the February midterm elections approached. Although Picado failed to persuade congress to revise the Electoral Code, it had passed a law in December 1945 providing for the representation of all principal parties on all local electoral boards. This did not quell the fear of electoral fraud, which was shared by Murray Wise of the Caribbean and Central American Affairs Division. This fear also contributed to a new round of rumors predicting a revolution before or after election day, February 10.

Two rumors received considerable attention. The first implied that Arturo Quiros was receiving arms in Nicaragua on behalf of the Calderón brothers, who reportedly enjoyed the financial backing of the Union Club, an organization of large coffee growers. The second rumor suggested that Quiros, Manuel Castro, José Figueres, Fernando Velverde, and Rafael Yglesias were working together to pull off a coup d'etat or engineer the assassination of Picado and Mora. Ambassador Johnson dismissed these rumors on the grounds that the opposition lacked leadership and sufficient financial backing. He also believed that only a "lunatic would attempt to implement a plot involving assassination in this peace loving and progressive country."[25] Apparently, he failed to understand the potential adverse impact a *Picadistas* victory would exert upon the upper and middle classes.

During the weeks prior to the close of voter registration, on January 14,

1946, the three main opposition groups—*Cortesistas, Ulatistas,* and Social Democrats—stopped their petty bickering and agreed on a united front, which enhanced their chances of victory. Tension within their ranks was further reduced when León Cortés announced he was not a congressional candidate and Otilio Ulate had his name placed low enough on the San José ballot in order not to be elected. Also contributing to a sense of confidence among the opposition was the National Republican party's failure to select strong candidates.

State's Research and Analysis Division observed a split within the opposition. It was a wide-ranging coalition fraught with diversity and personal conflicts, but was conservative in comparison to the Picado administration. This heterogeneity and conservatism caused the division not to share the opposition's confidence. For the National Republicans to maintain control of congress, twelve of their candidates needed to win. The election of nine deputies by the National Republican-Vanguard coalition would ensure its future legislative control. To win in either case, the opposition contended that the administration would have to resort to fraud.[26]

Thanks largely to Picado's efforts, the February 10 elections were relatively free of impartiality and almost devoid of disorder, in comparison to the 1944 presidential election. Consular officer Watrous dismissed opposition charges of fraud and vote-buying as public gestures caused by the election results. The final count gave the National Republicans twelve, the opposition nine, and Vanguard two winners. In congress, the National Republicans placed twenty-four deputies, the opposition seventeen, and Vanguard five.

The embassy staff, State's Research and Analysis Division, and Caribbean Defense Commander Willis D. Crittenberger were united in their view of the election results. All agreed that, despite an apparent working congressional majority, Picado continued to suffer from the fact that most National Republicans followed directives from the Calderón brothers. Conservative oppositionists offered to support Picado only if he broke with Vanguard, his only consistent base of congressional support. Otherwise, the opposition deputies tended to follow several different paths of action. Although Vanguard had failed to improve its voting strength since 1942, the party, with five deputies, was in a position to pursue a more independent path, potentially building a balance of power. Recognizing its independence, it immediately called for a comprehensive land reform program.[27] The election results offered little hope that Picado would effectively deal with several issues confronting him: inflation, national finances, governmental inefficiency, and corruption.

Calling the congressional elections fraudulent, several opposition leaders formed a so-called Tribunal of Honor and directed opposition delegates not to take their congressional seats on May 1, 1946. Ambassador Johnson believed that Ulate may have organized this "group of capitalists who refused to take cognizance of changing social conditions." Opposition delegates were split on the issue. Even without the attendance of the newly elected deputies, a congressional quorum was possible because the nine elected for the 1944 – 48 period were not obligated to boycott. Only the Social Democrats approved the boycott, but they had elected only one delegate in February 1946. By June 5 the boycott had ended.[28] The incident further indicated the disarray of the opposition and suggested its inability to prepare for the 1948 presidential election.

Traditionally, midterm elections were looked upon as a testing ground for the next presidential contest. Prior to the 1946 election, American officials maintained that a National Republican-Vanguard victory would guarantee Rafael Angel Calderón's 1948 candidacy, which would revive that of León Cortés. The results of the 1946 congressional election, however, gave no clear signals regarding the 1948 presidential contest. In a postelection analysis, Caribbean and Central American Affairs Division Assistant Chief Murray Wise noted that the government's failure to gain a landslide victory diminished the image of and presidential possibilities for Calderón. Cortés, too, suffered a loss of prestige because of the election of administration candidates in his home district, Alajuela. The situation was further clouded by his death in March 1946. Although the Democratic party quickly organized an executive committee consisting of Fernando Castro Cervantes, Fernando Lara, Eludo Trejos, Fernando Volio, and Ricardo Castro Beeche, it could not agree upon a new standard-bearer.

American officials in San José and Washington considered the Social Democrats to be less important. Their sole congressional deputy, Antonio Peña, subsequently organized an executive committee, including himself, Manuel Antonio Quesada, and Rafael Alberto Zuñiga, all of whom lacked charisma. The three were committed to restoring Costa Rica's political liberty "by whatever means it may consider advisable and necessary." The U.S. embassy staff was concerned with the party's linkage to revolt rumors. Ambassador Johnson judged Otilio Ulate's political star also to be in descent following the 1946 congressional elections. His lack of political acumen contributed to his small group of followers, and he therefore shifted his efforts to a personal attack upon Picado and his administration.[29] This lack of presidential front-runners contributed to the nation's outward political calm throughout the spring and early summer of 1946.

The serenity ended on August 5, when it was announced that the National Republican, Democratic, and Vanguard parties, after secret conventions, agreed on a three-point plan to achieve political liberty in the country. The program called for: immediate appointment of an impartial electoral tribunal, whose members were acceptable to all parties; distribution of photograph-electoral voting cards; and a new Electoral Code, which was not to be altered before the 1948 election. Each party remained free to select its own candidate. Picado applauded the pact as a step toward the elimination of political violence. The public also seemed pleased.[30] Where the 1946 congressional elections had failed, the August agreement set in motion the political manuevering pointing toward the 1948 presidential election.

The tempo of political activity immediately accelerated. In early September, Ulate denounced the August agreement, presumably because it did not aid his chance of becoming the 1948 opposition presidential candidate. Also, in September, "a handful of malcontents" under the leadership of Otto Cortés, son of the late president, and Robert Salazar and José Figueres formed the *Cortesista* Party. Figueres was considered to be the most dangerous because he was inclined toward revolution. Ambassador Johnson described the party "as a small group of hotheads without either popular appeal or political experience" who only wanted to be in a more favorable position to sell out to the highest bidder in 1948. Of even more significance was the October 18 agreement between the four leading opposition parties: Democratic, Social Democratic, National Union, and *Cortesista*. United only by their dislike of the Picado administration, they agreed to a future convention for the purpose of selecting a presidential candidate. This was a "move in the right direction," according to Murray Wise.[31]

Tension increased throughout the latter part of 1946 and into January 1947. The opposition increased its public criticism of the government's poor financial condition and called for the resignation of the electoral board and Picado's Cabinet because of his close association with the Calderón brothers. Rumors of impending revolution continued. In late December 1946 and early January 1947, a series of bombings took place in major cities. Both the rumors and the acts of violence were attributed to the opposition. Meantime, Picado had pursued a "weak" policy of minimal response. Ambassador Johnson noted that the verbal and violent attacks on the administration lacked a "cohesive plan," an indication of continued opposition factionalism. Furthermore, he found no cause for revolution because rural workers appeared to be content and the coffee growers, enjoying high prices for their produce, were in no mood to flock to a revolutionary banner. Johnson believed that only two opposition leaders—José Figueres and Alfredo Volio—were "capable of trying to promote a civil war," but not at this time.[32]

No front-runner was clearly apparent on the eve of the opposition convention, in February 1947. Although the Democratic party was the largest element of the opposition bloc, Ambassador Johnson found no guarantees that one of its three most prominent members would be the presidential nominee. Each suffered from obvious political liabilities.

Despite public statements to the contrary, Fernando Castro Cervantes was deemed to be the most likely choice, but his support of an income tax program raised doubts that wealthy planters would back him financially. Another possibility was Alfredo Volio, a wealthy agriculturalist, who reportedly had many enemies among the party's ranks because of his alleged financial support of recent subversive activities. The third possibility was Fernando Esquival, another wealthy farmer whose enemies were few, but he was little known throughout the country. José Figueres was judged to be the favorite among the *Cortesistas*. Suspicions that he had participated in the recent bombings and his wild charge that Picado's usurpation of power had turned Costa Rica into an "occupied country" created popular mistrust of his intentions. National Union leader Otilio Ulate was labeled as an unprincipled individual, whose personal ambitions often resulted in irrational political arguments. Although his party was small and lacked national support, his two newspapers, *Diario de Costa Rica* and *La Hora*, were valuable assets. Social Democratic leader Antonio Peña was considered to have the least chance of success on account of his small following. Ambassador Johnson believed that the Calderón brothers preferred Ulate as the opposition candidate because they felt he could be easily defeated.[33]

To Johnson's surprise, Ulate was selected as the opposition standard-bearer on February 13, 1947, receiving almost 400 more votes than Francisco Castro Cervantes. José Figueres finished a distant third. U-late's victory, however, failed to demonstrate opposition unity and caused Johnson to believe that the bloc would not remain unified. Only his own National Union party and the Social Democrats cast their support for Ulate. The *Cortesistas* threw their support to him only after it was evident Figueres would not win the nomination. Considered to be an "aggressive opportunist," Figueres was expected to exert strong influence over Ulate, further dividing the opposition. Fernando Castro Cervantes's Democratic party did not endorse Ulate. This caused speculation that Ulate would not receive financial and moral support from the upper class.[34]

As expected, Rafael Angel Calderón was named as the National Republican candidate on March 24, 1947. Ambassador Johnson immediately predicted his victory for several reasons. The party was efficiently organized and sufficiently funded. Calderón could appeal to labor on the basis of his own record, thus avoiding Vanguard, a move considered appealing to the wealthy landowners. Johnson, however, expressed caution in anticipation of a "violent political campaign." He also believed that, if the opposition became convinced it could not win free and fair elections, Ulate would "be tempted to forward any revolutionary activities."[35]

From the campaign's start, both Calderón and Ulate expressed confidence of victory. Calderón's optimism stemmed from his party's organization, adequate funding, disorganized opposition, and Ulate's small following. Ulate was convinced that he would win any free election and that Calderón could be elected only through fraud.[36] The campaign manifested two distinct characteristics: the dominance of personalities rather than issues; and a rash of violent activities, for which each side blamed the other.

Determined to prevent the other from capturing the presidency, both candidates resorted to bitter personal attacks. The personality issue contributed to movements toward a compromise candidate. Some *Calderonistas* were willing to accept an oppositionist, if victory were not within reach, provided: that Ulate not be considered; and that the Calderón brothers and their associates be guaranteed their safety and that their properties and resources not be confiscated. In the opposition camp, only the *Ulatistas* remained confident. Other elements continued to support their candidate because of their antipathy toward Calderón, but expressed a willingness to accept a compromise candidate. Trial balloons surfaced. The most important was the unsuccessful effort in behalf of Minister of Agriculture Joaquin Peralta. To vice-consul Cohen, a compromise candidate was not found because Costa Rica lacked a person "big enough to effect a conciliation," such as late Presidents Ricardo Jiménez, Cleto Gonzalez, or León Cortés. Cohen concluded that the "choice seems to be between a compromise candidate or serious bloodshed."[37]

Charging that their candidate, Otilio Ulate, was "the victim of government partiality in the campaign," the opposition led a general strike that lasted from July 23 to August 3, 1947. U.S. Vice-consul John Willard Carrigan, who had previously served in Nicaragua and Mexico, believed that most businesses closed out of fear, rather than sympathy for the protest movement. Whatever the reason, business and commerce were paralyzed; shortages of staples persisted that resulted in vandalism and looting in San José and Cartago. The government proved to be helpless. Its increased military visibility only "strengthened the movement." The strike ended on August 3, when both sides agreed to accept the national Electoral Tribunal's announced winner of the February elections. Also, it was agreed that the tribunal would be adequately funded to complete its task and that government workers would be permitted to join whichever political party they wished. Finally, both the president and public security minister agreed to turn over the armed forces to the successful candidate. Not all *Calderonistas* or *Ulatistas* were satisfied with the agreement. Some *Calderonistas* spoke out against President Picado's "appeasement policy," and opposition elements charged that they had been sold "down the river."

In April 1947 Walter J. Donnelly became the new U.S. Ambassador to Costa Rica. A graduate of the Georgetown University Foreign Service School, he had held assignments previously in Brazil, Panama, and Peru. He believed that the opposition had called off the strike "at the height of its effectiveness." If it had held out longer, the government would have granted even more concessions, thus enhancing the opposition's prestige.[38]

Sporadic bombings marred the campaign prior to the general strike in July. Following the strike's conclusion, rumors of possible armed violence by the opposition abounded. These rumors were dismissed by Vice-consul Cohen on the grounds that the opposition was no match for the government's armed forces. A relative calm prevailed through the fall, broken in early November with the bombing of Calderón's newspaper, *La Tribuna*, and the wrecking of the modern plant of Ulate's *Diario de Costa Rica*. As expected, each side blamed the other. President Picado remained silent. Thereafter, no major violence occurred until election day. Emotions ran high, however, in the closing days of the campaign. The opposition charged the government with illegal arrests, searches of private property without warrants, and general intimidation of the people. The National Republicans charged the opposition with provocation, fraud, and plots to disturb public order. The campaign violence, however, caused Cohen to believe that a confrontation between the competing groups was possible, particularly in the case of a Calderón election victory.[39]

The Vanguard party's role altered during the course of the presidential campaign. Throughout the spring of 1947, it remained on the sidelines of political controversy, pursuing a policy of watchful waiting, not attacking Ulate or Calderón. Rather, the party was content with its criticism of the government for its inactivity regarding the bombings as well as failure to curb inflation and control the coffee, sugar, and cattle industries. According to unconfirmed rumors, Calderón had divorced himself from Mora, and Ulate had turned down an alliance with him.

Apparently isolated, Vanguard registered itself as a political party on July 7, but did not name candidates. To Vice-consul Carrigan, Vanguard was still waiting "to jump on whichever bandwagon seems to give it the best opportunity to further its own ends." Although the party became increasingly active on the administration's side during the twelve-day general strike in July, it was notably absent from the agreement ending the crisis. Carrigan and Cohen were not sure if its absence was intentional or not, but correctly predicted that Vanguard would not "take this slight lying down." At the end of August, Vanguard changed its campaign rhetoric from seeking additional election guarantees to one of "open class warfare."[40]

U.S. officials' evaluation of the Vanguard party also changed during the course of the campaign. In May 1947 State's American Republics Affairs Division repeated previous evaluations, namely that Vanguard was communistic, hiding under the cloak of opportunism, and that

Manuel Mora recognized this weakness. The party appeared more interested in domestic reform than international communism, and, because of its undisciplined membership, did not appear to be militant. Mora was judged to be "sincere in his efforts to make the party a local reformist organization." Without Archbishop Sanabria's support, the party would be significantly weakened. Thus, the division concluded, "communism in Costa Rica is not now a force which ought to greatly concern this government."[41]

A month later, Vanguard issued a reorganization pamphlet calling for the application of "democratic centralism," which permitted a discussion of issues until a decision was reached, at which time all party members, majority and minority, would be bound to support it. A call was also made to imitate the Cuban, French, and Italian Communist parties in membership drives. To Carrigan, the reorganization meant that Vanguard was drawing closer to the communist line and taking on "a more essentially communist character." He also noted a cooling of Archbishop Sanabria's attitude toward Vanguard following the reorganization directive.[42]

Two communications from San José in October 1947 clearly reflected the changed assessment of Vanguard. The first cable came from the new ambassador, Walter J. Donnelly. It received high praise from the director of the Caribbean and Central American Affairs Division, William Tapley Bennett, who had returned to the State Department the previous year after military service during World War II. The second represented the consensus opinion of the embassy staff. Both documents described Mora as a devout communist whose following consisted of low-income wage earners. His popularity gave the party significant political influence. Presidents Calderón and Picado both "found it desirable to support and assist the communists" to keep them from going over to the opposition. As a result, communists received several governmental posts during both administrations and the embassy staff predicted that this influence would continue under either Calderón or Ulate because of the serious problems Vanguard could create. Thus, the Americans felt that Mora was "one of the big men" in Costa Rican politics. The collective embassy opinion added another point. Because Costa Rica was making no concentrated effort to eliminate communism, the republic could become a hemispheric training as well as message center and local communist leaders "may be of continually greater interest to Moscow."[43]

As the presidential campaign approached its conclusion, Vice-consul

Cohen noted that communism was an increasingly important ingredient to the traditional struggle for political power among the Costa Rican elites. Still, the National Republicans, or *Calderonistas*, were expected to win the February 1948 elections for several reasons. The party had maintained its successful election machinery since the 1940 and 1944 campaigns. It was efficiently organized under the control of the Calderón brothers, both experienced politicians. As the administration's party, it enjoyed nationwide governmental support. Another factor was that Calderón's 1940–44 record was credited with the advanced Labor Code. Finally, the armed forces and police were partial to the *Calderonistas*.

Although the opposition had a broad base of appeal—conservative landowners and businessmen, students, and professionals not employed by the government—Ulate did not enjoy their unqualified support because of his cunning attitude. Lacking a definite program, the opposition centered its attack upon Calderón and the communists. In fact, they classified Calderón as a communist.[44]

An assessment of the political situation was made by Vice-consul Cohen, who had been in the country longer than any other embassy staff member. He was not optimistic about the future. Were Calderón successful, he would not be able to govern because of a determined opposition. Ulate's personal ineptness, inefficient party organization, and the fact that the National Republicans would enjoy a congressional majority would prove to be equally disastrous. In either case, the years 1948–52 would see a continuation of the existing uncertainty, insecurity, and general disregard for the law, Cohen concluded.[45]

The February 8 elections were held without major violence. Hundreds of voters, however, were unable to cast their ballots because the cumbersome voting machinery proved to be time-consuming. Embassy officials dismissed allegations by both sides that the process worked against them. By February 13, all indications pointed to an Ulate victory. As Ambassador Donnelly conceded, for an individual who a year ago had only 15 percent support of the opposition groups behind him and was "violently disliked by many of his own political group, it must be admitted that he is at the very least an exceedingly clever politician."[46]

Fearful of defeat, Calderón requested the Electoral Tribunal to refrain from making a declaration until fraud charges could be determined. In reality, this was a delay tactic in anticipation of the elections being nullified by the National Republican-controlled congress. The Republican-Vanguard bloc charged that the opposition had violated the August 3, 1947, agreement and alleged that only congress had the right to certify the elections. On the other hand, the opposition, confident of victory, remained "dignified and restrained." President Picado kept silent, claiming his only responsibility was to ensure the peaceful transfer of power. U.S. Ambassador Nathaniel P. Davis did not expect him to intervene and felt that the Republican-Vanguard bloc would achieve its goal of congressional invalidation of the elections. Otherwise, Ulate would be unable to govern. Davis's perceptions of the political climate were quite sharp, despite his background. Appointed ambassador in September 1947, he lacked Latin American field experience. A career employee of the State Department, his most recent post had been in the Philippines.[47]

In the vacuum, secret efforts were made to reach a compromise. The Cortés element of the opposition, inclined toward this approach, favoring either Fernando Castro Cervantes or Fernando Esquivel. Calderón, fearing reprisals if Ulate succeeded to the presidency, and Mora, who was apprehensive about the loss of social gains, were "definitely not . . . adverse to a compromise." The Ulate camp, however, remained adamant in victory.[48]

In a 2−1 decision on February 28, the Electoral Tribunal declared Ulate to be the victor by a 54,931 to 44,348 vote margin. The tribunal also contended that its only responsibility was to count the votes and not deal with alleged irregularities. While the *Ulatistas* remained quiet in order to avoid confrontation, the government turned the capital into "an armed camp" by setting up street barricades to facilitate the searching of all vehicles. Each group accused the other of attempting to stir up violence while awaiting the congressional decision. Tensions heightened when the armed forces commander, General René Picado, announced that he would not turn the military over to Ulate as provided in the August 3, 1947, political agreement. Picado claimed that the non-unanimous nature of the tribunal's decision violated the agreement. Furthermore, if the contending factions wanted to "fight it out," he promised to exile the "survivors."[49]

The congressional decision was a foregone conclusion. Voting strictly along party lines, the deputies declared the presidential election to be null and void, but at the same time validated the February 8 congressional elections, which retained the administration's majority. Obviously, the

National Republicans had interpreted the February 8 elections to their "exclusive personal benefit." Significantly, because congress did not call for new elections, hope existed for the selection of a compromise candidate or permitting the first designate (yet to be determined) to assume the presidency.

Violence quickly followed the congressional decision. Two government guards and "lunatic fringe" leader Carlos Luis Valverde were killed. Rumors spread of assassination attempts on Ulate; two congressmen were kidnapped; waterworks, railroad tracks, and electric power plants were bombed. In response, businessmen boarded storefronts, and the government ordered the closing of banks and issued arms to cadres of Vanguard party members, the only organized group available to Picado.[50]

Throughout February and early March, Ambassador Davis expressed the hope that the issue would be settled constitutionally, meaning the validation of Ulate's election victory. To seat Ulate by force also was acceptable over the installation of Calderón under any circumstances because that would mean the continuation of communist influence in government. Such influence was not in the U.S. interest. Under the circumstances, Davis believed that a compromise candidate, acceptable to both the opposition and National Republicans, was the best solution.[51] Compromise, however, was not to be.

As early as March 7, the government was aware that "something serious was brewing," but was totally unprepared to deal with the situation. At San Isidro del General, on Costa Rica's central plateau, Figueres and his followers were joined by other disenchanted oppositionists. On March 12 Figueres led a revolt against the government, allegedly on the grounds that congress had failed in its responsibility by not validating the February elections. Government forces, poorly trained, led, and clothed, were not prepared for battle on the central plateau; and the irregular "mariachis" lacked teamwork and discipline. Following the failure of government troops in engagements on March 13 and 14, Figueres was content to fight a war of attrition. For the remainder of March, government forces appeared to be unwilling to face the insurgents in their haphazard attacks against San Isidro.[52]

Insufficiently prepared for the insurgents' military challenge, Picado turned to outside sources for assistance. Requests to Honduras and the United States went unheeded. Only Nicaragua's Anastasio Somoza expressed a willingness to send troops into Costa Rica to cooperate in turning "on the communists and remove them from power." Before the entry of Nicaraguan troops on April 17, however, Figueres's forces abandoned San Isidro on April 10, and within two days captured Altamiera, Port Limón, Cartago, and the government headquarters at San Isidro de Coronado. On April 12, Picado and his Cabinet resigned, placing the government in the hands of third presidential designate Santos León Herrera. The following day, the diplomatic corps negotiated a cease-fire that was extended until the final capitulation on April 21. Only Vanguard's forces ignored the cease-fire. Because of the Nicaraguan entry, Mora defected from the government cause and declared he was defending the homeland from a foreign invasion. Cohen credited Vanguard forces with wanton lawlessness in the major cities. President Picado, his cabinet, and the Calderón brothers and their followers left the country. Subsequently, from Nicaragua, Picado professed that the new government had been "formed by men of unquestioned honesty."[53]

On the civil side, once fighting had broken out, the Picado administration suspended several constitutional guarantees, including the right to free transit through the country, peaceful assembly, habeas corpus, inviolability of domicile, freedom of expression, and protection against detention without cause. Banks remained closed by executive order. President-elect Ulate called for a general strike when the uprising started on March 12. The strike failed to materialize when the government threatened to requisition supplies from merchants following his call. The opposition was credited with the bombing of electric and water supply systems for San José, Puntarenas, and Turrialba as well as the government-owned Pacific Railway. As the war of attrition continued, the enthusiasm of the public, a helpless victim of the political struggle, also waned.[54]

In reviewing events since election day, February 8, Ambassador Davis placed a large measure of responsibility for the civil war on President Picado because of his do-nothing policy. Picado repeated "almost *ad nauseam*" that he only wanted a peaceful transfer of government, but did nothing to facilitate it. Davis felt he wanted things to remain adrift so that Calderón would become president by congressional machinations. For fear of firing the first shot, Picado did nothing to halt Figueres's concentration of men and arms at San Isidro del General. Once fighting had begun, Picado relied upon Vanguard's forces, which formed their own general staff and issued military orders on behalf of the government.

After it became known that he had approved the entry of Nicaraguan troops, Picado was no longer "the patient . . . man of peace" against a misguided revolt.[55]

Davis noted that Rafael Angel Calderón's unending thirst for the presidency also contributed to the outbreak of hostilities. Following the election loss to Ulate, Calderón approved the maneuvering by his followers to have him named first presidential designate. This would enable him to move into the presidency without popular mandate. Once fighting erupted, the *Calderonistas* abandoned all pretense of compromise. With his brother and Picado's approval, Rafael Calderón negotiated Nicaragua's entry into the war, a move that discredited him, destroyed his party, and eventually forced him into exile.[56]

Once the civil war had begun, the National Republicans cast aside their pretended separation from Vanguard. Preaching a line similar to that of Mora, the administration stated that the current struggle was between "those who have the well being of the common man at heart and those who want to return to the former state of misery and oppression of the poor." Although Davis described Mora as a level-headed, intelligent leader "dedicated to a liberal and unobjectionable social legislation program," he was concerned only with saving his own party after February 8.

Mora's role in February's sequence of events was unclear, but he did use one of the "well known means of international communism," letting the ends justify the means. He took no part in the efforts to find a compromise candidate and professed support for anyone who would pursue the social gains he had labored for. For the same reason, he mobilized his forces on behalf of the government; spoke privately with Figueres during the peace negotiations; and at first supported the Nicaraguan intervention, which he used as a lure in dealing with both Figueres and the Calderóns. Vice-consul Cohen was not generous. He believed that Mora inspired the opposition to resist compromise and thus caused the civil war.[57]

According to Cohen, the opposition after the election supported Ulate. They hoped that, as president, he would protect their interests and eliminate "undue communist influence" throughout the country. Once war broke out, the opposition sought aid for Figueres, who allegedly was fighting for constitutional order, and led the opposition to believe that Ulate would be seated as president[58] when the fighting stopped.

Provisional President León Herrera was considered to be a figurehead, who provided the veil of constitutionality to the temporary government until May 8, when it was expected that Ulate would be inaugurated. That expectation was shattered on May 2, when Figueres and Ulate reached an agreement permitting the junta to govern for eighteen months. The agreement also provided for the election of a constituent assembly in six months. Ambassador Davis attributed the lack of adverse public reaction to Figueres's popularity and the general belief that he would put Costa Rica's political house in order. Davis also observed that the junta was "super-sensitive" to public opinion and for that reason could not afford to split with Ulate, considered by most Costa Ricans to be the rightful president.[59]

"To the victors go the spoils," Davis remarked as Figueres moved quickly against the *Calderonistas* and other National Republicans. The personal assets of almost all of them were frozen on the grounds that they had been guilty of corruption. The junta also dismissed National Republican bureaucrats, university professors, and labor leaders.[60]

More important was Figueres's claim that it was impossible to deal with communists as "normal people." Vanguard, as the only remaining organized political group, was next targeted for attack by the junta, despite, as Davis observed, a striking similarity in social philosophy and belief in authoritarian control between the two groups. Vanguard's social program spelled communism to Figueres, who had proclaimed a "war against poverty" so that the majority of the country's impoverishment would disappear. The younger men around Figueres were more intense and conceived their mission as a crusade against communism.[61]

In June, after the top thirty-five Vanguard officials refused to go into voluntary exile, the junta closed the party's offices, newspapers, and radio station, and forced many members into hiding. The leaders were arrested without preferment of charges and, when released on writs of habeas corpus, were immediately rearrested. Charged with being anti-democratic and dangerous to the nation's political stability, Vanguard was outlawed on July 17. In the future, its leaders charged with insurrection were to be subject to ten-year banishment. The favorable local reaction indicated to Vice-consul Cohen that communism was decidedly unpopular. He speculated, however, that the junta's action would only intensify Vanguard's hostility toward the government. Ulate's *Diario de Costa Rica* noted that communism would not be completely eradicated "as long as the causes which gave rise to it are not destroyed." The paper advocated that capitalists cease their resistance to needed economic and social changes.[62] The junta had eliminated the major source of political opposition and now directed its attention toward political reform.

The official campaign for the constituent assembly began on September 3, under unpopular conditions imposed by the junta. Only five parties were sanctioned to nominate candidates: National Union, National Republican, Social Democrat, Democratic, and genuine *Cortesistas*. With each party represented on all local election boards, the junta was in the favored position as it held dominance over the latter three parties. Once elected, the assembly was to deal with the following matters: ratification of Ulate's election; extension of the junta's term for another six months; ratification of supreme court justices who had been appointed in 1948; and "any other business which the junta may wish to place before it." The last potentiality paved the way for approving the junta's acts and keeping the assembly in indefinite session. In reality, the junta was resorting to pre-1948 political intrigue in an effort to attain its objectives. Popular reaction was swift and critical. The director general of the Electoral Register Ramón Arroyo resigned. Ulate instructed his *Diario de Costa Rica* to cease publication of editorials sympathetic to the junta. *Pensa Libre*, more outspoken, charged the junta with corruption. Only *La Nación* approved the measure.

The junta's decrees also opened the floodgates to attacks by the wealthy on Economic and Finance Minister Alberto Martén and Labor Minister Father Benjamin Nuñez. This group charged that Martén's economic policies would bankrupt the country and that Nuñez was interpreting the Labor Code solely for the benefit of the lower classes.[63]

Subsequently, other political parties were permitted to register, but Ulate's National Union, Figueres's Social Democratic, and the newly formed Constitutional parties dominated the campaign. The latter party was composed of "older and more mature" men who felt the need to take a stronger stand against the junta. The campaign, which was devoid of vilification and violence, was characterized by the "customary lack of enthusiasm." Only the younger members of the Social Democrats preached class warfare, which benefited the Constitutionalists.[64]

The National Union party swept to victory on December 8, winning 62,041 popular votes and giving it thirty-three congressional seats. The Constitutional party received 10,884 votes, which translated into six seats. Figueres's Social Democrats finished a distant third with 6,411

votes and four seats. The results confirmed the preelection opinion of
U.S. officials that Figueres needed Ulate to stay in power.[65]

The junta's honeymoon with the general public ended when Ulate and
Figueres agreed on February 4, 1949, to extend its term until May 8,
1950. Particularly repugnant was the idea that the constituent assembly
would remain on for consultation purposes. The agreement also resulted
in a number of charges against the junta. After ten months, it had failed
to provide an efficient, apolitical administrative machine. The junta's
"holier-than-thou" attitude, along with its inefficiency and nepotism
contributed to its unpopularity. Ruling by decree was unacceptable. The
business and financial community was uneasy about the junta's national-
ization of banks, taxation policies, control of currency exchange, and
continued inflation. Abortive labor strikes by shoemakers, stevedores,
and telephone workers served as symptoms of economic unrest. Vice-
consul Cohen believed that the junta's "blind adherence to its ideal"
significantly contributed to its own unpopularity. Its desire to remain in
power gave all appearances of returning to pre-1948 political behavior.
Despite the loss of confidence in the junta, Ambassador Davis believed
that Figueres still enjoyed widespread popularity, respect, and "even
affection."[66]

The constituent assembly completed its work in August 1949. The new
constitution, which replaced the 1871 document, was described by Cohen
as containing the "most advanced legal, political, social and economic
terms and principles." Checking the political vices of the past, at the same
time it strengthened individual and social guarantees.[67]

Politically, the constitution provided for a new congress and two vice-
presidents, who were to be elected in October. Campaigning for those
positions began in July. The political future of José Figueres and the
reemergence of the Vanguard party dominated an otherwise issue-free
campaign. The efforts by the Social Democrats to have Figueres run as a
vice-presidential candidate were rejected by the National Union party.
When plans to establish his own party were not well received, Figueres
withdrew his candidacy and cast his support behind the two National
Union candidates: Alberto Oreamuno and Alfred Volio. Other parties
entering the race included the Constitutional and *Cortesista* Democrats,
which put forward national lists of candidates, and two regional groups:
Alajuelense and *Unión Cartagensa*.[68]

Potentially more important was the reemergence of the Vanguard party. Beginning in March 1947, its paper, *Trabajo*, was clandestinely mimeographed. The paper attacked the junta and Labor Minister Nuñez for favoring capital, not labor. In July the organization registered as the National Democratic party. But its "frank admission of communist affiliation . . . opened the eyes of many" who in the past had regarded Vanguard as purely a local phenomenon. The Election Tribunal canceled the party's registration on August 16, 1949, because it violated Article 74 of the new constitution, which prohibited political parties whose "ideological program and methods of action or international connections" threatened Costa Rica's democratic principles. The tribunal pointed out that at least eighteen of the party's candidates were members of the previously outlawed Vanguard party. Thus the new organization was held to be illegal on the basis of personalities and their previous affiliation. Vice-consul Cohen believed that the tribunal should have let the National Democrats participate in the October elections. The communists would have been "resoundingly defeated" and their claims of political strength "put to rest."[69]

Communist threats to sabotage the elections failed to materialize. Throughout the day, October 2, fleets of cars flying the National Union flag scoured San José and nearby countryside rounding up an estimated 75 percent of the estimated 80,000 eligible voters. Ulate's party won an overwhelming victory, capturing thirty-three congressional seats. The Constitutional party won six and the Social Democrats three. Three other minor parties elected one deputy each. National Unionists Oreamuno and Volio were also elected as vice-presidents. Amidst an enthusiastic throng in the national stadium, on November 8, including U.S. Assistant Secretary of State, Edward G. Miller, Jr., and Ambassador Joseph Flack, Ulate was inaugurated as president for a full four-year term. The United States expressed public satisfaction that Costa Rica had solved its problems "in a democratic manner fully consistent with the country's long traditions of liberty and devotion to the principles of representative government."[70]

During Ulate's administration (1949–53), Costa Rica enjoyed peace and prosperity. His economic policies endeared him to the business community. Despite impressive progress in national and fiscal matters, he was a conservative and chose not to push forward with social reforms. This cost him the support of Figueres, who was victorious in the 1952 presidential campaign. His administration accelerated the furtherance of social reforms that had been promised in the 1948 revolution. Thereafter, until the 1970s, the Costa Rican electorate alternated conservative and liberal presidents.

The reports from Costa Rica and analysis in Washington validated consular officer Edward Trueblood's 1944 observation that the country was embarking on a new political path in which personalities were giving way to ideological differences. From this perspective, the Americans concluded that the 1948 revolution not only climaxed eight years of government corruption and maladministration, but also demonstrated the tightened lines between the conservative elements and others favoring rapid progress in social reform.[71] Both the 1944 and 1948 presidential campaigns illustrated the ideological conflict. Picado in 1944 and Calderón in 1948 were identified with reform elements, and Cortés in 1944 and Ulate in 1948 were conservatives.

The reforms—a Labor Code, social security, income tax, low-cost housing, education, and public health—were deemed to be reasonable and moderate by American policymakers.[72] To the upper class, however, these programs threatened its financial well-being and potentially its privileged social and political position. In the hope of gaining support for its cause, the elite labeled these reforms as communistic. So, too, did José Figueres, the 1948 civil war leader.

Figueres claimed that his forces "overthrew what actually was a Communist held [and] supported dictatorship."[73] He alleged that communism had permeated the Calderón and Picado administrations and that the 1948 civil war was a successful effort to purge Costa Rica of the dreaded ideology. Contemporary writer Samuel Guy Inman and later historians John D. Martz and Miguel Acuna made the same point.[74]

The communist issue must be considered both in its international context and as a domestic issue in Costa Rica. The two were intertwined. The perceptions of Costa Rican communism held by U.S. policymakers from 1944 to 1949 varied. Vanguard and its leader, Manuel Mora, were placed in one of three categories: legitimate representatives of the lower socioeconomic groups, political opportunists, or true Marxist-Leninist communists. As illustrated in the correspondence of Ambassador Hallet Johnson and Consuls Alex A. Cohen and Edward G. Trueblood, the general perception through early 1947 was that Mora and his followers were the sole representatives of the underprivileged and were pressing to correct their proper grievances. From this vantage point, the American policymakers understood that the government had been operated by and for the elite.

After May 1947, however, U.S. correspondence from San José compared Vanguard's activities to communist tactics elsewhere. Ambassador Walter J. Donnelly echoed Consul Cohen's belief that—despite the lack of clear evidence linking Vanguard to Moscow—the Costa Rican "situation of uncertainty and insecurity in many aspects [was] similar to that prevailing in Eastern Europe."[75] This harsher perception of Costa Rican politics coincided with the stiffening attitude of the United States toward the Soviet Union and the concomitant threat of international communism. President Harry S. Truman's call for aid to Greece and Turkey, Secretary of State George C. Marshall's proposed European Recovery Program, and the agenda for the 1948 Bogotá Conference illustrated the concern of the United States with the threat of expanded Soviet communism. From this point of view, the evidence suggests that U.S. perceptions of Costa Rican politics became entwined in cold war rhetoric.

U.S. policymakers clearly understood the oligarchical characteristics of those politics and recognized that Vanguard threatened their continued existence. Ideologically, communism was anathema to the country's socioeconomic elite. In a study of the 1948 Costa Rican civil war, based largely upon contemporary Costa Rican sources, John P. Bell clearly illustrated the manipulation of the communist issue by the elite.[76] The civil war provided a convenient mechanism to rid the country of the major nemesis to the status quo. U.S. diplomats clearly understood this issue.

Absent from the U.S. reports and analysis of Costa Rican politics was an understanding of the emerging middle sector, as found in the Social Democratic party. It was comprised largely of the nation's younger professional groups, who had tired of the personalism connected with Costa Rican politics and the elite's failure to come to grips with social problems. The Americans only identified the party as an opportunistic group wanting political power within the traditional framework of "outs" wanting "in." U.S. officials did not appear concerned with Figueres's philosophy, but rather with his willingness to use force to achieve political power. They apparently failed to perceive the middle sector's desire for democratic government.

Therefore, the United States was satisfied with the calm restored to Costa Rican life by the Figueres junta. In January 1949 the State Department recommended to President Truman that "we need badly to have this pleasant assignment [San José] . . . reserved for our use in taking care of deserving Chiefs of Mission who had done their stint in hardship posts."[77]

2

El Salvador

IN January 1944 El Salvador was deceptively quiescent. Actually, it was a potential powder keg. Since 1931, General Maximiliano Hernández Martínez had controlled the nation's life with an iron fist. Propped by the military, he politically isolated the landowning elite, which remained content so long as its wealth and status were not threatened. The middle sector was disorganized. The laboring masses were leaderless, in part attributable to the power of Hernández, who played upon their sympathies but did little to alleviate their poverty. Unexpected by U.S. officials, an eruption of the middle sector in the spring of 1944 paralyzed the nation with a general strike and forced Hernández to resign on May 8. The success of the middle sector, however, was short-lived. Following the election of General Salvador Castaneda Castro in January 1945, it was no longer a potent political force. The landowners aligned themselves with the older military officers and pressured Castaneda not to alter their status. From 1945 to 1949, the middle sector leaned toward the younger military officers, who rallied behind Major Oscar Osorio. This liberal element was primarily interested in constitutional government. The laboring classes remained politically dormant.

Salvador's economic evolution and political history explain the poten-

47

tially calamitous environment that had been created by 1944. The country's sharp social dichotomy was dominated by the so-called coffee aristocracy. Although some 11,500 coffee *fincas* were spread over 202,432 acres of land, 37 percent of these landholdings were divided among 192 large plantations and the balance among 11,353 small- and medium-sized properties. With nearly 140 people per square mile, Salvador was the region's most densely populated country. An estimated two-thirds of the population lived in the countryside and was tied to agricultural pursuits. Allied with the coffee industry was a small commercial group, composed mainly of Jewish merchants and bankers. Wealth clearly divided the "coffee aristocracy" from the masses of the people. The rich, who owned several cars and houses, made trips abroad, and paid frequent visits to palatial clubs, contrasted sharply with the worker, who possessed only a shirt and trousers, a wooden ox-cart, and a machete.[1]

Salvador was not a model of political stability. During its 125-year history, sixty-six changes in the presidency had occurred. Despite a constitutional provision for a four-year presidential term, only sixteen of the sixty-six presidents held office for longer than three consecutive years. Revolutions had become a norm of the political process in the nineteenth century. In the twentieth century, the "coffee aristocracy" sought an orderly and a protective government to ensure its interests. Supported by an efficient and well-trained army, the elite controlled the presidency until the 1930s, when the catastrophic effects of the Great Depression rattled confidence in the nation's economic, social, and political order. In 1931 General Maximiliano Hernández Martínez engineered a coup that inaugurated a thirteen-year dictatorial career. Constitutional provisions in 1935 and 1939 extended his term in office until 1944.[2]

Hernández, a believer in spiritualism and theosophy, was described as a "tribal chief to whom people bring their difficulties, both small and great." His administration was credited with advances in banking, education, labor, and resource development. Still, he was clearly a political dictator, even if he functioned "so discreetly that it [was] seldom manifested in any obvious or spectacular form." Deputies to the unicameral legislature and supreme court justices, despite election to office, were approved by the president for their nonopposition to the administration. In 1944 no political parties existed in the country. The *Pro-Patria* was Hernández's personal party, whose membership included present office holders and aspirants. The *Acción Democrática* was an opposition party without legal status. Its membership was unknown and its organizer, Francisco Lima, reportedly had little personal following or influence. Still, it was the only organization opposing the government within Salvador. In Mexico City, a group of exiles formed the Committee For Democracy in Salvador, but, like *Acción Democrática* lacked a negligible chance for success without support of the Salvadoran army, an element loyal to the president.[3]

Communist influence in Salvador was considered nonexistent in 1944. Its origins were traced to 1920, though not until 1925 was it judged to be significant. At that time, through the All American Anti-Imperialist League, communists blamed U.S. imperialism for the masses' plight. Communist agitators advocated land distribution and promised to improve wages and living conditions of the rural poor. After 1928, sporadic, but poorly organized, outbreaks occurred in the Sonsonate, Ahuachapán, and Santa Ana departments. Beginning in 1932, the government, ignoring legal process and finding mere suspicion of communist affiliation sufficient cause for action, suppressed everything communist. This program culminated in 1935, when President Hernández sent government forces into the countryside. An estimated 10,000 alleged communists were killed, including the party's leadership. The party was outlawed. In late 1943 the U.S. Federal Bureau of Investigation (FBI) was convinced that, as long as Hernández remained in power, "communism will never gain a foothold" in Salvador. The bureau also warned that, because "the conditions which made the country a fertile field for communism before 1932 still exist, a less vigilant regime would probably soon be faced by a communist menace."[4]

Thus, in early 1944 the potential for violence existed in Salvador. The disparity of wealth between rich and poor, the lack of constitutional government, and Hernández's repressive measures contributed to the threat of possible upheaval.

The crisis was precipitated on March 1, 1944, when the constituent assembly elected Hernández to another four-year presidential term. He was inaugurated on the same day, an event given little public attention. The critical editorial of José Quetglas in *La Prensa Gráfica* likewise received slight notice. Expressing disappointment in the United States for conducting World War II against dictatorships but elsewhere cooperating with dictators, he noted that "everything that is happening here has not the slightest point of contact with the practice of democratic ideals" and warned that "oppression causes violent explosions." The U. S. ambassador in San Salvador, Walter Thurston, felt these opinions were sincere, restrained, and "representative of the more literate section of the opposition." Nothing in the diplomatic pouch, however, warned of an impending crisis. Thurston, who had joined the State Department in 1916 and served in Costa Rica, Nicaragua, and Brazil, did not grasp the extent of middle sector opposition to Hernández. Thurston dismissed rumors of a possible uprising. Hernández appeared to be securely in control, bolstered by the army.[5]

Thurston obviously was surprised on April 2, when opposition groups took to San Salvador's streets while Hernández was at La Libertad, a coastal city southwest of the capital. The rebellion was suppressed within four hours, but not before 53 persons were killed and 134 wounded; two square blocks of the capital were destroyed when rebel pilots attempted to bomb police headquarters. Subsequently, 13 military officers were court-martialed and executed for plotting. Included were the commander of the First Infantry, General Alfonso Marroquín, and Colonel Tito Tomás Calvo, named as the plot's leader.

American officials in San Salvador concluded that the revolt failed not because of government strength, but because of the rebels' ineptitude.[6] Ambassador Thurston laid the immediate cause of the uprising to the extension of Hernández's presidential term, which meant continuation of civil rights violations and possible further curtailment of personal property and social rights through constitutional revision. Thurston maintained that the anxieties caused the business and capitalist elements to oppose the administration. In contrast, embassy consular officer Overton G. Ellis believed that the majority of Salvadorans supported the uprising. A former businessman who had joined the Foreign Service in 1932, Ellis was assigned to San Salvador in 1937, where he remained for ten years. He estimated that close to 90 percent of the professional class (doctors and lawyers), 75–80 percent of the middle class and white-collar groups, and 80–90 percent of the skilled labor groups opposed the Hernández dictatorship, but he could not judge the attitude of the "usually apathetic laboring and peon classes."

As a result of the uprising, American officials concluded that the president's confidence in the military was undoubtedly shaken and they were not sure he would remain in firm control of the government. The opposition was expected to try again, with a better planned insurrection.[7]

Following suppression of the revolt, Hernández's repressive measures did little to calm the tension. In addition to the execution of alleged revolt leaders, intellectuals, professionals, and businessmen were all suspect. Bank accounts were examined in an effort to determine the revolutionaries' financial sources. Civilians were subject to military brutality. For example, opposition spokesman Dr. Arturo Romero was seriously wounded by gunshot and machete while attempting to cross into Honduras. Incidents of the police torture of suspected insurrectionists were widely reported. There was a general uneasiness throughout the country. The large coffee growers were so apprehensive that they were reluctant to extend credit to small farmers. Citizens in the outlying towns of Santa Ana, Chalchuapa, Atiquizaya, Ahuachapán, and Sonsonate publicly expressed the hope of seeing the Hernández dictatorship end. In an effort to relieve the tension, the administration distributed handbills and had printed newspaper articles proclaiming that public order existed and that all elements throughout the country were collaborating for the common good.[8]

Later in April, the dissident professional groups pressured Ambassador Thurston to have the United States persuade Hernández to resign and to provide for general elections to choose his successor. Thurston resisted, pointing to the U.S. policy of nonintervention that had prevailed since 1933.[9] The Salvadorans were left to solve their own political problems.

In mid-April, San Salvador was beset by rumors calling for a general strike. A shouting match between students and police at the entrance of the National University on the morning of April 19 set in motion a chain of events that eventually forced the Hernández regime to crumble. Students organized several citizen groups to support a passive resistance movement against the government. In an effort to stave off the threatened general strike, fifty-four medical doctors visited President Hernández on May 2 and pleaded with him in vain to pardon all those under death penalties, grant general amnesty to all political prisoners, and restore democratic principles. The president appeared confident he could ride out the storm.[10]

On May 5 the student-initiated general strike began. Within a day, San Salvador was paralyzed and the strike spread to the cities of Santa Ana and San Miguel. There were reports of church support for the strike and of disaffection within the military. Ambassador Thurston reported that "the great majority of the inhabitants . . . are opposed to Hernández and support or approve of the current effort to depose him."[11] The United States would remain on the sidelines as an observer. Secretary of State Cordell Hull advised Thurston that, in committing itself to nonintervention, the nation made no reservations as to the type of crisis or issues, and the fact that it has "not voiced disapproval of domestic political developments . . . does not necessarily mean that it approves of those developments [but] . . . merely means that the United States feels itself bound not to express either approval or disapproval."[12]

Once the strike began, the Salvadoran Cabinet reportedly asked Hernández to resign, but he gave no indication he would leave office. In a May 5 radio address, he charged Nazi elements with trying to conduct a war of nerves in order to create panic. He also predicted that the crisis would pass in a day or two. On May 6 the president commenced a propaganda campaign by issuing leaflets and having editorials published in *Diario Neustra*. Appealing to the masses, he charged that the upper class— "the capitalists, agriculturalists, industrialists, merchants and professionals"—were responsible for the present chaos, but the workers apparently understood little about the theories or systems of government and how they related to the general strike.

According to some reports, Hernández was bringing farm workers into San Salvador, armed with machetes, to provoke violence that would provide an excuse for calling out the army to maintain order. These charges brought some 4,000 to 5,000 people to the streets demanding Hernández's resignation. Throughout the general strike, no violence occurred except the unprovoked police shooting of a seventeen-year-old boy on May 7.[13] Although Hernández was unable to break the strike or quell the demonstrations, he showed no signs of yielding to public pressure.

On May 8 a committee of opposition leaders rejected Hernández's offer to resign within thirty days, but under continued pressure he finally gave in. He announced his resignation in a short radio address that evening. National Defense Minister General Andrés Menéndez, one of three presidential designates, was selected by the Cabinet to succeed Hernández, who was permitted to leave the country for Guatemala on May 11. His departure was marked by popping firecrackers and screaming sirens in San Salvador. On the same day the general strike ended, businesses reopened and services were restored.[14] Thirteen years of dictatorial rule had ended.

There was ample evidence to indicate that the new government satisfied the demands of Salvador's middle sector. The only military officer in the Menéndez cabinet was National Defense Minister General Fidel Cristino Garay. Other members included medical doctors who were among the opposition leadership: Julio Enrique Avila, Joaquin Parada Aparicio, Hector Escobar Serrano, and Hermogenes Alvarado. The new administration granted complete political amnesty, released all political prisoners, granted free speech and press, and put out the welcome mat for political exiles. The government also announced that free elections would soon be conducted to choose a constituent assembly to modify the 1886 constitution. These actions contributed to the American belief that the Menéndez administration enjoyed popular support. The press, with its new freedom, was effervescent, but not vitriolic as had been expected. Two large demonstrations, on May 23 and 28, before the national palace provided a sense of confidence in the government.[15]

The new environment also provided the opportunity for political parties to organize. Eight new groups were founded. All advocated constitutional government and varying degrees of social reform. The chief of the State Department's Caribbean and Central American Affairs Division, William P. Cochran, judged two of the parties to be potentially significant for the scheduled October presidential election. The *Unión Democrática*, under the leadership of Dr. Arturo Romero, represented the rising middle sector. He was believed to be the only civilian capable of defeating a military presidential candidate. The other significant party was the *Partido del Pueblo Salvadoreño*, led by José Cipriano Castro. It offered a far-reaching social program that appealed strongly to the working classes. Considered of lesser significance were the *Social Republicans*, headed by Napoleon Vierra Altamarino, and the *Partido Unificación Social Democrática*, led by General Salvador Castaneda Castro.[16]

Behind these indications of political calm were signs of strain. Reportedly, some of the army's younger officers were engaged in conspiracies to overthrow the government. The church, which had supported the overthrow of Hernández, now appeared determined to take advantage of its newfound prestige and press for restoration of some of its privileges that were guaranteed in the 1886 constitution. Church officials publicly expressed concern about social issues, an indication they sought political leadership over the masses. The labor movement was split. The *Unión Nacional de Trabajadores* (UNT) called for conciliation committees among workers' groups to draft a labor code, and the *Agrupación Unión Nacional de Trabajadores* (ANT) advocated strikes to improve pay and working conditions. Finally, Menéndez was continually criticized for not having dismissed government officials appointed by former President Hernández.[17]

Communism emerged as an issue in June 1944, when Costa Rican Communist party Secretary Arnold Ferrato visited Salvador, apparently for "the purpose of organizing communist elements." He advised Alejandro Dougoberto Marroquín, who was deemed to be "the most capable Marxist" in Salvador, to imitate the Costa Rican communist tactic of forming a coalition with progressive groups. This would require the support of Romero's *Unión Democrática*, which had attracted the "progressive capitalists, professionals, students" and laborers from the UNT, an alliance that threatened the status quo. The union's social and economic proposals were regarded as "exotic and dangerous" by the capitalists, who believed communism threatened "the existing semi-feudal order of things." In their desire for a strong central government, the capitalists, mostly coffee growers, reportedly established a large fund for use by a conservative candidate to combat leftist ideologies. The church also campaigned against communism. Yet, the elite's fear of communism did not abate. In late August the Salvadoran government expressed its concern over the communist influence in the Romero camp.

Ambassador Thurston did not share the belief that communism threatened the country. He described the UNT's social program as "merely Mexican." Although the communist issue did contribute to Romero's decline in popularity, it was not enough to deny him an election victory according to Caribbean and Central American Affairs Division Chief Cochran. Given this political situation, however, Thurston expected the military to act. In addition to its dislike of communism and Romero's political liberalism, the military admired Argentina's survival without U.S. recognition and was confident Salvador could do the same.[18] The six short months of political freedom only brought into conflict Salvador's various long-suppressed self-interest groups.

On the morning of October 21, 1944, El Salvador was confronted with a fait accompli. At 7:00 A.M. President Menéndez resigned for "health reasons" and an hour later was replaced by third presidential delegate

Colonel Osmín Aguirre y Salinas after the national assembly declared the first two presidential delegates ineligible for office. The new U.S. ambassador to San Salvador, John F. Simmons, believed the coup was engineered by Aguirre in collaboration with the younger army officers. Aguirre apparently convinced the coffee growers that his group was a reasonable alternative to the "increasingly radical and communist support" Romero had gained. Aguirre's cabinet reflected this military-landowner connection. Posts were given to either military officers, who shared the Nazi-Fascist ideas of Aguirre, or the older reactionary landowners, who were "afraid to give a man what he deserves because he might ask for more." To bolster its position, the new government imposed martial law and jailed upward of 3,000 people.[19]

In reality, the military and elite were fearful of a Romero election victory. His *Partido Democrático Unión* represented the articulate middle sector, which consisted of business and professional groups whose "vision extends beyond the need of order and security by the old methods of violence and military dictatorships familiar in the history of Central America," Simmons cabled Washington. But the ambassador noted that the disorganized opposition was incapable of bringing Aguirre down and that his continuance in power would encourage the crushing of liberalism elsewhere in Central America. For the moment, the United States withheld recognition of the Aguirre regime.[20]

Political calm existed in the country through the remainder of 1944. Simmons, however, did not believe that Aguirre had firm control of the government. He was pressured by the older military officers, distrusted by the elite, and unwanted by the middle sector. His political isolation was evident by his failure to persuade seventy-year-old landowner Francisco Dumas to serve as provisional president. Salvador's economy also worsened. Under such conditions, Simmons anticipated a coup at any moment, but not within the "well worn pattern" of Central American squabbles for power among different factions. Rather, he believed that "the present struggle is one in which idealism and the broader social concepts actually play an important role" and the demands were not exaggerated or unreasonable.[21] He understood the need for both political reform and satisfactory answers to the plight of the Salvador masses. His perceptions of the political dynamics were quite accurate, even though he had arrived in the country only one month prior to the coup. A Princeton graduate, he had joined the State Department in 1916 and had served in Europe and Latin America.

Amidst the political uncertainty and economic adversity, Aguirre continued with plans to hold elections on January 14–16, 1945. Leading opposition candidates Arturo Romero, Antonio Claramont, and Napoleon Viera Altamirano withdrew from the race in anticipation of a government-controlled election. Claramont and Romero issued instructions to their followers to avoid the polls. Only the administration's candidate, General Salvador Castaneda Castro, remained. Without opposition, he received a reported 312,754 votes, more than a third of Salvador's male population! Cynically, coffee grower Carlos Menéndez Castro remarked to a U.S. embassy staffer that only 60,000 votes were cast, but the inflated figures were used to show Castaneda's "hold on the popular will of the country." A confident Castaneda proclaimed a general amnesty on March 3 and invited political exiles to return home. To Simmons, the electoral farce was no demonstration of the popular will. Reluctantly, the United States extended diplomatic recognition on February 19, 1945.[22]

As scheduled, Castaneda was inaugurated on March 1, 1945. Simmons did not believe that the president possessed the qualities and abilities the office required and recognized that his only support came from the coffee growers and a major portion of the army. His Cabinet reflected this makeup. Reportedly, skilled and experienced civilians refused to serve and Castaneda was forced to select men who had been previously "aloof from politics" and of mediocre quality. The supreme court appointments were associated with the Hernández regime. Under such conditions, Simmons maintained that the opposition would need to keep a low profile, for any activity on its part would only solidify the army factions. A strategy of quiescence might lull the administration into a false sense of security and then into factional strife.[23] In less than a year, Salvador had come full circle. The overthrow of Hernández in May 1944 stirred hope for political reform, but the Castaneda administration gave no promise of providing it.

The outward political calm was only superficial, according to Simmons, because of the "subterranean activities" of the various military and civilian opposition groups, who themselves were factionalized.[24] During its first nineteen months, March 1945 to September 1946, the administration was confronted with intermittent revolts and constant political crisis. Throughout, Castaneda attempted to conciliate all factions: the army, landowners, and liberals.

The army was clearly split. Some of the older officers followed the leadership of National Defense Minister Peña Trejo in support of Castaneda. Others followed former President Aguirre, who desired to return to power. In both instances, the older officers wanted to maintain their traditional influential role in politics. The younger ones, led by Assistant Chief of Staff Major Oscar Osorio, realized that "history is changing and that El Salvador cannot continue indefinitely as a more or less disguised military dictatorship."[25] Each military faction exerted pressure on Castaneda.

From the outset of his presidency, Castaneda appeared determined to eliminate the political influence of the coffee growers, their Agrarian party, and its leader, Carlos Menéndez Castro. Crafty and intelligent, Menéndez Castro allied himself with the Aguirre military faction against the administration. Ambassador Simmons felt that the conflict was the most important one confronting Castaneda in the early days of his administration. After refusing a diplomatic post in Brazil, Menéndez Castro was ordered out of the country in July 1945. His departure for Mexico City temporarily discouraged the coffee growers, but it did not eliminate the possibility of some political disturbance, Cochran opined.[26]

American officials in San Salvador sensed a contradictory attitude among the liberals. On the one hand, they appeared willing to give President Castaneda a chance to succeed in establishing some sense of national unity, but, on the other hand, they were unwilling to accept his conciliation offers. During Castaneda's first nineteen months, the liberals remained on the political sidelines, biding their time before taking an active part in politics. They continually expressed their dissatisfaction with Castaneda's conservative policies despite his continued efforts to bring them into his administration, overtures opposed by all military factions. By August 1946, the administration had decided that the liberals were a real threat to its existence.[27] Thus, all three elements—military, landowners, and liberals—exerted constant pressure on the regime.

Castaneda's political plight was worsened by the nation's continued economic woes: inflation, shortages of basic foodstuffs, depletion of the national treasury, and unsatisfactory working conditions. The only legislative act of 1945 lowered the coffee export tax, but this adversely affected the national treasury. Retail merchants charged whatever the sugar market would bear despite government-controlled wholesale prices. Investigations in May and June 1945 revealed that the economy minister was keeping portions of the customs duties for his own use. Scandals and graft were so common, Ambassador Simmons reported, that they were "too numerous to detail individually."[28]

The much-maligned Castaneda administration survived several crises during its first nineteen months. Three confrontations with the military alone occurred in 1945. The first was an unsuccessful coup in April 1945 that involved the president's son-in-law, Artilio Garcia Prieto, ten army officers, and several moderate liberals. Little publicity was given to the incident because of Prieto's involvement, and he subsequently left the country secretly, but with the president's knowledge. More significant was the second attempt to oust Castaneda in June. Led by former President Aguirre, generals Francisco Emilio Ponce and Peña Trejo, and Major Oscar Osorio, eighty-three younger officers demanded that Castaneda make several cabinet and constitutional changes. They insisted on the ouster of Adolfo Perez Menéndez, Efrain Jovel, and Dario Flores from the Cabinet. The group also contended that the president should be divested of control over the army and that it ought to be vested in a military general staff, whose power should be raised to the presidential level. Castaneda refused and ordered the arrest and deportation to Guatemala and Honduras of those responsible.

The third confrontation with the military came in September 1945. Castaneda wanted to replace Police Chief Dario Flores with Chief of the Presidential Staff António Castaneda. Flores refused to relinquish his post, and instead suggested that Castaneda resign. Only maneuvering within the army saved the president. Both the Aguirre and Osorio factions preferred Castaneda over Flores. The landowners were aligned with the Aguirre military faction, which was responsible for Cabinet changes in June 1946. One rumor was that the old Hernández groups were coalescing with the disgruntled landowners.[29] Singularly or in combination with the landowners, the military remained a dominant force in politics.

Several crises involving the liberals contributed to placing Castaneda squarely in the conservative camp. According to him, an alleged "left wing plot" was "nipped in the bud" on July 24, 1945. The government accused liberal Augustín Alfaro and his followers of engineering the aborted plan, but failed to prove the allegation. Rumors of a revolt by the younger army officers, favored by the liberals in July 1946, made the administration nervous enough to arrest and interrogate several lieutenants. The same two groups planned a coup for August 4, 1946, but the government learned of it in advance and suppressed it.

Liberal pressure peaked in August and September 1946, when a campaign against the supreme court was launched. It originated with university students, but gained support from the middle sector. The protesters charged the court with being reactionary and associated with the old Hernández regime. A massive demonstration on August 24 forced all the justices to resign, and they were replaced by a group of undistinguished lawyers not identified with either liberals or conservatives. Locally, it was described as "a court of non-entities."

Castaneda further succumbed to liberal pressure on September 21, when he changed three of his Cabinet posts: Foreign Minister Hector Escobar Serrano was replaced by Manuel Castro Ramirez; Interior Minister Juan Benjamin Escobar by General Manuel António Castaneda; and Economy Minister Napoleon Viera Altamirano by Max Patricio Brannon. Although these replacements satisfied the liberals' immediate demands, Ambassador Simmons noted that none of the political groups were satisfied. The conservatives believed they had lost government influence, the army was disgruntled without control of the Defense Ministry; and the liberals were disappointed at the shallowness of their victories.[30] Castaneda's reprieve was only temporary.

Two days later, on September 23, 1946, a seven-day general strike beleaguered the nation and threatened the collapse of the government. The causes were varied: continued protest against the supreme court by the university students, a strike by bakers and textile workers that resulted in sympathetic labor demonstrations, police brutality against labor demonstrators, and the steady condemnation of government officials. In response, the government imposed a state of siege and martial law. When the strike ended on September 30, martial law was lifted, but the state of siege remained, mostly for the purpose of government control of the press, censorship, and the restriction of public meetings. An estimated one hundred persons were deported for their role in the strike.

Castaneda emerged in a stronger position, but his dependence upon the military was more visible. The Cabinet changes announced on October 14 reflected the army's belief that Castaneda demonstrated "tendencies too liberal for their tastes." Two generals, Mauro Espinola

Castro and Manuel António Castaneda, were appointed respectively as Interior and Defense ministers. The civilians—José António Quiroz, Max Patricio Brannon, Ronulfo Castro, and Trinidad Romero—lacked public stature, but received their posts in an effort to curtail political strife. Simmons observed that Castaneda's increased dependence upon the military meant that Salvador was "settling down into the more usual Central American pattern of the past."

That the nation was tired after nearly two years of political violence was evident by the absence of enthusiasm during the celebration of its 400th anniversary during the period November 3–11, 1946. By the year's end, antigovernment activity had ceased, but not because of public confidence in the administration, Simmons concluded. Rather, this was brought about by the increased presence of the military. A superficial calm permeated the political atmosphere. Castaneda enjoyed no widespread popularity, and his administration was marked by indecision and vacillation.[31]

Since the fall of the Hernández regime in August 1944, Ambassador Simmons believed that the inarticulate laboring masses were gaining a class consciousness and were becoming more aware of the rights and privileges due them. Even during periods of apparent prosperity and calm, he observed their discontent with the status quo. Events during the first half of Castaneda's term illustrated the ambassador's point.

A series of strikes or threats of strikes in the industrialized sector took place from mid-November through December 1945. Well organized and without violence, they affected the cotton mills, hemp factories, and railroads. The government mediated an end to the strikes, and labor gained improvements in wages and working conditions. When a strike threatened San Salvador's light and power plant, the government, by decree, banned strikes in public utilities, which were defined as "any corporate or private enterprise which the government considered essential to the economy." Labor unrest threatening agricultural production was described by landowners as "radicalism and communism," an opinion not shared by U.S. embassy officials in San Salvador.[32] Labor made progress by striking and gaining benefits in the manufacturing sector, but the obstinate landowners still presented an enormous obstacle.

At the time of Castaneda's presidential election, in January 1945, a constituent assembly also had been chosen. Castaneda deputies outnumbered those representing the Aguirre faction 42–5, which meant the assembly would be subservient to the new president's wishes. Its potential, however, was unlimited because it could modify the constitution "any way it may see fit, as well as declare all previous constitutions null and void."[33] For several months, the body worked in secret. Almost all socioeconomic groups, from the laboring masses to the landholding and business elite, feared the results. On November 30, 1945, all the country's newspapers carried a surprise government statement, without comment, regarding the assembly's decision to continue the 1886 constitution with certain modifications.

One of the most important of these was the reestablishment of the legal position of the church, the implication being that it would control public education. The supreme court's power was enhanced by granting it the right to judge the constitutionality of legislative laws and rulings. The people were empowered to petition the court on constitutional issues. The state was authorized to confiscate property without prior indemnification. Ambassador Simmons observed that adverse reaction was confined to the provisos regarding the church only. Otherwise, these constitutional changes went almost unnoticed.[34]

Potentially more important were the modifications giving the state sweeping powers over labor. The constitution's section entitled "Family and Life" called for minimum wages, control of child and women labor, social security, regulation of the hours worked per day, construction of rural and urban housing, and promotion of social welfare institutions. The details remained to be defined, but these generalizations represented government recognition of the needs of the underprivileged. As expected, landowners and businessmen criticized these provisos. Although the critics agreed that Castaneda had influenced the assembly's work, Ambassador Simmons applauded the results for being more responsive to public opinion.[35]

For the two years following the fall of the Hernández regime, President Castaneda piloted a ship through unstable political waters. The older army officers and landowners were in constant conflict with the liberals, who demanded political reform at the expense of the elite. The limited expression on behalf of labor's needs brought harsh reaction from the elite, which branded social reforms as communistic. Under constant pressure, Castaneda failed to conciliate all sides. His political weakness only served to increase the military's influence over his administration.

Thus, at midpoint in his term, Simmons noted that the president lacked any strong group upon which he could rely in case of crisis. The younger and older officers were growing further apart. The liberals were casting about for a rallying point. The landowners preferred the status quo. Castaneda survived, Simmons believed, only because each group preferred to oust him politically rather than "assassinate a man of . . . essentially mild and inoffensive character."[36]

The nation's political atmosphere was relatively calm from 1947 to 1949, largely because of a government-imposed state of siege, which kept public and newspaper discussion of issues to a minimum. Yet, Castaneda was beset by several serious problems. Government expenditures reached $24 million, a staggering figure by Salvadoran standards. Such a debt created constant fear of a tax increase. Continued inflation and alleged government graft, combined with the suppression of civil liberties associated with the state of siege, provided potential crisis situations. These problems may have been offset by apparent prosperity, which contributed to a sense of political stability. For whatever reasons, a general apathy toward politics prevailed, as was evident in the January 1947 congressional elections. Under censorship, the press failed to discuss the elections, and in many outlying areas people were even unaware of them. Amidst a low voter turnout and without any opposition, Castaneda's *Partido Unificación Social Democrática's* slate of candidates continued their control of the legislature.[37]

Despite the appearance of political calm, public apathy, and apparent prosperity, rumors of coup attempts continued. Castaneda's reliance upon the older conservative army officers was under constant threat from other groups. According to the embassy's third secretary, Overton G. Ellis, the wealthy landowners and farmers turned to former President Aguirre for leadership because their own spokesman, Menéndez Castro, was in exile, residing in California. A group of "high quartel chiefs" in the military wanted to place Colonel Rodolfo Morales in the presidential palace. Reportedly involved were middle-grade and younger officers who showed reactionary tendencies.

Finally, there were the liberals, who were traced to the attempted coup in April 1944 and the general strike a month later. This group remained split into two factions. One consisted of civilians of liberal persuasion and democratic beliefs who were estimated to include some 25 percent of the landowners, 80 percent of the doctors, engineers, architects, lawyers, and the like, and 50 percent of the Chamber of Commerce membership. The more militant liberals were organized in cellular form and included members of the middle class, skilled labor, and scattered groups of the elder elements of the peasantry. Associated with both of the broad factions were university students and all the young army officers on inactive duty. A plot to overthrow the government in July 1947 combined a group of inactive officers led by Major Humberto Peneda Villarta and militant liberals headed by lawyer Ricardo Arbizu. Government knowledge of the plan thwarted its realization.[38]

American policymakers held varied views of Salvadoran politics. Ambassador Simmons concluded that, though the army remained loyal to Castaneda, it was so split that officers spent most of their time watching each other. Furthermore, Simmons noted, the military was pacified by pay increases and unchecked graft. The constant shifting of personnel hampered possible centralization. Central America and Panama Affairs Divison country specialist Murat Williams believed that Castaneda's increased dependence upon small cliques of officers contributed to the republic's "lapsing definitely back into its former status of military dictatorship."[39]

Embassy secretary Ellis maintained that neither of the liberal factions was capable of action at any time, an opinion not shared by others. Ambassador Simmons believed that the liberals were not only badly divided, but also lacked leadership and that many of them preferred the financial gains that were possible by joining the Castaneda circle. When new Ambassador Albert Nufer arrived in San Salvador in the late summer of 1947, he found it difficult to define a liberal. He believed that Central Americans of this persuasion opposed a military government, but in Salvador they required military assistance to change governments. For those honest and sincere liberals, devoted to general social betterment, Nufer believed that their criticism had been quieted by the work of Culture Minister Ronulfo Castro, who had undertaken successful projects in health, sanitation, and education.[40] Nufer's perception was similar to the Cuban model, the country he had just left.

Historically, the dominant force in Salvadoran politics had been the large landowning coffee growers, who in alliance with the military were a major force in any noncommunist revolutionary activity. Provided Castaneda did not move on two sensitive issues affecting them—tax increases and improved labor conditions—this wealthy class saw no need for change, Ambassador Nufer explained. Because high coffee produc-

tion more than offset the mounting cost of living, its income was not
threatened. When the government increased the coffee export tax in
October 1947, many people in this class called for a change in government. Castaneda quieted the situation with a Cabinet shake-up. By the
appointment of new Agricultural Minister Francisco Orellana Valdez,
whose qualifications were minimal but who was described as "one hundred percent farmer," he further conciliated the coffee growers.[41]

The incessant rivalries and maneuverings of these various political
groups—liberals, military, and wealthy—was nothing more than an "ins
vs. outs" struggle, concluded embassy secretary Leslie A. Squires.[42] Such
an interpretation gave little indication that political or social reform
would be forthcoming in the near future. Squires's opinion may have
been influenced by his lack of Latin American experience. He had joined
the State Department in 1942 and served only in Europe prior to his
appointment to El Salvador in 1946.

In the country's politics, its largest socioeconomic element, the laboring class, was ignored. Yet the modified 1886 constitution of November
1946 contained broad statements about its needs. In January 1947 Castaneda took the opportunity to flesh out those generalizations with a
specific Labor Code. A five-man committee was appointed, consisting of
two government representatives, one each from the organized industrial
and commercial workers' groups, and one representing employers. None
were of outstanding caliber because Castaneda's advisers did not "relish
the idea of any really honest and able men" getting too close to him. For
the next five months, the committee worked with no apparent haste.
Castaneda showed no real inclination to push the issue. In late October
1947, he promised that a new Labor Code was forthcoming and hoped it
would be in place before the next president took office, two years hence!
No code was adopted.

By April 1948, Ambassador Nufer had noted a rise in resentment by
the laboring masses against the upper class. "Most intelligent Salvadorans
are conscious of the discontent," he continued, but "there has been no
effective effort in the past year to alleviate the conditions of those who are
existing at the base subsistence levels."[43] The elite, still the dominant
political force, remained opposed to change.

The wealthy landowners and old line military officers branded as
communist any effort directed toward the workers. The Communist
party was outlawed in Salvador, and U.S. policymakers saw no evidence

of any extensive underground organization. The conditions favoring "the development and spread of the communist doctrine" were apparent in the disparity of wealth, Nufer explained, and therefore it would be "overly naive not to assume that there is some communist agitation going on undercover" and that help was being received from abroad. The ambassador concluded that the communists had so cleverly concealed their efforts that they defied detection.[44]

Other officials shared Nufer's opinion that the "semi-feudal economy" made the country ripe for social revolution, but disagreed on communist exploitation. Embassy secretary Squires believed that inasmuch as Salvador was not an area of importance to the Soviet Union, any local communist activity would receive little outside assistance. Within Salvador, he noted several factors that militated against the growth of a communist movement. The typical citizen was apolitical, and, with few exceptions, people entered politics solely for financial or personal advantage, as was illustrated by the historic absence of political parties. Rather, politics represented a struggle between "various military and monetary groups" that negated allegiance to any political ideology.

Given "his lack of political development and his disinterest in political theory, the Salvadoran may not be ready for social revolution," as it appeared on the surface, Squires added. The nation's social structure was also inimical with communist influence. To be successful, outside forces would need to neutralize the allied wealthy coffee interests and military establishment. Squires deemed this to be an impossible task. The middle class, small in size and for the most part related by blood to the elite, was considered to be unimportant. Economically, Squires believed that the "trickle down" exerted a positive effect upon the worker, whose food, clothing, and shelter were adequate. Although these necessities were at the subsistence level, "by his standards [they represent] as much, if not more, than he has found customary in the past." Squires concluded that the country's political character, social structure, and economic prosperity negated the growth of communism there.[45]

Central America and Panama Affairs Division political adviser Robert E. Wilson rejected Squires's conclusions. Wilson, who had joined the Foreign Service in 1936, possessed a better knowledge of Latin America than did Squires because he had previously served in Argentina and Bolivia. He accepted Squires's opinion that the low level of communist activity was primarily attributable to the lack of outside influence. Otherwise, the conditions that had provoked the 1932 communist revolt remained. This made the country a fertile field for communist activity. Appropriate leadership could exploit the situation. Wilson took issue with Squires's allegation that the elite's alliance with the military guaranteed the status quo. Rather, as in Czarist Russia in 1917 and in Salvador before, such political situations contributed to the growth of communism.

Wilson further noted that Salvador's middle sector, consisting of government employees, clerks, teachers, merchants, artisans, journalists, students, and small farmers, was also tied to the lower classes. Although small in size, this group provided potential leadership, particularly because of the absence of traditional political parties. The middle class was capable of recognizing communism and explaining it. In a country where *personalismo* was the rule, politicians spoke with men in the street who accepted or rejected their ideology. In such an atmosphere, Wilson reasoned that "if the majority of the people . . . got the idea they really want communism, they have the power and know-how to achieve it." Wilson also countered Squires's notion that "trickle down" economics had benefited the lower classes. If prosperity had been transmitted in the form of better education, living conditions, food, clothing, and shelter, "the country would not be so receptive to a radical political philosophy," Wilson concluded. Unlike Squires, he believed that Salvador was easy prey for communist exploitation.[46]

Events at the Bogotá Conference in March 1948 momentarily raised the communist specter in Salvador, though the country had shown a general lack of interest in the conference when it opened. The assassination of Jorge Gaitán and subsequent violence in Colombia, however, gave the Salvadoran *finquistas* a "bad case of the jitters" and an increasing awareness that "it can happen here," observed Ambassador Nufer. Rumors about communist activity increased markedly, but there still was no evidence of an organized communist movement. The leftist-leaning labor union, UFT, gained greater prestige and was far more active than its 400–500 dues-paying members could sustain. The government became more suspect of the union, as it did a group of intellectuals led by university professor Ricardo Gallardo and the university student organization AGEUS. Both reportedly espoused communist thought.

Although the nation remained under a state of siege, making it almost impossible for communists to operate, Ambassador Nufer did not doubt that some communist-leaning individuals were fanning the flames of discontent. He cautioned his superiors in Washington, however, that all the local capitalists branded as communists any person or group that sought to improve social conditions. Until those conditions improved, the communist threat remained. Nufer concluded that "many of the reported communists or fellow travelers in El Salvador would probably be considered left of center in other countries."[47] According to the consensus of American opinion, no current communist threat existed in Salvador, only the conditions that created an appeal for this doctrine.

The modified constitution, announced in December 1945, stipulated a four-year presidential term. This was commonly interpreted to mean that a presidential election would take place in January 1949, which may have contributed to the altered opposition tactics after 1946. Rather than concerning itself with bringing down the administration by force, this group concentrated on capturing the presidency by election. In a country that lacked a history of political parties, several persons appeared to be potential presidential candidates. American officials in San Salvador identified several of these, but none of them seemed to have broad-based support.

One was Interior Minister José Angel Avendáno, whose 1946 campaign for reelection as mayor of San Salvador had been blocked by President Castaneda. His subsequent appointment to the Cabinet was a conciliatory gesture by the president. Unidentified sectors of the military and business community reportedly supported Avendáno. Another prospect was former economy minister and 1944 presidential aspirant Napoleon Vierra Altamirano, who called for a "democratic alliance" to support his candidacy. U.S. officials in San Salvador did not believe he could muster a sufficient following.

Supporters of General Peña Trejo advanced his name in early 1948. His alleged ties to the local labor movement and administration charges that Nicaraguan dictator Anastasio Somoza was contributing to his financial coffers diminished Trejo's chances. Other possibilities included Economy Minister Max Brannon, believed to be one of the nation's best politicians; Agriculture Minister Francisco Orellana, who was linked to some of the army's dissident younger officers; and, latecomer Colonel Asinso Menéndez, who appeared to be popular among the masses, but was viewed as a political opportunist seeking personal gains only.[48] None of these aspirants, however, had support from the administration or its main props: the landowners and the military.

Most prominent of the prospective candidates was Osmin Aguirre, who shifted his tactics from potential revolutionary to presidential candidate in early 1947. In January and February he demonstrated that he had significant backing from the older officers in the army and national guard, who were discontent with Castaneda's inefficiency. The wealthy capitalists and coffee growers also favored Aguirre's candidacy because they wanted firm leadership over Castaneda's vacillation in order to have peace and order among the laboring classes. The younger military officers and civilian liberals disliked Aguirre because of his association with the older conservative elements, but they lacked enough power to prevent him from becoming the major opposition candidate to challenge the "official" presidential nominee, whoever that might be. In late 1947 Aguirre's political strength was estimated to be so strong that rumors persisted to the effect that Castaneda wanted him removed from the country. Beginning in January 1948, Aguirre campaign buttons and handbills began to appear in San Salvador, much to the administration's dislike. By late May 1948, three months before becoming the Social Democrat's presidential candidate and the official opening of the campaign, Aguirre spoke confidently of an election victory.[49]

The search for an "official" candidate began in mid-1947, when Castaneda reaffirmed his intention not to remain in office beyond inauguration day, March 1, 1949, but he hoped "to have an active voice" in naming his successor. The army rejected Castaneda's suggestion that Culture Minister Ronulfo Castro, also the president's cousin, become the official candidate. Claiming support from the "honest members of the military" and against the president's advice, Castro advanced his own candidacy. Ambassador Nufer dismissed him as a serious prospect because the coffee growers disliked his liberal views on social legislation and his idealism would diminish his force as an administrator.[50]

President Castaneda suggested another cousin, General Mauro Espinola Castro, who suffered from several handicaps. His previous association with former dictator Hernández caused general concern. His alcoholism raised questions about his ability to function normally. On the positive side, he had repaired his differences with the church over his divorce, and he enjoyed the backing of the younger officers allied to exiled Major Oscar Osorio. Also, Espinola seemed to be acceptable to a segment of the coffee growers because he was the candidate least likely to disturb their position. But he never received the administration's official blessing.[51]

The presidential campaign opened in October 1948. Despite Ambassador Nufer's prediction to the contrary, the campaign was free of violence, but also absent was an "effective and articulate feeling either among the rich or poor, which could develop into a truly popular movement to bring about a change in government." The opposition remained disunited, the candidates pursuing their own campaigns. The coffee growers and businessmen were prospering and it was unlikely they would participate in a political venture that would disturb their situation. As one businessman remarked "Let this fellow [Castaneda] continue if he wants to . . . we are just as well off if there is no change."[52]

The first speculation that Castaneda intended to remain in office came in November 1947, when he took to the countryside to counter Aguirre's popularity. This resulted in persistent rumors that he intended to continue in office beyond the legal term. By August 1948, the rumors had become so widespread that they seemed to have an air of authenticity. Some believed that Castaneda engineered the rumors as part of a scheme to test public opinion on *continuismo*. Although he declined to comment on the subject, he took time to proclaim his own achievements: "Behind me I leave schools, higher salaries, roads, hospitals, electric light and markets. Behind me are no stains of blood, no widows, no orphans." Handbills bearing the same adulations were distributed throughout the capital. The failure to designate Espinola as the "official" candidate, even after the campaign opened in October 1948, heightened speculation that Castaneda would continue. Aguirre's apparent strength may have encouraged Castaneda to stay on by legal means or otherwise.[53]

Talk that the national assembly would alter the constitution to extend the presidential term from four to six years began in August and continued throughout the campaign. Discussion of this subject had intensified by December because of the assembly's failure to fix an election date. The rumors proved to be true. On December 13, 1948, President Castaneda convened a special session of the national assembly, which rushed through legislation calling for a constituent assembly to consider the legality of extending Castaneda's presidential term an additional two years.

This maneuver was the catalyst for a military coup. During the siesta hour on December 14, a group of five young army officers headed by Manuel J. Córdova ousted Castaneda from office. The former president was arrested, and held for trial for "flagrant violations of the laws of the land and misuse of the national treasury." Subsequently, Aguirre was arrested and jailed. The coffee growers, caught by surprise, failed to react. The populace, unaffected by the coup, returned to normal activities on December 15.[54]

Córdova quickly formed a junta of three military officers, including himself, and two civilians. The other officers were Major Oscar Boloñas, who had been in the Defense Ministry, and Oscar Osorio, who immediately returned from Mexico. The two civilians were highly respected lawyers, Reynaldo Galindo Pohl and Humberto Costa. Designated as the Council of Revolutionary Government, the junta abrogated the existing constitution and promised to call soon for a constituent assembly to write a new document. In an apparent appeal to the coffee growers, the junta also promised to suppress communism throughout Salvador.[55]

Ambassador Nufer described the coup as "strictly a local show," which was justified given Castaneda's intention to remain in office. Nufer believed that the council was fairly well balanced between the political left and right and that it had the support of Salvadorans from all walks of life. However, he dismissed as overly optimistic the popular view that the junta "would usher in a period of honesty and integrity."[56]

Córdova's nepotism and alleged leftist leanings caused a split in the junta. Most flagrant was the appointment of his father-in-law, Alberto Ildefonso Castellanos, to the presidency of the government-owned Mortgage Bank, and his brother, Major Carlos Córdova, as subdirector of the Military School. Alleged leftists Raul Ayana and Julio Eduardo Jiménez were appointed to lesser government posts, and reportedly Córdova permitted unidentified communists to return from abroad. He was forced to resign on January 4, 1949, in order "to equalize the civilian and military elements in the government."

Oscar Osorio emerged as the leader of the four remaining junta members. Ambassador Nufer expected that Osorio would broaden the junta's political base beyond the university professors and students, professionals, and labor groups. A week after Córdova's resignation, this occurred when San Salvador's most influential businessmen hosted a reception for the junta. Such support, Nufer noted, stabilized and strengthened the government, but also caused public speculation that some secret "mutual understanding" was reached between the two groups. For the next four months, the junta attempted to steer a middle course, as evidenced by the elimination of extreme leftist and rightist elements from government circles. Ambassador Nufer noted that communist influence was lacking in the junta, whose actions were credited with restoring national calm.[57]

The junta, however, was not without opposition or problems. It appeared to be nervous about several rumored plots. Nufer believed that the concern was legitimate because several persons were willing to supply funds to back a coup. Followers of Castaneda and Aguirre were frustrated by the loss of political prominence, and within the military ambitious officers awaited an opportunity to gain power.[58]

A major concern to the population was the convening of the promised constituent assembly. Critics charged that the junta did not want to do so, fearing a loss of power. Its members were afraid that a constituent assembly might provide a radical document, but were split on how to deal with the problem. One element proposed canceling the decree calling for an assembly, and the other wanted only to modify the 1945 document. Nufer attributed the junta's delay to public disinterest in the subject by late August 1949.

Only the coffee growers and businessmen continued to express concern, but largely over potential nationalistic economic provisions. The delay, coupled with the junta's failure to write an Electoral Code, caused Nufer to speculate that it would be at least mid-1950 before Salvador's political process would be restored.[59]

An air of excitement gripped the nation on September 5, 1949, when the junta permitted the registration of political parties with the Interior Ministry, provided each one identified 2,000 members from five different departments. Such a requirement, along with the government's continued ban on political activity and the traditional practice of following caudillos, caused Nufer to doubt that any nationwide parties could be formed. He also dismissed the notion that the decree was intended to eliminate the caudillos from politics and prevent extremist groups, such as the "clandestine communist party," from coming forward. Rather, Nufer believed that the decree further indicated the junta's determination to delay the convening of the constituent assembly or to hold presidential elections.[60]

The first political party to register was the *Partido Revolutionario de*

Unificación Democrática (PRUD), in late October. It was formed by Osorio and Galindo Pohl, both of whom had resigned from the junta, and Humberto Romero, one of Salvador's original liberals. The support base included the army, government workers, students, professionals, and the bulk of labor—enough to be successful in any election. Osorio, PRUD's standard bearer, proposed "to balance the needs of capital and labor, assuring a genuine social harmony by means of equality and justice." He described critics of the current government as wealthy power seekers. George P. Shaw, who was appointed as ambassador to El Salvador in June 1949, believed that PRUD provided the junta with confidence to hold elections for both the constituent assembly and the president.[61]

By the year's end, five other political parties had been formed: *Nacional Republicano, Constitucional Demócrata, Demócrata Salvadordo, Social Democrática Independiente,* and *Acción Renovadora*. Each called for a return to constitutional government before any presidential election were held. Chargé d'affaires William A. Wieland described the opposition as "a pack of hound dogs milling around to rediscover a lost scent. All the political groups know well what they are after, but none seems to know how to find it." PRUD swept to victory in the March 1950 elections and remained as Salvador's dominant political party for the next ten years.[62] During his six-year administration, Osorio oversaw significant social advances, including urban housing, legislation on labor unions, and expanded social security. But the military remained the predominant political force.

Since the beginning of the twentieth century, U.S. officials had perceived Salvador as a relatively stable, though dictatorial, government. An alliance between the military and the landowning elite had dominated the political process at the expense of the middle and lower sectors. The events of April and May 1944 that brought down the Hernández regime demonstrated the emergence of the liberal middle sector, comprised of professionals, intellectuals, white-collar groups, and skilled labor.[63] Ambassador Walter Thurston, Consul Overton G. Ellis, and State's Caribbean and Central American Affairs Division Chief William P. Cochran understood this.

Middle sector pressure was largely responsible for the 1945 Cabinet changes. Afterward, liberal pressure for political reform decreased as President Castaneda came to rely upon conservative military officers. Unable to make further gains, the liberals withdrew to the sidelines or contented themselves with personal financial gain by accepting government positions. By 1947, the liberals were in a difficult position, according to Ambassador Nufer. As advocates of political and social reform, they risked military reprisals for wanting to restructure Salvador's system. Yet, to effect change, the liberal middle sector needed military support.

At the start of his administration, Castaneda appeared determined to eliminate the coffee growers' influence, illustrated by the exiling of their leading spokesman, Carlos Menéndez Castro. Cochran correctly predicted that his exile would not diminish the power of the landowners, who now turned to the conservative military officers, headed by Osmín Aguirre. Cabinet changes in 1946 and 1948 reflected the increased sway of the conservative factions over the administration. Ambassador Nufer concluded that Castaneda's political life was safe provided he did not deal with the two most sensitive issues affecting the landowners: raising taxes and improving labor conditions.

According to Ambassador John F. Simmons, the laboring classes gained new public expression after 1944, and some gains were registered in the nation's manufacturing industries. Potentially more important were the sweeping generalizations in the 1945 constitution that granted the government authority to improve labor's lot. Castaneda's promise of a Labor Code never materialized. On account of conservative pressure, he never pushed the issue beyond the establishment of a study committee. The conservative elite labeled as "communistic" any proposals that threatened their economic and social status. Liberal Arturo Romero, for example, who advocated social change, was described as a communist.

Most of the Americans disagreed. Ambassadors Thurston and Nufer, embassy secretary Leslie Squires, and State Department analyst Frederick B. Lyon did not perceive a communist threat. Squires was convinced that, despite the dichotomy of wealth, the laboring class was content with its status and ignorant of political philosophy. Only political adviser Robert E. Wilson believed otherwise. He maintained that the poverty conditions made the country ripe for communist exploitation. After the rioting at Bogotá in 1948, Ambassador Nufer became convinced that a communist underground existed in Salvador, but admittedly could not prove his point.

To American policymakers, the 1944 revolution unleashed forces of political liberalism demanding constitutional and representative government, including free elections. From this perspective, Squires described Salvadoran politics as the "outs" wanting "in." The liberal middle sector, however, sought more than political reform. The 1944 revolution awakened interest in the needs of the laboring classes, but minimal progress was made in meeting them during Castaneda's administration. The Americans failed to perceive the significance of the largest socioeconomic group and did not understand the importance of the middle sector and younger officers rallying behind Oscar Osorio in 1949. The Americans were content with Salvador's outward political tranquillity.

3

Guatemala

SINCE 1931, Guatemala had endured the repressive military dictatorship of Jorge Ubico. The landowners, middle sector, and lower classes were not represented in government. Middle sector opposition to Ubico first appeared in 1941 and erupted in 1944 following the downfall of Hernández in Salvador. Following Ubico's forced resignation in July 1944, a struggle for political power ensued for the next five years. The landowners, in alliance with old line military officers, sought to preserve their privileged status. The middle sector joined forces with the younger military officers to achieve constitutional government. Both groups opposed President-elect Juan José Arévalo, whose social and economic programs for the poor were labeled as communistic. Isolated from the traditional political groups, he increased his reliance upon local communists. From 1944 to 1949, the country moved from the political right to the political left.

The explosive nature of Guatemalan politics in 1944 was caused by several factors. Coffee and bananas accounted for approximately 90 percent of the nation's income. As elsewhere in Central America, the nature of the economy forged two distinct socioeconomic groups: the small, wealthy upper class; and the poverty ridden, illiterate, and inert masses, comprised chiefly of Indians. Politically, this dichotomy meant that the government was controlled by a minority that demonstrated little concern for the general welfare of the people. In practice, politics tended to perpetuate the privileged position of the ruling class and to keep the largest sector of the population politically helpless, which bred in it a sense of hopelessness. The small middle sector was frustrated in its desire for political participation.[1]

Guatemala's political history illustrates the evolution of an elitist government. For 72 of the 104 years since independence in 1839, politics had been dominated by four dictators: Rafael Carrera, Justo Rufino Barrios, Manuel Estrada Cabrera, and, since 1931, Jorge Ubico. Based upon the 1879 constitution, last amended in 1935, Guatemala considered itself a democracy, but was described in 1943, by the U.S. State Department as a "benevolent military dictatorship" under General Ubico. The unicameral chamber of deputies was a "rubber stamp" congress, which met occasionally to approve decree-laws promulgated by Ubico. The national judiciary hesitated to oppose his wishes. Guatemala's twenty-two departments, or states, were administered by a political chief (*jefe político*) who was appointed by Ubico. This official also doubled as military commandant.[2] Central authority characterized governmental administration.

Historically, political parties were unimportant in the country, particularly during military dictatorships. Dictators suppressed the opposition and took complete control of their own parties. Ubico was no exception. Once in power, he outlawed all political parties except his own, the Liberal Progressive, which he controlled. Those not supporting him were eliminated from political participation. Open disagreement often resulted in exile, imprisonment, or execution. Several parties allegedly operated clandestinely, the most important being the Conservative, or Union, party, which represented the landowning upper class.[3]

Despite the government's repressive measures, active opposition began to surface in 1941, when university students cheered the only member of the national assembly voting against the extension of Ubico's term. Subsequently, many of them, picking the name *Esquilaches*, organized a plot against the government. Several of the individuals later played a significant role in the nation's politics: Mario Méndez Montenegro, José Manuel Fortuny, Jorge Luis Arriola, Manuel Galich, Julio César Méndez Montenegro, and Mario Efraín Nájera Farfán.

An antagonistic attitude arose among those who were capable of holding public office but who were doomed to oblivion because their political views differed from those of the administration. In 1943 the Federal Bureau of Investigation reported to Presidential Assistant Harry Hopkins the existence of considerable sentiment against Ubico. He reportedly feared three groups: lawyers, skilled labor, and the Masons. Many of the populace resented the public and private expenditures for the alleged "spontaneous" celebration in Guatemala City on the twelfth anniversary of Ubico's presidency, on February 14, 1943. At the same time, the Division of American Republics assistant chief, Gerald Drew, noted the marked increase in revolt rumors and political tension. To the Americans, the country was threatened by political instability because Ubico's political and military strength had lessened over the years.[4]

The pressures for change did not erupt until 1944, following the downfall of Salvadoran dictator Maximiliano Hernández Martínez. Ambassador Boaz Long believed that Ubico must "realize that every successful revolution in Central America would be likely to give encouragement to the anti-government factions" in Guatemala because of the similarities in political experience. Long's analogy was based upon his lengthy experiences in Latin America. Previously, he had served as minister in El Salvador, Cuba, Nicaragua, and Ecuador. Ubico did not help his own cause by permitting Salvadoran exiles into Guatemala, a departure from the traditional practice of Central American dictators working in close harmony to prevent local disturbances. Although the opposition regarded the welcome mat as a sign of Ubico's weakness, Long did not detect any immediate signs of danger.[5]

In mid-June, 1944 a group of university students demanded the ouster of the dean of their medical school. At first considered an innocuous protest, the incident became the catalyst of events that resulted in Ubico's resignation. The government's capitulation encouraged the students to agitate for further changes. On June 21 they presented the government with a list of twenty-four demands and threatened a sit-down strike if the administration failed to react. In response, Ubico convened the first full Cabinet meeting in thirteen years, where it was decided to suspend certain constitutional rights: right of assembly, freedom of speech and press, protection from illegal arrest, inviolability of correspondence, and freedom from search of domicile. None of these liberties had been practiced during his regime, but some of his advisers considered the action "a political blunder of major importance."[6]

Ambassador Long concurred. The constitutional suspensions converted the student movement into a political issue. Guatemalans who had applauded Ubico for his "efficient and reasonably honest administration" joined others in charging him with the "ruthless suppression of civil liberties and the exercise of despotic repressive measures." Long correctly judged that the students had unleashed latent hostilities that Ubico would not be able to control. Students made good their promise to stay away from classes and not engage in other educational experiences, such as teachers' aides, law court employees, and hospital interns. The presence of police and cavalry limited the scope of a general sit-down strike on June 26 and caused cancellation of a planned demonstration on June 29. The presidential palace was placed under heavy guard, and plans were made for the military's supervision of essential services in case the general strike materialized. The military's continued loyalty, however, gave the impression that the government would "ride out the storm."[7]

Throughout the week, other groups joined with the students in calling for political democratization of the country. A group of prominent lawyers and businessmen presented Ubico with a petition that applauded his record of material progress in the country but called for a repeal of the decree suspending constitutional guarantees and urged restoration of the guaranteed civil liberties. Two additional memorials, one signed by Guatemala City's leading physicians and the other by more than a thousand women of the city's "so called society," protested Ubico's repressive measures and implored him to resign. The Caribbean and Central American Affairs Division assistant chief, William P. Cochran, noted "discreet criticisms of Ubico by younger [military] officers . . . something heretofore unheard of" in Guatemala. Despite the wide surge of protest groups, the opposition lacked central direction because none of its leaders enjoyed popular support, Long observed.[8] Thus, what had begun as a student demand for university reform grew into a call for Ubico's resignation by the upper and middle sectors.

Reportedly, Ubico had told his closest advisers that he would not stay on as Hernández had in Salvador once he had determined that the populace was against him. The first indications that he planned to resign came on June 29, when his personal papers and government confidential files were burned and money was transferred into his wife's account in the Bank of London. Still, Long was surprised when he learned of his resignation. On June 30, at the presidential palace, Long found Ubico "calm but deeply disillusioned and hurt with the realization that the majority of the country was against him." In his public resignation statement, however, Ubico charged that only a minority of people were dissatisfied with his administration and responsible for his resignation. Cochran agreed that the pressure to oust Ubico came from a small group, notably "the upper portion of the pyramid," which included several of the president's closest friends.[9]

Although in high spirits from its victory, the opposition accepted the need to protect Ubico's life and property. Lacking leadership, the opposition also had no choice but to accept a military triumvirate selected by the general staff: Generals Buenaventura Pineda, Eduardo Villigran Areya, and Federico Ponce Vaídes. Guatemalans greeted the change with "restrained jubilation." Ambassador Long said the junta consisted of "relatively innocuous career military officers, none of whom has any antidemocratic background."[10]

Although the junta improved its public image by lifting the suspended constitutional decrees, Long observed a sense of anxiety throughout the capital until July 4, when the national assembly convened to select a provisional president. Public deliberations were suspended because gallery spectators constantly interfered with the deputies' discussions. Reassembling in closed session and protected by the military, the body selected junta strongman Federico Ponce as provisional president. A day later, public disgruntlement disappeared, and it was business as usual for the government. Local newspapers applauded Ponce, who walked the streets freely without the pomp and ceremony that had surrounded Ubico. Ambassador Long optimistically anticipated that the presidential election would be free. U.S. recognition of Ponce came on July 7, largely because of Long's observation that the "change of administration had been carried out without violence and appears to be accepted in Guatemala as in legal form."[11]

Despite the appearance of political calm, Ponce was faced with several sources of potential confrontation. The three major factors involved in the June 1944 crisis were still present: former President Ubico remained in the capital; many of his appointees stayed in office, notably Foreign Minister Carlos Salazar and private secretary Ernesto Rivas; and Ubico's Liberal Progressive party not only maintained its position but also was expected to represent the interim administration. Embassy second secretary William C. Affeld, who had come to Guatemala in 1941 following Far Eastern duty tours, believed that no candidate would be acceptable to this party unless Ponce exercised strong political control and pursued policies favorable to the army, particularly the older generals. Ambassador Long held a similar opinion.[12]

The students also continued to agitate, confident that "as they had succeeded in removing Ubico, they could do the same with Ponce or anybody else" until their demands were met. At first, they clamored for the dismissal of all Ubico supporters from public office. Ultimately, they wanted assurances that no official candidate would take part in the December presidential elections. Long expected the students to "give the government quite some headaches" before the December contest.[13]

The lawyers, other professionals, and businessmen who had asked for Ubico's resignation in June formed the Social Democratic party. Although deemed to be competent individuals by the U.S. embassy staff, they lacked experience in public administration. Whoever their candidate, Cochran concluded, he would not "meet the necessary requirements of a good president." Furthermore, without military support, the party's chance of success was remote.[14]

Ubico's resignation also unleashed political groups of various persuasions that had been suppressed since 1931. By September 1944, seven other political parties had been formed, but, according to embassy officials in Guatemala City, they lacked singular strength and did not demonstrate any willingness to cooperate behind a common candidate. Forty-year-old educator Juan José Arévalo, who had been in Argentina for the last eight years, was the choice of two groups. One party, the Popular Liberation Front (FPL), was described by political affairs adviser Laurence Duggan as a group of "noisy scalawags" that did not deserve any particular attention. He had joined the State Department in 1930, eventually becoming chief of the Office of American Republic Affairs. He was sympathetic to the needs of the lower socioeconomic groups. Comprised largely of educators and university students, the FPL exerted little influence outside the capital. The National Reform party, also consisting of students, was the second group backing Arévalo's candidacy.[15]

Other parties advancing individual candidates included: National Action, Jorge Gregorio Diaz; National Democratic Front and Democratic,

Adrían Recinos; and the Constitutional Democrats, Teodoro Díaz Medrano. These four parties represented the middle sector. Two parties did not name candidates, but issued manifestos only. Both appealed to the laboring class. The National Workers party called for the improvement of living and working conditions of the masses. More important was the National Vanguard party, which had been founded in July for the announced purpose of uniting all groups opposed to the Liberals. The party was alleged to be communistic because two of its leaders, Alfonso Solózano and Miguel García Granados, had been exiled to Mexico, where they were linked with Marxist labor groups. Others within the party were not extremists but rather "starry-eyed" idealists, according to Long, who also believed that the party's platform "makes some sense," particularly the call for the establishment of wage floors, price ceilings on essential commodities, large-scale agricultural production, and the organization of all sectors to contribute to the growth of the national economy.[16]

Cochran, assistant chief of the Caribbean and Central American Affairs Division, maintained that the plethora of political groups and the desire for a civilian president were natural reactions to a hundred years of military domination. He further contended that the election of a civilian president was dependent upon securing support from the Indians, who were tied to the large *finca* owners, already possessing political power. The importance of the underprivileged did not go unnoticed by five of the new parties: Social Democrats, National Action, National Democratic Front, National Workers, and National Vanguard. Each issued various statements advocating improved welfare and working conditions for the masses.[17]

Events in September and October led Long to conclude that Ponce intended to remain in power until 1949. The momentary popularity of any candidate always made the administration nervous. Arévalo's return to Guatemala on September 2, 1944, and the fear of student groups influenced by Mexican-based communism became major irritants to the government. Embassy officials had, since July, judged Arévalo to be the strongest civilian candidate, and his growing popularity struck sensitive government chords. Officials claimed he was an Argentine citizen and thus was not constitutionally eligible for the presidency.

Ubico and Ponce met separately with Long on October 2 and 5, each placing similar charges against Arévalo: that his support did not come from the country's wealthy people but those who intended "to upset the normally quiet life" and sponsor student unrest, such as pro-German Argentine or even communist groups. Each of the men also discounted the qualifications of the other presidential aspirants and claimed that the majority of Guatemalans were too incompetent to understand the issues at stake. Finally, Ubico and U.S. officials representing the United Fruit and W. R. Grace companies told Long that Ponce would continue in office.[18]

The government also took measures limiting opposition activities. Strict regulation of tire and gasoline distribution was followed by a ban on night driving in an effort to halt the alleged movement of arms. The delivery of newsprint to the opposition press was sharply curtailed. The marked increase in larceny throughout Guatemala City was attributed to Indians who had been brought in deliberately from the countryside by the government in an effort to cause a popular demand for order. Liberal party candidates easily captured the five congressional seats available in the October 13–15 elections, which further strengthened the administration's hand if it chose to legalize its extension in office. In an effort to avoid disorder and possible martial law, the opposition remained determined to avoid confrontation with the government. The assassination of well-known journalist and deputy Alejandro Córdova did not bring disorder. Discussion of his death quickly dropped into the background, despite his stance as the strongest opponent to constitutional change, which would permit Ponce to remain in office.[19]

In the face of such tactics, Long believed that the opposition leadership lacked sufficient political acumen to meet the challenge. "There is youth and enthusiasm aplenty," he noted, but no ready formula was available for upsetting the established order. Despite Arévalo's apparent popularity, his divergent sources of support—the church (covertly), moderate reformers, old line conservatives, students, and leftists—raised doubts about his real political strength.[20]

Shortly after the congressional elections, the embassy began to receive reports of an imminent insurrection led by younger army officers. Dismissing the rumors, Long attributed them to long-standing differences between the army's younger and older officers. The rumors proved to be correct, however. On October 19, 1944, as the government initiated steps to control the situation, insurrectionists led by Major Francisco Javier Araña, Captain Jacobo Arbenz, and businessman Jorge Toriello seized the capital's forts of San José and Matamoras. Ponce was left in the presidential palace protected only by his honor guard. Using the U.S. embassy as a meeting place, the rebels conveyed their demand to Ponce that he resign and threatened to bomb the palace if he did not. By 5:00 P.M. October 20, the revolt was over, Ponce had resigned, and order had been restored.[21]

Embassy second secretary Affeld was favorably impressed by the junta that replaced Ponce. Thirty-five-year-old Jorge Toriello, though quick-tempered, managed the revolt well. Thirty-two-year-old Jacobo Arbenz was a career officer who represented the younger progressive officers. Thirty-year-old Francisco Araña also represented the younger officers, but he was not believed to be personally ambitious. The junta's Cabinet, also young, inspired confidence because its members were felt to be sound and responsible. Included were Juan Córdova Gerna, Government Minister; Rafael Perez Deleon, Public Works; Pedro Cofino, Agriculture; Gabriel Orellana, Finance; Enrique Muñoz, Foreign Affairs; and Jorge Luis Arriola, Education. Araña assumed leadership over the War Ministry.

"I am pleasantly impressed with the broad basis and apparently sincere purpose of the present organization," cabled Affeld to Washington. Unlike the people of Salvador, earlier in the year, the Guatemalans demonstrated widespread support for the junta. The stage was also set for an ideological change. Leaders of the Liberal Progressive party were gone; Ubico fled to Mexico; justices resigned from the courts and some left the country; and old line officers were retired with generous pensions.

The diplomatic corps in Guatemala City expressed a common view:

> Who would have thought it possible that a few inexperienced young men would have thrown out the corrupt Ponce regime so quickly and thereafter have expeditiously uprooted the Liberal Party which has been in power more or less since 1870. The people support this movement and seem to idolize its leaders. The corrupt policemen of the past administrations are replaced by school boys, many of them not over ten years of age, who guide the traffic in the streets successfully. Many a year has past since we have experienced such a feeling of optimism as that of today.

Ambassador Long also was confident that the junta members were devoid of personal political ambitions. The reports led Secretary of State Edward

R. Stettinius, Jr., to conclude that the junta was of uncertain leftist orientation, but liberal not radical.[22]

The junta immediately dissolved the legislature and set dates for three elections: congressional, November 3 – 5; presidential, December 17 – 19; and, constituent assembly, December 28 – 30. Several nonproductive decrees were issued against Ubico, Ponce, and their associates. Long believed them to be warning signals to would-be dictators. More important were several decrees that benefited the Indians: elimination of forced road work when unable to pay taxes, arbitrary police courts, and *finca* owners' ability to punish thieves and trespassers arbitrarily. Long did not feel that any of the decrees were radical, and, compared to U.S. liberal standards, they were "quite moderate and middle of the road."[23]

Several factors contributed to the anticipated *Arévalista* congressional election victory in November. Liberals were in exile or hiding. Conservatives, hopeful of not being victimized by the political change, supported Arévalo. Although no guns were "sticking in the backs of voters," all ballots were cast openly in front of government-appointed electoral boards. Convening on December 3, the legislature rubber-stamped the junta's decrees. Its only self-initiated act modified citizenship laws to ensure Arévalo's presidential eligibility.[24]

Major Araña insisted that the upcoming presidential elections be free and that the junta not sponsor or back any candidate, despite statements by its civilian member, Jorge Toriello, that Arévalo was the best man available to establish the nation's first truly democratic government. Arévalo remained the most popular presidential candidate, though he was no longer a rallying point against dictatorship. Embassy second secretary Affeld estimated that 80 percent of the people supported his vague promises of "Spiritual Socialism," in which he promised a new order in building Guatemala's resources without foreign capital and a "square deal" for the common man. The two reform-minded parties, the Popular Liberation Front and National Reform party, remained committed to Arévalo. Subsequently, five opposition parties agreed to support the candidacy of Manuel María Herrera.[25]

Ambassador Long did not share the local popular view of Arévalo. Long sensed that the emotional support surrounding him at the time of Ubico's overthrow was being replaced by more sobering judgments as elections approached. Despite the recent legislative act, serious doubts about Arévalo's eligibility remained. As an educator, Long noted, he was a theorist who lacked governmental experience, and his lengthy absence from the country contributed to his ignorance of local matters. Many Guatemalans believed that Arévalo's advisers were undependable radicals who would endanger future government stability. These factors, Long concluded, caused many original supporters—business and professional men as well as wealthy people—to seek a compromise candidate.[26]

The brief presidential campaign was unscarred by violence and the election was free. As expected, Arévalo won, capturing more than 80 percent of the popular vote:

Juan José Arévalo	255,260
Adrían Recinos	20,749
Manuel María Herrera	11,062
Guillermo Flores	8,230

The third election decreed by the junta, that for a constitutional assembly, was also devoid of violence, and also went to the *Arévalistas*, who captured fifty of the sixty-five seats. They had swept all three political contests: legislative, constitutional assembly, and the presidency. The scope of their victory indicated to Secretary Stettinius that the new president enjoyed widespread popular support and that his administration was "authentically democratic." He was inaugurated on March 15, 1945, at the same time a new constitution went into effect.[27]

Prior to the inauguration, Ambassador Long spoke with several of his political rivals. Manuel María Herrera, Guillermo Flores, and José Gregorio Díaz doubted that the common people understood the significance of events since June 1944 and believed that the country would return to its old political habits. Adrían Recinos, who was extremely critical of Arévalo's advisers, suggested that their lack of experience would result in political chaos. The landowning elite let it be known that it expected its interests to be protected. The ambassador believed that the army still had the last word in politics. These factors resulted in Long's conclusion that the "change to a more democratic procedure will undoubtedly take time." The same reasoning caused the embassy's second secretary, Robert F. Woodward, who had previously served in Argentina, Brazil, and Bolivia, to expect political unrest in Guatemala for at least the next two years.[28]

At the center of political controversy was Arévalo's benevolent attitude toward labor's needs and his appeal to the Indians. Property owners described such appeals as socialistic. The term "socialism" was soon replaced by "communism," but State Department officials at first dismissed charges of communist influence in the administration. In August 1945 the Federal Bureau of Investigation (FBI) reported that Arévalo was becoming friendly with communist sympathizers who were stirring up labor troubles. "Phooey," commented Frederick B. Lyon, chief of State's Foreign Activity Correlation Division. The ambassador to Guatemala, Edwin G. Kyle, dismissed Jorge Toriello's allegation that "this country is going communistic fast under the influence of the Mexican government." Kyle, an agricultural expert who held Arévalo in high regard, interpreted Toriello's charge to be part of the elite's effort to discredit him.

The evidence was sufficient to support the views of both Lyon and Kyle in 1945. Following the example of Maximiliano Hernández Martínez in Salvador in 1932, President Ubico had crushed the communist movement in Guatemala. Some two hundred alleged leaders were either jailed or exiled. Since 1934, communist activities had been negligible because of continued repressive measures. Article 28 of the new constitution, promulgated in March 1945, forbade the forming of political parties possessing an international or foreign character. At best, Guatemala's communist movement was a clandestine and underground operation.[29]

The ground was fertile, however, for communism to take hold. The disparity of wealth and land ownership, which made life difficult for the masses, facilitated the reception of a new ideology. It was easy for leftists of all shades to support the 1944 revolution against the Ubico dictatorship. The postrevolutionary atmosphere tolerated liberalism and desire for reform. In this environment, Marxist theories infiltrated into the political scene. During the first two years of Arévalo's administration, the U.S. embassy in Guatemala City received several reports of communist infiltration into government circles, but, given the sources of information, found it difficult to judge their validity.[30]

Most of the country's alleged intellectual communists were abroad, including its ambassador to the United States, Miguel García Granados; its minister to the Soviet Union and later ambassador to Chile, Luis Cardoza y Aragon; and its secretary at the Moscow legation, Manuel Pellecer. The U.S. consul, Andrew E. Donovan, noted that García Granados was of Mexican background and believed it was "fair to say that his 'communism' is more local than international and that in other circumstances and countries he might be named an 'advanced liberal.'"

Donovan had witnessed similar reform movements at his previous assignments in Colombia, Mexico, and Bolivia.

The number of identified communists in Guatemala increased throughout Arévalo's term in office. In 1946 the FBI identified the two most important ones to be José Manuel Fortuny and Alfredo Pellecer. Described as an extreme leftist, Fortuny was a member of the directing committee of the Revolutionary Action party (PAR), the official government party founded in 1945. He spoke and wrote against "foreign imperialism" and "foreign monopoly capitalists," which meant U.S. firms in Guatemala. He also applauded the Soviet Union's international policies. Pellecer, who had been active in local communist organizations since the 1930s, became a leader in the Marxist-leaning Confederation of Guatemalan Workers (CTG) in 1944 and was the recipient of communist propaganda from abroad.

Carlos Manuel Pellecer was appointed as chief of the Traveling Cultural Mission by Arévalo despite his communist philosophy. The mission was charged with stamping out Indian illiteracy in the countryside, which meant the Indians not only learned "their A.B.C.'s [but] they also got a shot of communism," according to the embassy's first secretary, Milton K. Wells. Wells, who had come to Guatemala City from the State Department in 1948, reflected the changing U.S. attitude toward communism. Other notable communist appointments included Economy Minister Augusto Charnaud MacDonald; the press attaché to the embassy in Chile, Manuel Eduardo Hubner; and the organizer of Guatemala's school for diplomats, José León Deputre. Important foreign communists, including Chilean Virginia Brave Leterlier, Salvadoran Pablo Neruda, and Cuban Blas Roca, were welcomed by Arévalo and permitted to lecture widely throughout the country.[31]

Although the 1945 constitution banned political parties having international affiliation or characteristics, two efforts were made to organize communist parties: the Socialists in 1945 and the National Vanguard party in 1947. The embassy staff concluded that both efforts failed because the communists were content to work within the existing labor organizations and government agencies. The estimated two hundred actual communists in 1948 worked under the camouflage of other groups, and their influence was believed to be far out of proportion to their numbers. Assistant Secretary of State for Latin American Affairs Spruille Braden, suspicious of all leftist movements, believed that the communists had a secret agreement with Arévalo that permitted their participation in labor organizations and government agencies. The communist objective had been to take advantage of the revolution, which was not communist motivated, and to direct the source of revolutionary reforms.[32]

Labor was a chief target of the communist leadership and quite early appeared to gain control of the CTG. In July 1945 the CTG opened a "Clarity School" to educate laborers in political economy, unionism, and union administration. Known local and Central American communists were affiliated with the school's administration, including Alfredo Pellecer, Antonio Obando Sánchez, Pedro Geoffrey Rivas, Sebastian Ferrara, and Edmundo Suárez Barrios. Much of the educational material, or propaganda, was traced to the Soviet embassy in Mexico City. Such contacts were in violation of the 1945 constitution and provided the government with legal grounds for closing the school in January 1946. At that time, Arévalo referred to the school as "another communist attempt to disrupt social and political harmony."

Closing the "Clarity School" did not prevent communist propaganda from coming into Guatemala from Mexico as predicted by Foreign Minister Silva Peña and army Colonel Francisco Araña. Several Guatemalan labor leaders of Marxist persuasion—Armor Velasco De Leon, Edmondo Suárez Barrios, Alfredo Pellecer, and José Luis Soto—were linked to the distribution of this propaganda. De Leon also called for the expropriation of private land and its distribution to the farm workers, a proposal that was considered to be communistic by every landowner.[33]

By early 1947, the embassy staff doubted the government's ability to control labor for several reasons. The communists had made serious headway into the leadership of both the CTG and the Committee of National Syndical Unity (CNUS) as well as several lesser labor unions. The leadership was known to have been in contact with the former Communist International and the communist-oriented Confederation of Latin American Workers (CTAL). CTG was under the direct influence of Mexico's Marxist labor leader Vincente Lombardo Toledano, and CNUS was dependent upon the advice of Cuban communist Blas Roca, both of whom advocated Marxist-oriented labor laws and supported the Soviets in world affairs.

Four important communist front organizations identified by the embassy staff included: STEG, a teachers' association; SAKIR-TI, which brought together writers and intellectuals; STIAR, artists and intellectuals; and the Alliance of Guatemalan Democratic Youth, a student group organized by and affiliated with the communist-front World Federation of Democratic Youth. Another front organization, the Committee for Peace and Democracy, was organized by CTAL member Roberto Moreno and demonstrated "all the well known earmarks of a typical communist group." It sought to bring the diverse elements of Guatemala's intellectual community into one organization.

Backed by such a broad-based following, labor constantly pressured Arévalo to deliver on his promises to improve workers' conditions. For example, in its 1947 May Day proclamation, CTG called for union unity under its direction, national leadership under the current administration, and agrarian reform by breaking up landed estates for distribution to farm workers. Central America and Panama Affairs Division country specialist Murat W. Williams did not believe that the Arévalo regime could survive if it gave in to such demands. Embassy secretary Wells cautioned that the communist agitators, in the future, might force the government's hand regarding private enterprise in Guatemala.[34]

Fear of communist-instigated violence was ever present. In January 1948 *Pariesta* leaders were blamed for pushing the peasants in El Tumbador, El Progresso, and Asunción Meta into civil disorders. Residents and newspapers in each community and United Fruit Company officials identified the leaders and charged them with using Marxist demagoguery to incite the Indians. The official government investigations cleared the *Pariestas* of any wrongdoing, a decision not accepted by the residents of each town.

The rioting in Bogotá during the March 1948 Inter-American Conference caused serious alarm in Guatemala. Colonel Francisco Araña, chief of the armed forces, believed "it could happen here." Acting Foreign Minister Carlos Hall Lloreda was more specific with the charge that "professional agitators of communist inspiration" could provoke riots in Guatemala. The propertied class, which already believed Arévalo's administration was communistic, became noticeably more nervous. Embassy secretary Wells, however, did not believe any immediate danger existed because the army supported the status quo.[35]

In addition to pointing to the alleged and known communists within government and labor circles, the landowners used a number of legislative acts to support their charge that communism was a real threat to the country. The objectives of the 1944 revolution to bring about badly needed social and economic adjustments were easily susceptible of being distorted by Marxist dialectics into instruments of class warfare. According to an embassy staff report in 1948, the administration's reform programs went beyond the objectives of the 1944 revolution and in many cases sounded like "attempted advances toward a dictatorship of the proletariat." Government activity favoring the interests of organized labor and the underprivileged at the expense of the landowners as well as local and foreign capitalists alarmed the upper and middle classes.

These reform efforts alone did not constitute a communist threat according to Central America and Panama Affairs Division political adviser Robert E. Wilson, but when considered with the "unmistakable proofs" of communism there was cause for concern. Wilson, after several years in Latin America, returned to the State Department in 1947, at a time when U.S. suspicions of communism in Central America were causing concern. He used several administration proposals to support his argument. The bill providing for the Department of Intervened Farms was amended to provide for the land's ultimate collectivization. The 1947 Labor Code was judged by the embassy staff to be a "drastic document" that contained unusual labor benefits at the expense of capital. If literally enforced, it "would greatly facilitate the communist objective of state or worker control of industry." The April 1948 Rent Law was actually a form of confiscatory taxation, which, if enforced, would result in financial ruin for many landlords. The 1946 Social Security Law taxed businessmen unreasonable amounts. The Petroleum Law militated against U.S. investment.

Such programs, the embassy staff concluded, were similar to those of the former Communist International, which meant dictatorship of the proletariat. Only the tactics differed: in Guatemala the communists worked under cover. However, the embassy staff could not establish any direct links between local communists and Moscow. Direct relations with the Soviet Union never materialized because that nation did not reciprocate recognition in 1945. Thus, any contact with Moscow was suspected to be through Mexico City and Paris.[36]

The popular concern with communist influence in government was responsible for the founding of the Guatemalan Democratic League against Communism in July 1948. It charged Arévalo with initiating a class struggle and pitting worker against capitalist while masquerading the movement as one for the betterment of the working class itself. The league denounced labor's ties to CTAL and Arévalo's known friendship with Vincente Lombardo Toledano. The Rent Law as well as proposed income tax and agricultural reforms were described as steps leading to state subjugation of the whole economy. In March 1949 the Anti-Communist Unification Party was formed. It hoped to mobilize large public demonstrations against the government and thus force Arévalo to take a strong stand on communism. After its initial protest demonstration failed on April 28, 1949, the party faded from the political scene.[37]

The communist issue drew major attention in June 1948, when the Guatemalan archbishop, Monsignor Mariano Rosell Arellano, issued a pastoral letter that was read in all churches and published in leading newspapers. He urged Catholics to support congressional candidates in the November 1948 elections whose ideas "most advanced social justice," but, without mentioning names, he warned that Catholics could not support communist candidates without suffering severe church condemnation. Leading newspapers applauded the letter, which included a plea for all to vote, because absenteeism was one of the nation's most serious weaknesses. Following the letter's release, there was an immediate increase in the number of women, mostly upper class, who registered and also made house visits to urge others to register.

PAR recognized the strength of church influence. On June 19 it warned of great danger if the church held the reins of government power. Despite the absence of a Catholic political party, PAR threatened to amend the Electoral Law so as to outlaw all parties having religious connections. Rumors subsequently spread that Arévalo's Cabinet considered deporting the archbishop, but the tension eased when Colonel Araña assured the public he would not permit that to happen. In a second pastoral letter, on August 5, Rosell reminded Catholics to perform their civic duty in November, but "deny their vote to communists and communist sympathizers."[38] The government did not react publicly to the second letter.

Arévalo consistently dismissed allegations that his government was Marxist or of extreme character. In press conferences throughout his administration, he denied the existence of communism in the country. He explained that the government argricultural reforms could not be communistic because private property was protected by the nation's constitution. He maintained that the results of the 1944 revolution had made the country more "Rooseveltian."[39]

The opinion of U. S. policymakers concerning the extent of communist influence from 1945 through 1949 varied. Ambassador Kyle, in 1945, dismissed charges of communist influence in the government as an attempt by the elite to discredit Arévalo. A year later, the State Department indicated that the small group of communists in the nation received support from and were in contact with the Soviet embassy in Mexico City, but that communism was still not "a particularly important factor" in Guatemala. In 1947 Chargé d'affaires Andrew E. Donovan questioned President Arévalo's sincerity when he denied that communism existed in the country. At the same time, first secretary Milton Wells expressed serious concern over the extent of communist influence in the labor movement. He believed that communist agitators might force the government's hand regarding the future of private enterprise in Guatemala. Ambassador Kyle's opinion also wavered. He noted that Arévalo continued to advocate policies dictated by PAR's radical element, including "some of undoubted communist sympathies."

A consensus embassy opinion in May 1948 concluded that Arévalo himself was not a communist, but that communist and Marxist doctrines had unquestionably exerted a strong influence upon government policies since 1944 and that the communists had increased their hold on the number of government posts. This view was shared by the Central America and Panama Affairs Division's (CPA) acting chief, Robert Newbegin. "More surprising" the embassy staff noted, "is the fact that the [communists] were not even more successful." This was probably attributable to several factors. The masses did not demonstrate real want despite their low standards of living. The Catholic church and Guatemalan army were staunchly anticommunist, both of which exerted a moderating influence upon government policies in 1947. The effects of the Bogotá Conference and drift of world events that exposed the dangers of communism served to strengthen the local anticommunist movement.

In view of these factors, the embassy staff predicted that the prospects for the "communization" of Guatemala were on the downgrade. Ambassador Kyle was more optimistic. In September 1948 he believed that Guatemala was in "excellent economic condition and . . . politically stable." He maintained that President Arévalo was not a communist, but rather was sincerely interested in developing Guatemala along constructive lines. The criticisms of the government's reform policies reminded Kyle of "opinions expressed by some of his wealthy fellow Texans relative to President Roosevelt." Although the ambassador favorably viewed Arévalo's intentions, he doubted the sincerity of several government officials, including alleged communists Muñoz Meany and García Granados. Assistant Secretary of State for Latin American Affairs Spruille Braden did not share Kyle's sympathetic opinion of Arévalo. Braden never accepted Arévalo as a democratic crusader and judged him to be more than a communist sympathizer. Rather, he was "an agent of Stalin."[40]

The continued conflicting opinion from the embassy and the unraveling of political events in Guatemala caused political adviser Raymond K. Oakley to harbor "reasonable doubt" concerning the extent of communist influence. His previous assignments had been in Mexico, Colombia, and Argentina before returning to the department in 1948. A hard-liner on the communist issue, he urged that the United States make it clear to the world that it would not tolerate Soviet control of any Latin American government. Assistant Secretary of State Edward G. Miller, the CPA chief, Willard F. Barber, and his assistant, Murray A. Wise, rejected the recommendation of a strong public statement about Soviet influence in Central America, but asked only for an updated analysis of the Guatemalan situation by State's Research Division.[41]

That report, completed in October 1950, supported many of the interpretations that had been held by the embassy staff in May 1948. Namely, the communists had seized upon the 1944 revolutionary fervor and found a sympathetic Arévalo, who tolerated their existence and permitted their entry into government agencies and labor circles. The estimated five hundred communists or alleged communists had exerted influence out of proportion to their numbers, particularly in the labor unions. Still no concrete evidence indicated the existence of an underground communist organization or that the Soviets were attempting to establish a base of operations in Guatemala. Issued prior to Colonel Arbenz's presidential election victory in November 1950, the report predicted that communist influence would continue to be dominant in government circles because none of the leading politicians had sufficient appeal to the laboring masses.[42]

Arévalo's "Spiritual Socialism" contributed to his administration's inauspicious start in March 1945. During the next four years, government policies and sponsored legislation further alienated Arévalo's relationship with the disorganized elite. Embassy secretary Robert F. Woodward believed that sufficient opposition would arise to counter the revolutionary zeal and force of the administration to become "moderately progressive" and "more conventional." The junta itself was deemed to be moderate, and its only civilian member, Jorge Toriello, was named as finance minister in Arévalo's Cabinet. Although not personally liked by the agricultural and business community, he appreciated and represented their views. According to Woodward, Toriello considered himself the force behind the throne and after June 1945 attempted to exert even more influence over Arévalo, whom he respected little. Ambassadors Long and Woodward both concluded that Toriello exerted less influence than military officers Araña and Arbenz.

Toriello's consistent pressure made him unpopular with other government officials, which further hurt the landowners' cause. Woodward correctly expected a showdown between Arévalo and Toriello. It began in August 1945, when Arévalo did nothing to discount the military's investigation of a brawl between police plainclothesmen and leftists Michael Galich and Hiram Ordoñez that traced responsibility for the incident to Toriello. Rebuffed by the president, Toriello subsequently formed a group to discredit him publicly. Because of his continued adversarial role, Toriello was dismissed as finance minister in January 1946 and was replaced by conservative Eugenio Silva Peña. As expected by embassy secretary Donovan, Toriello was subsequently linked to antiadministration activities.[43]

The moderating trend expected by Woodward was reflected in the June 1945 administrative changes that were made to satisfy the army's conservative elements, which were supported by the landowners. National assembly President García Granados was named ambassador to Washington; labor leader Alfonso Solórzano to Mexico City; and deputies Carlos Manuel Pellecer and Juan Umberto Sosa were assigned to the legations in Moscow and Mexico City, respectively. To Woodward, the elimination of leftists demonstrated the influence of the army's moderate conservative element, headed by Armed Forces Chief Araña. As a result of these changes, Woodward expected Arévalo to carry out moderate reforms without disturbing the agricultural proprietors and business entrepreneurs. Cabinet changes in July 1946 and December 1948 were made in deference to the army's wishes.

In July 1946 Araña privately told Donovan that most Guatemalans were opposed to the "advanced theory" expounded by some congressmen. Publicly, at the same time, Araña remarked that "the present situation is intolerable." Congressional leaders understood this to mean that they were in no position to legislate reform programs. Araña's continued assurances that the army was committed to the establishment of a democracy provided Donovan with confidence in government stability and continued moderation.[44]

Arévalo could not help but be cognizant of the elite's determined opposition to his socialistic philosophy. In an effort to secure its position politically, the most important segment of influential landowners and business elements formed the National party in January 1946. Among the organizers were Alejandro Arenales, Juan Ernesto Perez, Pedro G. Cofino Duran, Carlos O. Zomora, and Leopoldo Berger. Although the members numbered only about a thousand, the party influenced a large number of voters. It called for sound monetary and fiscal policy, further economic development, and improved working and living conditions for laborers, but disapproved the "extra social and economic policies followed by the present government . . . [which] are leading to an unjustified class struggle." The party was threatened with extinction in July 1946, when a new Electoral Code was passed. It stipulated that no party could call itself "national" until it received 90 percent of the registered voters and that a party consisting of less than 3,000 members had to go out of existence.

The *finca* owners were also distraught over government restrictions on newsprint allotted to opposition newspapers, which limited their ability to protest government activities. Political tension increased over government allegations that the United Fruit Company was not treating workers fairly. The *finca* owners feared they would be attacked next. The conservatives were also disturbed in 1946 by the resignation of Minister of Agriculture Robert Guirolla, who opposed the government's proposal to distribute privately owned lands among the workers.[45]

Political tension was so severe in September 1946 that the Social Democrats and the National, Revolutionary, and Worker's Republican Democratic parties formed a coalition to confront Arévalo. It made four demands: remove the restrictions on newsprint distribution, revise the July 1946 Electoral Code, stop identifying the church as a political body, and halt police harassment of opposition leaders. This effort failed to budge Arévalo, but the incident caused the moderates within the administration to warn him that if he moved further left, the Cabinet would resign en masse.[46]

The government's failure to discuss the opposition's demands contributed to abstention from the January 1947 congressional elections by the Social Democrats and the Revolution, Liberal, and Constitutional (formerly National) parties. Only the Worker's Republican Democratic party remained in the contest, though it failed to challenge PAR. Public discussion of issues and interest in the election was limited. The opposition's petition for government nullification of the election proved to be futile. A March 16, 1947, public demonstration against the existing electoral law was forcefully broken up by government civilian supporters "in a quite apparently planned manner." Arévalo's firing of Department Governor Juan Mazorga Franco for failing to protect the demonstrators did not prevent the opposition from placing blame upon the administration for the violence.

Frustrated in their efforts to change the Electoral Code and nullify the congressional elections, the Social Democrats and the Constitutional party withdrew from political participation. Although both represented the upper class, Donovan believed that the Constitutional party was potentially the most dangerous because of its wealth and experience, and he expected it to come forward again in a more organized fashion.[47]

In mid-1948 the opposition became more active. Embassy secretary Wells and State's political adviser Wilson gave several reasons for the revived activity. Government expenditures had gained little return. In three years, the Arévalo administration spent more than $100 million, compared to annual prewar budgets of $10 million. The proposed income tax, whose rates ranged from 3 to 41 percent, created fear in a country that previously had been debt free and that had found customs and stamp taxes sufficient to meet government expenditures. The Rent Law, which severely limited landlords' profits, and the proposed Housing Law, which would require that 10 percent of all annual profits be used for workers' houses, were considered discriminatory against the upper class. The Labor Code allegedly ignored realities and the capabilities of the economy. The political inexperience of Arévalo and all the government officials was regarded as appalling, and the failure to check alleged government graft at all levels was repugnant.[48]

The attacks upon Arévalo's political programs were not limited to opposition groups. PAR, itself, was divided into two factions. One was labeled the "government in exile" because its members—Secretary-General Alfonso Bauer Paíz, Finance Secretary Julio Rivera Sierva, and Propaganda Secretary Marco A. Villamar—wanted to oust the so-called radicals: Fortuny, Gonzalez, Juarez, and Charnaud MacDonald. Donovan agreed with Foreign Minister Silva Peña that the split was so wide it was "practically impossible to bridge."

On May 31, 1947, a large group bolted the party and formed the Popular Liberation Front (FPL). Included in FPL were Cabinet members Roberto Moran (Public Health) and Julio Bonilla Gonzalez (Education). The primary objective was to liberate the country from "governmentalism," which meant cleansing government of employees whose personal gain came before service. Pledging to carry out the aims of the October 1944 revolution, the FPL promised improved working and living conditions for the laboring class, but only after a lengthy government study of national needs. Communists were barred from the party because they were believed to be a threat to the country's security and democracy.

Local political observer Morroquín Reyas believed that no real change was involved; most Guatemalans recognized the split represented internal infighting, not a battle against communism or any other ideological struggle. Embassy second secretary Donovan agreed, but embassy first secretary Wells came to view the FPL as a rallying point for moderates and felt that this trend toward the semblance of a two-party system was a good sign. [49] Apparently Arévalo was not involved in the split.

It gave FPL thirty-five congressional seats, compared to nineteen for PAR. The unfavorable imbalance contributed to Arévalo's charge in March 1948 that congress no longer represented the people and therefore should be dismissed. In mid-March he discharged all FPL members from his Cabinet. This dashed all hopes of conciliation between the two parties. Arévalo also gave every indication that he would turn PAR into a personal political machine for the November 1948 elections. The split also prevented any constructive legislation during the 1948 session. The sweeping FPL municipal election victories in June were interpreted by Wells as a rejection of Arévalo's program, but the president refused to adjust his policies to accommodate public opinion. Rather, he remained committed to PAR's radical element. [50]

Embassy officials attached significance to the November 1948 elections for half of the congressional seats because, for the first time since coming to power in 1945, the Arévalo administration was confronted with organized opposition. FPL was the most prominent opposition party. It was considered a moderating influence, a move toward the center, but not reactionary. Many Guatemalans viewed FPL as a legitimate protest against the "threatening steady march toward Marxism."

In late September the National Electoral Union (UNE) was formed by several opposition groups. The most important was the Worker's Republican-Democratic party (PTRD). Because of its five congressional delegates, it was the only party that possessed any political experience. It previously had received church support and had undoubtedly benefited from Archbishop Rosell's pastoral letters in June and August 1948. The diversity of interests among the UNE factions made victory almost impossible, but it hoped to capture enough seats to retard, if not reverse, the "radical [and] hastily conceived legislation which has shaken the confidence of business and propertied classes." Its long-range goal was to prepare for the 1950 election, which was believed to be the first real opportunity to remove the leftists from power.[51]

In August, PAR reached an agreement with the National Renovation Party (RN), the third leftist party in Guatemala. The agreement was a determined effort to destroy FPL's congressional majority.[52]

Not until January 31, 1949, were the November 26–28, 1948, election results confirmed by the National Election Board. The PAR-RN "Victory Block" captured fourteen seats, the FPL nine, and UNE eleven. These results gave FPL twenty-seven seats in the next congress, UNE twelve, and the "Victory Block" twenty. This caused FPL to lose its congressional majority and UNE to increase its strategic importance, particularly if the PAR-FPL split continued.[53] Given the course of events in 1948, pressure appeared to be mounting against Arévalo's policies.

The allegations of communism within the government, which had alarmed the upper class and were responsible for the constant political tension, also had contributed to much of the violence since Arévalo's inauguration. During his five years in office, he had survived twenty-two military revolts. Many of the attempted coups linked the landowners with the military, the former understanding the need for the latter in order to be successful. Recognizing that violent change in government was a distinct possibility in Guatemala, Secretary of State James F. Byrnes advised Ambassador Edwin Kyle to use his "discreet influence" to express the hope of the United States that Guatemala continue to practice constitutionalism.[54]

During the first year of Arévalo's presidential term, three unsuccessful coup efforts were reported. The first, in February 1945, was headed by defeated presidential candidate Adrían Recinos, who subsequently was deported for disturbing the "political tranquility of the country." During the first week of April, twenty-two persons were arrested and later deported for the same reason. All were ideologically linked to Ubico's Liberal Progressive party. Three were unsuccessful presidential candidates: Ovidio Pivaral, José Gregorio Díaz, and Manuel María Herrera. In late September 1945, a group of obscure army officers was linked with reactionary civilians, including Carlos Solazar, son of Ubico's foreign minister, and Manuel Coronado Aguillar, who represented German business interest in Guatemala. They, too, were deported. Embassy consular officer Woodward believed it important to understand that the government, threatened with revolutionary plots, was forced to take such drastic actions. William Cochran, chief of the Caribbean and Central American Affairs Division, disagreed. He argued that such repressive measures only increased the elite's hostility toward the government.[55]

From April to June 1946, Central Bank official Jorge Pelacios spearheaded a revolt attempt that never materialized because the government was fully informed. Importantly, however, he represented the country's economic and social hierarchy, which feared that Arévalo's programs frightened away foreign investors and caused the flight of capital. The whole incident passed without much public fanfare, but Chargé d'affaires Andrew Donovan warned that, so long as the government cleavage with the elite continued or widened, revolts remained a real possibility.[56]

Constitutional guarantees were suspended in September 1947 in the wake of another anticipated coup. Subsequently, twenty-four prominent persons "voluntarily" left the country, including Jorge Toriello, Guillermo Echeverria Izarralde, Carlos Gutierrez Custudio, and Guillermo Flores Avendaño. All were members of opposition political parties, "whom the government found inconvenient." Embassy secretary Wells correctly predicted that those exiled would return without much fanfare.[57]

Following the breach between Arévalo and congress in March 1948, rumors of a possible coup abounded. Wells noted that the number of dissidents had sharply increased, which added a sense of validity to the rumors. A March 1948 decree permitting the return of political exiles and the effect of the Bogotá rioting intensified the situation. By the summer of 1948, political adviser Robert Wilson of the Division of Central America and Panama Affairs (CPA) believed that Guatemala's elite was prepared financially to support a change of government. In late July the cabinet debated deportation of opposition leaders, including Archbishop Rosell. Neither a revolt nor the prelate's deportation materialized. Rumors continued, however, only exacerbating an already tense political situation. In January 1949 an uprising at Puerto Barrios was linked to a larger plot, but was cut short by government action.[58]

At the start of Arévalo's administration, Ambassador Boaz Long identified four distinct factions within the army. The first consisted of conservative officers who disliked Arévalo's liberal ideas and any linkage with Mexico. The second faction was made up of the old line officers, who had not graduated from the military academy. This group not only detested liberalism and ties to Mexico, but also feared the loss of jobs to the younger and educated officers. The third element believed that the army was not adequately represented in the national Cabinet or legislature. Finally, personal jealousies among officers over political power continued within the army ranks. Throughout Arévalo's administration, various members of these factions were linked to attempted coups d'etat.

Important to the failure of the alleged plots was the continued loyalty to Arévalo of War Minister Jacobo Arbenz and Chief of the Armed Forces Francisco Araña. Both enjoyed support from the army's rank and file. Arbenz told Woodward that all the younger officers abhorred "the idea of traditional Latin American revolutions" whereby the military continued as a major force following the overthrow of a dictator. Arbenz, however, expected that Arévalo's administration would need to depend upon the goodwill and character of the men who reorganized the system. Obviously Arévalo's tenure in office depended upon his granting favors to the army, which would speak the last word in politics. During the four years following Arévalo's inauguration, embassy cables consistently reported the loyalty of Arbenz and Araña to the president. Their control of the army was believed to be the most significant factor in preventing his ouster.[59]

Although Arbenz and Araña were both graduates of the military academy, their philosophies and objectives were different. Ambassador Long judged Arbenz to be an idealistic crusader who had political ambitions. On the other hand, Araña was deemed to be as conservative as any officer who had come up through the ranks. Content with his position, Araña was interested only in preserving the nation's newfound democracy. Because of these differences, Ambassador Kyle, in 1948, placed the men in the separate camps of Arévalo's followers. Arbenz was identified with PAR's more radical elements, whose sincerity was questionable. Araña allied himself with the moderate elements interested in developing Guatemala along constructive lines.

The belief that Araña lacked political ambitions was shattered in November 1948, when a congressional resolution charged that the military was interfering with the congressional campaign in the Department of Quiche. The resolution, signed by forty delegates of PAR, RN, and FPL, was intended to discredit Araña, who was suspected of having 1950 presidential ambitions. Araña confirmed those suspicions at a November 1948 news conference when he announced "that should there develop a popular demand . . . he would answer the call to run for president." He also expressed support for the moderate FPL over the PAR and RN parties. Woodward noted that, in early 1949, Araña-for-President groups began to appear throughout the country, "presumably with his encouragement if not his actual instigation."[60]

The big question was whether Araña would become the official candidate, once identified with the moderate elements. Arévalo's recent statements that a military man should not be eliminated from the presidency were interpreted as a green light for Araña. Others mentioned as possible official candidates were Jacobo Arbenz and Jorge García Granados, both representing the administration's radical supporters. The latter was supposedly Arévalo's choice. Embassy secretary Wells believed that García Granados would do anything to keep the nomination from Araña.[61]

The political situation had intensified by early July 1949, when reports pointed to a power struggle between the Araña and Arbenz cliques within the military. According to other rumors, Araña planned a coup for the afternoon of July 18, which caused Wells to speculate that the "government would take advantage of this story as an excuse for the assassination of Araña." He was killed that same afternoon, July 18, under mysterious circumstances. The immediate cause was traced to the power struggle within the military, but Wells and the embassy's second secretary, Ernest V. Siracusa, believed it was "a carefully engineered attempt on the part of Colonel Arbenz, President Arévalo and the leftist elements . . . to eliminate the growing opposition movement" headed by Araña. On July 20 the government ordered the arrest of pro-Araña officers and opposition leaders. Except for Colonel Castillo Armas, U.S. officials in Guatemala maintained that the government prosecuted only "small fish" in connection with the Araña assassination. Armas was not only connected with that act, but also with émigré groups in Nicaragua that promised to oust Arévalo eventually, by force if necessary.[62]

Ambassador Richard C. Patterson and Siracusa held similar opinions about Guatemalan politics, despite different backgrounds. Patterson's diplomatic career had begun in 1920. After several European assignments, he was appointed as assistant secretary of commerce and later as a trustee of the Export-Import Bank. From 1944 to 1947 he was ambassador to Yugoslavia. Siracusa had started his foreign service in 1941 at Mexico City. He also served in Honduras and Guatemala before returning to the department in 1949. Both agreed that Araña's death represented the loss of the most influential moderating force in Guatemalan politics and the strongest presidential candidate. Both expected the government to move further leftward in its policies and warned that, if the opposition failed to plot earnestly against the government, risking its resources in the near future, it faced the possibility of not having any to risk at a later date.

A subsequent Siracusa memorandum concerning Arbenz was given considerable merit by CPA Assistant Chief Murray A. Wise. According to Siracusa, Arbenz emerged from the July 18–20 events as the leading military figure, but he lacked a deep-seated intellectual alliance with the left and sympathy for the lower classes or the communists who had infiltrated the government. Rather, he was a political opportunist who had strung along with Arévalo for his own political purposes. His feud with Araña was personal and arose out of the latter's growing popularity. Because local and foreign opinion was moving against Arévalo, Siracusa doubted that Arbenz could win any election. Thus, the crafty Arbenz was isolated. Under such conditions, Siracusa considered it "more than a real possibility" that he might engineer a coup, claiming to save the country from communism.[63]

Araña's assassination significantly affected the various political groups. Prior to Araña's death, Arévalo's efforts to bring the FPL together with the PAR and the PN to select a presidential candidate had failed, largely because FPL preferred to remain alone, even in the face of defeat. Following Araña's death, Milton Wells noted an increasing tendency on the part of the opposition parties to unite. If this failed, he concluded "the future would look extremely dark for the now harassed and intimidated opposition." In November the path was cleared for Arbenz to become the official candidate. The three *Arévalista* parties issued a joint statement eliminating Jorge García Granados as a possible united front candidate. This placed him with a large number of former revolutionary leaders outside the fold. Among them were Colonel Miguel A. Méndoza, former Cabinet members Pedro Cofino and Eugenio Silva Peña, and party stalwarts like Mario Menendez Montenegro as well as a long list of army officers. [64]

Arbenz announced his presidential candidacy in early 1950. He enjoyed the support of the extremist political and labor leaders, but never received a public endorsement from Arévalo. Arbenz's campaign, however, emphasized a continuation of programs Arévalo had begun. The election was never in much doubt. The opposition was in disarray because its two leading candidates were eliminated. Miguel Ydígoras Fuentes was exiled, and Miguel García Granados was forced into hiding a month prior to the 1950 presidential election. Under such conditions, Arbenz won easily. During his administration, the fragmented political opposition could not stem the expanded communist influence in government. No restrictions were placed on the Communist party, which was legally registered in 1952 as the Guatemalan Labor party. Internal discord grew, exile groups organized, and the United States became increasingly concerned about the direction of Guatemalan politics. These forces came together in 1954 to bring down the Arbenz regime. [65]

Until the election of Arévalo in 1944, twentieth-century Guatemalan politics was dominated by the long dictatorships of Manuel Estrada Cabrera (1898–1920) and Jorge Ubico (1931–44). Little progress was made toward democracy. Although Ubico instituted some economic and social reform programs for the poor, "readjustments were badly needed" when Arévalo assumed office in March 1945. [66]

During its six-year term, the Arévalo administration was responsible for legislation favoring the poor at the expense of the rich. A Labor Code, a Rent Law, and a social security program illustrated the application of his "Spiritual Socialism." Such measures were anathema to the landowning elite, which labeled them as communistic. The question of communism became the centerpiece of politics during the period 1944–49.

Ubico, like Hernández in El Salvador, was brought down by the force of political liberalism best expressed by the middle sector. Once its goal was achieved, however, this group was unprepared to deal with the economic and social needs of the nation's poor. In 1944 and early 1945, American policymakers, including Ambassador Boaz Long and Secretary of State Edward R. Stettinius, Jr., did not seem concerned about the leftist-leaning ideology of the Toriello-Arbenz-Araña junta or president-elect Juan José Arévalo. Their ideas were categorized as liberal, not radical. New Ambassador Edwin G. Kyle, in 1945, shared this opinion. The Americans concluded that the landowners branded the four men as communists solely because the established order was threatened.

By 1948, however, U.S. opinion had changed. Known Marxists found their way into government posts, and, though they numbered only an estimated two to three hundred, the embassy staff concluded that they wielded influence out of proportion to their numbers. The Americans never believed that Arévalo was a communist, but, as embassy secretary Andrew Donovan and CPA Chief Robert Newbegin illustrated, they did not accept his denials of extensive communist influences in government and labor circles. Assistant Secretary of State Spruille Braden was more adamant when he charged that Arévalo had a secret agreement with the communists. Only Ambassador Kyle remained sympathetic to the Arévalo administration.

No threat of international communism existed in Guatemala. Moscow did not reciprocate recognition in 1945. Contact with the Soviet embassy in Mexico City was known. The travels abroad by Guatemalan Marxists and the visits of Latin American communists to the country provided guidance and inspiration, "but not proof [that] direct control has yet been established."[67]

Opposition to Arévalo's regime was expected to come from the land-owning elite. Disorganized, however, it failed to counter Arévalo's programs. Increasingly, it turned to the military for support, and the two groups were linked to several alleged coup attempts. Until 1949, the embassy reported that the military exerted a moderating influence upon the government, as illustrated by the several Cabinet changes throughout the period.

Within the military, two distinct factions emerged. The liberal, even radical, element rallied behind Captain Jacobo Arbenz; the moderate, or conservative, element, behind Major Francisco Araña. Embassy secretaries William C. Affeld and Robert Woodward believed that Arbenz entertained personal political ambitions and that Araña was content with Guatemala's newfound democracy. Thus, the Americans were surprised in November 1948 when Araña announced his interest in the nation's presidency. His assassination in July 1949, concluded embassy secretary Ernest V. Siracusa, was engineered by Arbenz in order to clear his own path. Subsequently, Siracusa and Ambassador Richard C. Patterson expected the politics to move further left.

From 1944 to 1949, the Americans watched Guatemala swing from the political right to the political left. The 1944 revolution was judged to be a legitimate liberal movement against a dictatorship. At the same time, the revolution opened the floodgates to leftist-leaning individuals. Facing no organized opposition, the leftists, or communists as they came to be called, gained dominating influence over the political scene.

4

Honduras

MORE than any other Central American nation, Honduras best fit the popular, but misunderstood, concept of the "banana republic." Tiburcio Carías had ruled as dictator since 1933. His two main support groups— the landowners and the military—desired no change. Most political opposition was eliminated or exiled, and the small middle sector was disorganized. Like Hernández in Salvador and Ubico in Guatemala, Carías played upon the sympathies of the poor, but did nothing to improve their status. Despite these conditions, U.S. officials were convinced that most of the people were satisfied with Carías's rule, as evidenced by the meaningless demonstration in the spring of 1944 following the fall of Hernández and the isolated revolts instigated by Honduran exiles until 1949. Carías remained entrenched in power until his resignation in 1949. He faced no serious threat.

Several factors contributed to the Honduran image of a "banana republic." Rugged mountains and inadequate transportation meant that contact was limited among the towns and villages, each of which acquired its own sense of self-sufficiency. Knowledge of or interest in people living only a few miles away was restricted. The differences among towns was

107

best illustrated by comparing the quiet, isolated capital of Tegucigalpa, in the mountains, with the spirit of San Pedro Sula, the busy port city on the northwest coast.

The dichotomy in society was sharp. An estimated 90 percent of the population was Indian or mestizo, the remainder being divided among white, Black Caribs, and Antillean Negroes. More than 50 percent of the population was illiterate. Landownership and family lineage played the most important role in determining social status, but education and wealth were contributing factors. Society was divided into four groups: urban upper class, local upper class, local middle class, and lower class. Thus, an individual's status depended upon his or her qualifications and those of other community members. For example, a schoolteacher's education or amount of a merchant's wealth may have placed him or her in the upper class of a rural village but only in the middle class of a large town or city.

The upper class consisted of the old families whose wealth was based on landownership. This group had traditionally provided the nation's political leadership. There was a distinction between the cosmopolitan upper class in Tegucigalpa and San Pedro Sula and the local, or provincial, upper class, which made up the largest segment of the elite. The middle sector was an amorphous group, whose wealth separated it from the upper and lower strata but which lacked the required lineage to be accepted by the elite. Included in this sector were the merchants, technicians, schoolteachers, and government officials; and, in urban areas, skilled labor, doctors, lawyers, and university professors. The lower class was the largest socioeconomic element in the country. It was comprised of small landowners, tenant farmers, squatters, and unskilled laborers, most of whom were engaged in subsistence agriculture. This group was distinguished by its extreme poverty and lack of education.[1]

The Honduran economy was the least mature of the Central American nations. Agriculturally based, it produced mainly bananas, cattle, and coffee. The United and Standard Fruit and Steamship companies developed the banana industry. Honduras was the world's leading producer of that crop, which provided for the largest share of the national income. Trade depended on the United States, which in the year ending June 30, 1944, took 85 percent of exports and supplied 67 percent of imports.[2]

Honduras endured a tragic political history, characterized by chronic instability and acute civil strife. Politically, it was labeled as the most backward of the five Central American states. Until 1933 the various administrations (the presidents had numbered 118) possessed little stability and adhered to constitutional forms only sporadically. The government was inefficient, graft assumed wholesale proportions, and law enforcement was lax. Chaotic conditions were the result.

The political picture changed with the February 1933 presidential inauguration of General Tiburcio Carías. As the National party candidate, he had defeated Liberal Angel Zuñiga Huete, who went into exile that same year, following an abortive revolution allegedly sponsored by his followers. Through constitutional manipulation in 1936 and 1943, Carías extended his term in office until 1949. Assuming dictatorial powers from the time of his inauguration, he incarcerated or exiled opposition leaders and restricted freedom of press, speech, and radio. Congressional, judicial, and municipal government decisions were subject to his approval. Although some labor and social legislation was passed, it was not enforced. Despite vociferous opposition from exiles abroad, Carías was firmly entrenched. Illiteracy and poverty remained the most serious barriers to the country's progress.[3]

Officially, the U.S. government did not approve of the Carías dictatorship, and therefore relations were formally correct but lacking in cordiality. Unofficially, he was considered less deplorable than Anastasio Somoza in Nicaragua and Rafael Trujillo in the Dominican Republic. Despite the dictatorship and the poverty, many Foreign Service personnel felt that Honduras was a "delightful place." The Honduran-Nicaraguan desk officer, Gordon Reid, noted in 1949 that "the Eden-like qualities of the place have had a tendency in the past to create the impression in the minds of the personnel, that the State Department was the snake offering in the form of instruction the apple of temptation."[4] Reid, who had joined the department in 1942, was never assigned to Honduras. In Washington, he served as assistant director of the Institute of Inter-American Affairs and then as a country specialist in State before his assignment in 1949 to the Central America and Panama Affairs Division.

Reid's favorable impression only reflected the views of U.S. diplomats assigned to the country. Ambassador John D. Erwin, a former journalist, who served for ten years (1937–47) at Tegucigalpa, was the most positive emissary. He agreed with an unidentified foreign banker that Honduras was wonderful: "no volcanos, no earthquakes, no Communists, no labor unions, no wage or social security laws, [and] no income tax." Erwin attributed the tranquillity largely to economic prosperity. The national budget was balanced, and the national debt was half that of 1933. The country was on a "pay as you go basis," accomplished through "old fashioned orthodox virtues of hard work and frugality, without recourse to screwball economics," which meant not tinkering with prices or spending money not in hand or in sight.

Virtually no unemployment existed among the laboring class, whose wages were higher than elsewhere in the region (50–75 U.S. cents per eight-hour workday for a common laborer and $1.25–$1.75 per hour for skilled labor). Small businessmen were free to pursue their own interests unencumbered by government or labor interference. This group expressed confidence in Carías. Politically, "the Nazis have gone [and] the Communists have not yet arrived," Erwin noted. He dismissed the occasional armed conflicts as raids on rural villages by bandits who described themselves as revolutionaries. The economic prosperity and political tranquillity caused him to conclude that Honduras was the "only country on earth better off today than in 1933," and that "future generations will probably credit Carías with having done more good than harm."[5]

Others also recorded favorable impressions of Carías. Paul Daniels, a career Foreign Service officer with a long record of Latin American experience, succeeded Erwin as ambassador in April 1947. He concluded that the Carías regime, "particularly when judged by Latin American standards," had an excellent record in the financial arenas and in the maintenance of relatively peaceful and stable conditions. Chargé d'affaires John B. Faust, who had come to Tegucigalpa in 1942 from Santiago, Chile, believed that Carías was "a great and patriotic Honduran, entirely without ambitions beyond his own frontiers" and therefore deserving of "more sympathy than has been given him."[6]

Erwin, Daniels, and Faust were fully aware that Carías was a dictator. Erwin and Faust, however, remained positive. Erwin did not believe any other Honduran could rule as well as Carías and that chaos would follow his departure from the presidency. Faust noted that recorded history provided few examples of democracy emanating directly from chaos; the usual sequence of events were chaos, dictatorship, and then a gradual softening toward democracy. "President Carías is at least moving in the same direction, and . . . nothing better is in sight," Faust concluded.

Daniels was less optimistic. He believed that continued political suppression coupled with the low level of social and economic conditions, served as "a breeding ground" for political unrest. Allen Dawson, assistant chief of the Division of American Republics who had served for nearly two decades in Latin America, made the same points directly to Carías during a January 1947 visit to Honduras. Dawson came away confident that Carías got the message and "that a wedge has been inserted which . . . might be possible to widen at a later date."[7]

Although no open revolution had occurred in Honduras since 1932, the U.S. Federal Bureau of Investigation (FBI) was convinced in 1944 that there was a "strong undercurrent of unrest and dissatisfaction rapidly approaching open manifestations," both in the Liberal and National parties. The acting military attaché, Captain Thomas D. Burns, disagreed. He claimed that the discontent with Carías was simply the "fact that the 'outs' want to get 'in'" because the only political issue between the two parties was patronage.[8]

The National party split was traced to 1936, when Carías had illegally extended his presidential term and opponents were forced out of office. Although many considered Carías a poor administrator, the primary charge against him was that he had surrounded himself with a small group of trusted advisers who were more interested in personal gain than public welfare. Included in this group were: Carlos Izaquirre, Andres Reyes Moyola, Fernando Zepeda Duran, Esteban Díaz, and Andres Rodríguez. All had allegedly vastly increased their personal wealth during the Carías administration. Even his wife was accused of increasing her own fortune.

Military officers allegedly reported more soldiers than they actually commanded and pocketed the difference in financial allocations. Included in this group were General Rufino Solis and district commanders Carlos Sanabria, Alonzo Caln Oliva, and Marcial Lopez Nuñez. In addition to charges of nepotism and graft, the National party dissidents contended that Carías had failed to make important improvements in the country during his administration. By 1944, the FBI believed that this group represented the majority of the National party members who were rallying behind two prominent, honest, and capable men: Vice-President and General Abraham Williams and War Minister Juan Manuel Gálvez.[9]

The Liberal party list of grievances against Carías was long: illegal tenure in office, political prisoners jailed without trial, flagrant graft and corruption among government officials, and curtailment of free speech and organized opposition. The imprisonment and exile of party leaders since 1932 had left the Liberals in disarray, and Carías's continued repressive measures prevented the party's reorganization. Its poorer members favored Angel Zuñiga Huete, who was exiled in Mexico; and the intellectuals and professional men came to support the more militant groups, located in Costa Rica, Guatemala, and Salvador.

The principal objective of all his opponents was to force Carías's resignation and to replace him with a provisional president who would arrange a free election. The propaganda from abroad was distributed largely in Tegucigalpa by the Federation of University Students. Failing to achieve their objective, the exile groups claimed to be prepared to risk a long and costly civil war. Rumors of revolution often circulated throughout the capital. Captain Burns and Chargé d'affaires John B. Faust disagreed with the FBI opinion that Carías's resignation or a revolt against the government were real possibilities because of the opposition's disorganization and fear of reprisal. Rather, Faust speculated that the assassination of the sixty-eight-year-old dictator was a distinct possibility.[10]

The overthrow of Maximiliano Hernández Martínez in Salvador in May 1944 was given little attention in the Honduran press, which reported only that he had resigned and been replaced by General Andres Menéndez. The fall of Hernández, however, contributed to a marked increase in propaganda from the exile group in San Salvador and added impetus to the fear of revolutionary action. The rumor that Zuñiga Huete's group in Mexico was moving to join forces with the exiles in Salvador increased anxiety in Tegucigalpa and caused reinforcement of the border along the Inter-American Highway. Faust discounted the rumors because he doubted that the two groups could coordinate their efforts. Furthermore, he and Ambassador Erwin doubted that a general strike, or any form of passive resistance, as in Salvador, could take place in Honduras. Noting that such a concept was new to Central American politics because previous strikes had been by laborers, not the middle sector, Honduran conditions militated against the organization of such a movement. The country also lacked dense population centers and adequate transportation between cities. Also, a general strike required open organization, something not possible because Carías was in firm control.[11]

If Honduras was secure from a general strike, it was not from demonstrations. On May 28, 1944, an estimated 300 women marched on the presidential palace demanding the release of political prisoners and the holding of free elections. The group was led by Carlota de Vallardes, widow of a prominent newspaperman; Visitación Padilla, a teacher; and Argentina Díaz Lozano, a prize-winning novelist. Carías promised only to review the matter and subsequently explain the reasons for holding political prisoners. On July 4, 1944, a well-organized group of some 200 students and women marched through the capital to the presidential palace asking for Carías's resignation, free elections, the release of political prisoners, open frontiers for the return of exiles, free press, and a revision of the 1936 constitution.

Later that same day, a more rowdy group, estimated at 2,500, demanded that Carías resign when it made an attempt to enter the grounds of the presidential palace. The government described the demonstrators as fascist sympathizers. Carías ignored a petition presented to him on the evening of July 4 that was signed by about 200 professionals (lawyers, physicians, dentists, and some engineers) and that asked him to resign in order to save the country from bloodshed. During the suppression of antigovernment demonstrations on July 6 at San Pedro Sula, "wholesale slaughter" occurred. The Honduran United Democratic Front, based in San Salvador, criticized the United States for not aiding its cause and permitting Carías to use American military equipment to suppress Honduran people. The group also contended that Ambassador Erwin maintained a pro-Carías attitude.[12]

In response to the protest, the administration took several actions. Carías's supporters organized a demonstration on his behalf on July 10. Utilizing the "usual measures" to provide good attendance, some 8,000 people, mostly women and students, carried placards honoring Presidents Carías and Franklin D. Roosevelt. Carías and Vice-President Abraham Williams addressed the marchers, asking them to maintain order. Congressional President Plutarco Muñoz was dispatched to the north coast to lead proadministration demonstrations, which were highly exaggerated in the government-sponsored newspaper *La Epoca*. For example, it claimed that 16,000 turned out at Puerto Cortes, where the area population was estimated at only 10,000.

Government officials stated that such large turnouts clearly indicated that the opposition groups were a small minority. The administration also released propaganda pointing to its progress with new schools, hospitals, roads, and eleven years of continued peace—all of which would be jeopardized by internal strife. Subsequently, the government confined dissidents to their homes and denied them public services in an effort to prevent their scheming. On the surface, the crisis apparently had passed because they needed better organization. Finally, Franklin D. Roosevelt's reelection further strengthened the Carías regime because it meant no immediate change in U.S. nonintervention policy.[13]

By summer's end, American officials in Honduras believed that Carías had weathered the crisis and reaffirmed his political strength. Vice-consul Lee Hunsaker, who had been in the country since 1939, predicted that the opposition would remain suppressed so long as Carías stayed in power because local officials, all loyal to him, could continue their corrupt practices. Ambassador Erwin, although cautious about possible violence from exile groups, was confident that the military would maintain allegiance to Carías. Honduran landowners and North American capital—the United Fruit and Standard Fruit and Steamship companies—would also resist change. Finally, unidentified neutral observers noted that Carías was the only choice for providing order and the semblance of a unified government. Without him, unrest would be rampant.[14]

On the other hand, exiled opposition groups remained confident that Carías would be deposed by revolution if necessary. In August both the FBI and the ambassador to El Salvador, Walter Thurston, reported that the Salvadoran government was willing to assist with the overthrow of Carías, but that an agreement could not be reached between the Honduran National and Liberal factions. Through early October 1944, the two groups attempted in vain to unify their efforts. Their divisiveness contributed to political calm in Tegucigalpa.[15]

The silence was broken in mid-October, when revolutionaries made an incursion from Salvador and captured San Marcos before retreating back to their base. Seven rebels were killed and twenty wounded; the government lost fifteen men and twenty-five were wounded. Apparently, the rebels expected an internal uprising, which never materialized. Subsequently, other isolated attacks were made at Santa Rita, La Bria, Danlí, El Corpus, and Angria Fría. None of these indicated to Erwin that an uprising of any substantial proportion was in the making. He expected sporadic outbreaks to continue at remote points and that they would often be confused with bandit activities.[16]

Throughout the first quarter of 1945, Erwin reported no visible opposition movement. The Liberals had abandoned their war of nerves. "The plain fact is," Erwin observed, "that there is no present 'ambiente' [atmosphere] for a revolution in Honduras; [and] as is well known, nothing moves in Latin America in the absence of a favorable 'ambiente.'"[17]

The tranquillity ended on April 10, 1945, when two armed groups, totaling 300 men, entered Honduras from Guatemala into Copan State. The chief danger was the possibility that they would sustain themselves in the Espiritu Mountains long enough to attract support from anti-Carías elements in the country. The rebels' defeat by government forces gave Tegucigalpa "a feeling . . . that a big victory had been won," though confirmed casualty reports were never published.[18]

Fearing the "imminent hatching on Salvadoran territory of revolutionary plots against him," Carías persuaded the Salvadoran regime in 1946 to place close surveillance on Honduran exiles there. In particular, Santos Chinchilla, who had plotted the 1944 revolt, and Toribio Ramos, leader of Honduran Indian groups, were closely watched.[19]

On August 14, 1946, the FBI reported to the State Department that Honduran exiles were planning an invasion with the assistance and approval of the Guatemalan government, including President Juan José Arévalo. A month later, twenty Hondurans were arrested following the government's discovery of an arms cache in Tegucigalpa. Reportedly, Guatemalan Minister Carlos Zachrisson and his secretary, Alfredo Chocano, collaborated in the plans to instigate an uprising. Although it was generally believed in Tegucigalpa that Arévalo was actively interested in deposing Carías, Erwin could find no evidence to link the crisis to Guatemala.[20] Tensions soon eased, but the concern about Guatemalan support of a revolution in Honduras remained.

In December 1947 General Solis's son-in-law, Juan Laffite, went to Cuba reportedly carrying a $200,000 letter of credit to purchase arms to be used by the combined forces of Solis and exiles Zuñiga Huete and Alfred Trejo Castillo. Although nothing materialized, embassy second secretary Harold E. Montamat noticed an increased apprehensive attitude among administration officials.[21]

In the years 1944–47, the exiles also appealed for U.S. intervention. During the public demonstrations in May 1944, Ambassador Erwin, refusing the invitation to play a role in the negotiations for the release of political prisoners, cited the nonintervention policy. In October 1945 the

Honduran Democratic Front, based in San José, Costa Rica, appealed with no success to Assistant Secretary of State Spruille Braden to help alleviate the political crisis in Honduras. The Front, directed by former Honduran President V. Mejía Colindres and congressional President Venancio Callejas, compared Carías to Juan Perón in Argentina. Although details of Carías's oppressions were known, the Front alleged that Ambassador Erwin never fully reported them to Washington and also asked for the enforcement of various Central American treaties signed in Washington that provided for the nonrecognition of illegal governments.

In December 1947 Liberal exile Angel Zuñiga Heute visited Washington to call upon the acting chief of the Central America and Panama Affairs Division, Robert Newbegin, and later with the former ambassador to Honduras, Paul C. Daniels. Zuñiga Heute expressed the belief that "a gesture" from the United States would alleviate the Honduran political tension, and contribute to the release of political prisoners, and encourage free elections. Both Newbegin and Daniels repeated the policy of nonintervention in the domestic affairs of Central American nations. [22] The Hondurans were left to solve their own political problems.

On several occasions from 1944 to 1947, the Honduran government made allegations of communist influence in the country. In 1944 it charged that Zuñiga Heute was in collusion with alleged Mexican communist Miguel Angel Vasquez. Also in 1944 it contended that one Graciela Bogran had organized labor groups on the north coast for the purpose of teaching communist beliefs. Although Mexican labor leader Vicente Lombardo Toledano was denied entrance into Honduras, Bogran had visited Mexico on several occasions. Erwin conceded that it was not unreasonable "to suppose he [Toledano] has agents at work here." In February 1945 the government-sponsored newspaper *La Epoca* conducted a vigorous campaign against the alleged distribution of communist propaganda along the north coast and charged that it was coming from the Russian embassy in Mexico City via Guatemala. United Fruit Company representative Antonio Mata told Erwin that Mexican communist agent Jaime Ballesca was laying the groundwork for anti-Carías demonstrations on July 4 in several towns outside of Tegucigalpa. Government actions thwarted the alleged demonstrations.

When the wartime state of siege was lifted on January 21, 1946, three antigovernment publications immediately appeared: *Orientación* and *El Libertador* in Tegucigalpa and *La Tribuna* in La Ceiba. To the editor of *La*

Epoca, Zepeda Duran, this was an indication that "Communism has raised its ugly head." The newspapers' appearance was given credit for a March 1946 congressional law designed to discourage totalitarian and communist activities by providing imprisonment or exile for those convicted of engaging in them.

On August 16, 1946, the government-controlled *Honduran Nueva* editorialized about the threat of communism to Central America. The editorial charged that Russian communism threatened the region, praised Carías as a bulwark against it, and, claimed his opponents were communists. In July 1947 Carías spoke to Ambassador Daniels about the dangers of this doctrine in Costa Rica. Carías criticized previous presidents of that country for permitting communist elements to penetrate it and claimed that it "was now reaping the awkward harvest." He also charged that European communists were seducing local student groups, as was evident in Guatemala. Carías promised never to permit such infiltration into his country.[23]

American officials never shared Carías's view regarding a communist threat to Honduras, which had no diplomatic relations with Russia. Ambassador Erwin noted that "any person who agitates for improved labor conditions is often classified as a communist." Erwin could not so classify Graciela Bogran in 1944. A year later, Erwin reported the absence of any active communist activity in Honduras and that conditions were not favorable for it. Unemployment was not much of a problem and economic distress was not very apparent. The "workmen are reported to be well pleased." In response to the 1946 *Honduran Nueva* editorial, Chargé d'affaires John B. Faust agreed that Carías would counter communism, but, unlike Erwin, concluded that Carías's enemies would accept communist assistance and that the nation's illiteracy and poverty were breeding grounds for communism. Still, no organized Communist party operated there. In August 1948 Ambassador Daniels noted a "marked coolness" toward the Soviet Union by Honduran officials and people.[24] The Americans in Honduras did not perceive a communist threat to the country, and only Faust appeared to recognize that social and economic impoverishment potentially provided the opportunity for penetration.

From 1944 until 1947 U.S. officials did not believe that Carías would be brought down by violence. Unity among the fractured political opposition was unlikely, and leadership with an appeal to the lower classes was lacking. Carías could not rule forever, and the question of his successor became an important topic.

The first indications that Carías anticipated ending his political career came in August 1945. Rumors circulated in Tegucigalpa that he was considering retirement in the United States, where he would pursue farming "merely to have something to do." Subsequently, *La Epoca* editor Zepeda Duran confided to Faust that Carías was hesitant to do so because of limited investments outside of Honduras and his inability to liquidate his domestic properties quickly to acquire the cash he needed to take the step. Dismissing the retirement rumors, Faust believed Carías would remain in office until the expiration of his term, on January 1, 1949. "This would, perhaps, merely postpone the evil day," but provided additional time to develop an acceptable candidate, Faust concluded.

But Carías was serious, as Liberal party member Mario Valenzuela learned in early 1946. Although Valenzuela typified the young business-men in Tegucigalpa who wanted a change in government, Erwin noted a desire for a peaceful transition. Members of both political parties ex-pressed a belief that Carías had set a pattern for stable government which "will be followed in the future." Erwin attributed this attitude to the fact that each side feared confiscation of property if chaos followed. In April 1946 the respected man of Honduran letters, Rafael Helidoro Valle, spent a week in Honduras on behalf of several exile groups in Mexico City to investigate the political situation. He spent several hours with Carías and with political leaders, both pro- and anti-Carías, in Tegucigalpa and San Pedro Sula. Valle came away confident that Carías was serious about retirement. He was so impressed with the "enormous material and moral progress" of the country under Carías that he advised the exiles against revolution in order to avoid national chaos.

In August 1946 the United Fruit Company president, Samuel Zemur-ray, told Erwin that, though "no one could have done any better" for Honduras than Carías, free elections and the peaceful transfer of power were necessary in 1948 to avoid bloodshed; otherwise, he speculated that "no private property or concessions would be safe." He added that the Bolivian and Guatemalan revolts "will be like pink tea" compared to any in Honduras should the situation get out of hand.[25] Such exhortations indicated that each group was concerned with protecting its own interests in the post-Carías era. Still, the opinions of the middle sector and lower socioeconomic groups were not measured. Political rivalry remained a struggle among the elite.

The question of Carías's successor had long been a subject of speculation. Within the fractured National party, the Americans identified four potential leaders in 1944. War Minister Juan Manuel Gálvez was most prominent. Although loyal to Carías, he was critical of his administration. Still, some people suggested that he would be Carías's handpicked successor. Gálvez had been a lawyer for the United Fruit Company, which in the past had "made and broken Presidents," and its influence was expected to continue. Gálvez was more of a company favorite than Second Vice-President Abraham Williams, who was considered more ambitious and desirous of the presidency than Gálvez. A third possibility was the commandant of La Ceiba, General Rufino Solis, an educated and ambitious person, who was expected to make a bid for power. Finally, Carías's nephew, Calixto Carías, a known killer, unscrupulous and ambitious, was expected to seek the office. Of the four, only Calixto had strength among the lower classes, but death in October 1944 removed him from consideration.[26]

When it became clear that Carías had no intention to remain in power beyond January 1, 1949, the political jockeying among Gálvez, Williams, and Solis intensified. The rivalry for the National party candidacy narrowed to Williams and Gálvez in 1947 because Solis had been linked to the Liberal party, both as a potential revolutionary leader and possible presidential candidate. Solis resigned his military post in April 1947 to pursue his candidacy. Thereafter, he demonstrated no real strength outside of his region of La Ceiba. His popularity waned and his promise of government for the people was taken as window dressing because he allegedly had amassed personal wealth as the commandant of La Ceiba. Chargé d'affaires Montamat observed that the Solis candidacy was "usually greeted with a superior smile signifying a willingness to accept a joke."[27]

In 1947 Gálvez also promoted his own candidacy, and evidence indicated he would be the National party nominee. In August, Congressional President Plutarco Muñoz told Ambassador Paul C. Daniels that Williams would not be the Nationalist candidate, but that Williams would support whoever was nominated. Williams, however, approved his supporters' work on his own behalf and would not resign the vice-presidency for fear of losing his immunity. The government-controlled press made glowing comparisons between Gálvez and Carías. In San Pedro Sula, the Gálvez campaign was already underway with the distribution of campaign buttons and broadsides. The embassy second secretary and vice-consul, Harold E. Montamat, who had come to Honduras in April 1947, believed that a Gálvez presidency would "not be an unhappy one for the United States," but felt the Honduran path toward democracy would be impeded. Gálvez, who was considered to be weak, was expected to be a "marionette handled by Carías," and things would continue as they were under Carías, whose wealth would be protected. Not only would graft and corruption continue, but a Gálvez victory would ensure the "selling of Honduras" to the United Fruit Company. Throughout September and October, government newspapers extolled his virtues.

From unidentified government sources, Montamat learned that former Minister of Finance and Minister of Foreign Affairs and now Minister to the United States Julio Lazano was the vice-presidential choice. Thereafter, Lazano also received accolades from the government press. By the year's end, it was clear that the Nationalists would nominate Gálvez and Lazano, and they did, at their convention on February 20, 1948. The twenty-four-point party platform called for continued progress on all fronts: education, civil rights, tax reform, transportation, and industrial and agricultural progress. Montamat, doubting that the poorly drafted platform would be honored, noted that it appeared "harmless to external interests and political benefit of the country."[28]

The Liberal party had been severely factionalized since 1932. Most of its leaders were in exile in Costa Rica, El Salvador, Mexico, and, after 1944, Guatemala. The most active émigré was Angel Zuñiga Heute, whose Honduran Democratic Front, or Liberal Committee of Hondurans, was based in Mexico. His long-term absence from the country diminished his following among the middle sector, and thus in 1944 he was not judged to be a strong presidential candidate. When new Ambassador Paul C. Daniels arrived in Tegucigalpa in July 1947, he found the Liberal party still split over the selection of a presidential candidate. The director of the newspaper *Diario Del Norte*, Enrique Ortiz, was leading a party faction advocating support for General Rufino Solis, the Nationalist promoting his own candidacy. Still, exiled Zuñiga Heute was the "unlikely white hope of the Liberals."[29]

The Liberals also sought U.S. assistance to increase their chances for political success. On August 11, 1947, party leaders Antonio R. Reinab and Federico A. Smith transmitted a party position paper to Ambassador Daniels. It repeated the long list of Carías's oppressive measures and went on to ask that President Harry S. Truman withdraw his moral support of all dictators, which would be consistent with his international attitude in support of democracy. The paper also asked that the U.S. embassy in Tegucigalpa use its influence to bring political freedom to Honduras. In December 1947 Zuñiga Heute traveled to Washington, D.C., to meet Robert Newbegin, acting chief of the Central America and Panama Affairs Division, as well as Daniels, who had just relinquished the ambassadorship. Zuñiga Heute suggested that the United States make some "gesture" to ensure free elections in Honduras. Newbegin and Daniels reiterated the American policy of nonintervention.[30] The Liberal appeals were reminiscent of previous times, when political parties out of power appealed for U.S. assistance.

In February 1948, two months after his return from Mexico, Zuñiga Heute and Liberal party president Reinab called upon the U.S. embassy in Tegucigalpa to repeat the charges against Carías and beg for U.S. intervention. Although there were good grounds for such charges, Montamat, the embassy consul, again repeated the American position of nonintervention. He also came away with a favorable impression of Zuñiga Heute. Rather than a headstrong and disagreeable person, Montamat found him to be intelligent and tolerant, and knew that his position "was one of resignation and possibly the realization of the grave difficulty, or even impossibility and hopelessness of what he was attempting."[31]

At the party's convention on May 16, 1948, 200 Liberal delegates nominated Zuñiga Heute for the presidency and Francisco Paredes Fajardo of San Pedro Sula for the vice-presidency, the same ticket that had been put forward in 1932. The platform reiterated much of the National party's proclamations. Montamat described it as "one of those political documents which mean very little if anything." When new Ambassador Herbert Bursely arrived from Ankara, Turkey, in December 1943, he noted a sense of pessimism among the Liberals. He cabled Washington that this pessimism "could well have its foundation in their [Liberal] failure, possibly inevitable, to produce anything more stimulating than a warmed over 16 year old dish."[32]

Immediately following the Liberal party convention, a flurry of revolutionary rumors emerged. However, Ambassador Bursely could find no internal group in favor of violence. The most prosperous groups preferred the status quo; and, though the major portion of the intellectuals opposed the government, Bursely believed they too shied away from violence. The small farmer, who had made great progress during the last fourteen years, was considered a "stabilizing influence" that would be one of the last elements to participate in any revolution.[33] Bursely knew nothing about the attitudes of the common man except that he looked to Zuñiga Heute as a symbol of his desire for more freedom. Bursely concluded that the nation would avoid revolution for now, but it seemed "almost inevitable that the elections will be accompanied or followed by bloodshed in some parts of the country." Within a month, Tegucigalpa became particularly quiet, but Military Attaché H. S. Isaacson reported political activity in the cities along the north coast.[34]

As the presidential campaign got underway, the opposition failed to make the most of alleged government corruption, possibly because, like many Latin Americans, they were "unfortunately rather hardened to this aspect." On the other hand, the government was not very efficient in pointing out its accomplishments: public works, road building, a solvent treasury, and lack of excessive inflation. The campaign degenerated into a vicious name-calling crusade. In July, Zuñiga Heute presented Bursely with a list of ninety-five alleged instances of government interference with the Liberal party. Some of the charges were true, Bursely concluded, but "the bill of particulars reads just like what the Liberals used to do when they were in power." In turn, the government press attacked Zuñiga Heute as an "ignominious traitor" for his alleged 1932 understanding with Guatemala's Jorge Ubico, which weakened the Honduran position regarding the Guatemalan boundary question. The charges and countercharges of graft and corruption intensified to the point where the rhetoric was almost unrestrained vilification of each candidate.[35]

The Liberals did not give full support to Zuñiga Heute, who reportedly was becoming arbitrary and intransigent in his leadership. This resulted in an effort to have him withdraw from the race and be replaced by either Ramon Villeda Morales or Abraham Bursco. In August a splinter group of the Liberal party formed the Honduran Democratic Revolutionary party. Bursely found some "slightly diluted Communist phraseology" in its attacks upon foreign investment and interference with Honduran sovereignty, but the party recognized the need of foreign assistance for economic development. Such rhetoric reminded Bursely of the Mexican "double talk" regarding foreign interests. Still, he cautioned that it was not in the U.S. interest to have "such ideas propagated even to a limited audience since the crop from such seeds may eventually be abundant." By late September, Zuñiga Heute's position was so weak, there was speculation that the Liberals would propose that both candidates withdraw and a compromise candidate be found. The Nationalists, expecting a victory at the polls, refused to even consider the idea.[36]

  While the Liberals despaired, the National party became more confident of victory, largely because of the ineffectiveness of the opposition. In late August, Gálvez spoke publicly of his anticipated presidency. He proposed revising the "antiquated, inequitable, ineffective and immoral" tax structure that had oppressed the workers while being lenient upon the wealthy. Vice-President Williams instructed his followers to vote for Gálvez, though as a government officer he was prohibited from campaigning.[37]

  The Liberals "at long last realized the helplessness of the situation" and that they could not win a free election. Rumors began circulating in early September that they would withdraw from the race and boycott the elections, which occurred on September 22, when the party's supreme council decreed its abstention from the polls because of the "atmosphere of oppression." Ambassador Bursely thought the action "may be a smokescreen" for something more ambitious, like a revolt. The Carías administration shared that view and became more apprehensive as rumors of an invasion from Guatemala circulated. Subsequently, quiet prevailed. The consensus in Tegucigalpa agreed that the opposition action was taken in light of anticipated defeat.[38]

  On election eve, October 9, 1948, Zuñiga Heute and eight other prominent members of the Liberal party became "guests" in the Chilean, Guatemalan, and Mexican legations. Although Ambassador Bursely speculated that the Honduran government probably welcomed having these persons out of circulation, the widely held opinion was that, in the face of anticipated electoral disorder, the leading Liberals, not wanting to "face the consequences of . . . [their] direct or indirect activities in encouraging outbreaks, chose the coward's path and took cover."

  The election, however, went quietly. Reports of shootings in the countryside were "attributed to paying off personal grudges" rather than calculated revolt plans. Official results gave Gálvez 255,000 of the 300,000 votes cast. The Nationalist victory was attributed to the widespread fear of disorder that might follow a change of political power. Zuñiga Heute remained in hiding for some time, and the government attributed Liberal revolt rumors to the election defeat.[39]

Gálvez's inauguration, on January 1, 1949, went smoothly and Ambassador Bursely was impressed with the warm reception given Carías as he walked among the people. This was "a most interesting incident," Bursely observed, "when it is considered that he is so widely known as a 'dictator.'" Bursely was disappointed, however, that no American correspondents were there to report the event, which offered "a lesson which could well be emulated in other lands."[40]

The Cabinet appointees—Leonidad Pineda, War; Julio Lazano, Government; Marco Batres, Finance; Eduardo Valenzuela, Foreign Relations; and, Marcos Carías Reyes, Education—were deemed to be Gálvez's alter ego and were judged to be only temporary. The populace, content with the prosperity inherited from the Carías regime, contributed to the serenity. Carías retired to his *finca* and gave every indication of remaining aloof from politics. The return of political exiles throughout January and the release of political prisoners from jail demonstrated Gálvez's conciliatory attitude. Police carried billies instead of rifles. Gálvez accepted a petition signed by two thousand persons asking for a congressional amendment to permit women the right to vote. These factors gave Bursely confidence about the future of the country. He saw the possibility of "an increasingly enlightened administration" that would become more democratic in "the absence of violent opposition."[41]

Throughout May, the political scene remained calm as the government continued to make reorganization plans and propose future government-sponsored projects. Public criticism of the administration emerged in June and continued throughout the summer. Gálvez was attacked for appointing too many Liberals to government posts and dismissing long-term loyal Nationalists. Discontent with various ministers also surfaced. Valenzuela was criticized for his antiforeign business attitude and his lack of brilliance. Reyes, in addition to being a poor administrator, also was considered unqualified for the Education Ministry. Lazano was linked to the previous administration, and questions were raised about his competence.

Public patience was wearing thin awaiting promised government reorganization and reform plans. Unemployment increased, and a general downturn occurred in business activity. Although the economic problems were not attributable to the government, they only served to increase public dissatisfaction. Disconcerting rumors also abounded, ranging from friction between Gálvez and Carías as well as local commandants and other Nationalists to assassination plots against Gálvez and/or Carías. Bursely dismissed these rumors as "representative of political gossip" common to Central America.[42]

The optimistic anticipation Bursely expressed in January failed to materialize during the first year of Gálvez's administration. His lengthy state of the nation address on December 5, 1949, was an "unanalytical and uninspiring" speech that "dealt largely with details and avoided some of the more basic aspects of national life."[43]

Gálvez proved to be more independent of Carías than most political observers had expected. During the next five years, he accomplished more than Carías had in the preceding fifteen. Financial and tax reform stimulated the economy. Coffee became an important export, ending the nation's dependency on bananas. Roads were built to connect outlying villages and towns. A concerted effort was made to improve the nation's literacy rate. A believer in constitutional government, Gálvez prepared the people for free elections in 1954, in which Carías again sought the presidency. His poor showing demonstrated that Hondurans had outgrown their caudillo.

Honduras, like its neighbors El Salvador and Guatemala, had endured a dictatorship since the early 1930s that was threatened in 1944. Unlike the dictatorial regimes in San Salvador and Guatemala City, where Maximiliano Hernández Martínez and Jorge Ubico were deposed, Tiburcio Carías remained in power in Tegucigalpa. The protests against Carías from May to July 1944 were conducted by small groups of the middle sector: students, writers, and professional people. Ambassador John D. Erwin and consular officers John B. Faust and Lee Hunsaker gave several reasons for the group's failure. One of these was its disorganization, and, given the country's poor communications system, unity appeared unlikely. The military remained loyal to the president and, along with the landowning elite and the United and Standard Fruit companies, resisted change. Government bureaucrats, enriched by graft, also did not favor any political alteration. The exile groups in Costa Rica, El Salvador, and Mexico were in disarray and failed to contribute to the

1944 protest movements. The Americans found little chance for success of a national uprising against Carías.

From 1944 until 1947 sporadic exile incursions into Honduras failed to gain internal support because, as Erwin believed, of the lack of desire for change attributable to economic prosperity. No one was willing to risk the loss of wealth and property. Paul C. Daniels, who succeeded Erwin in April 1947, agreed that the stable conditions contributed to political tranquillity. For the same reason, economic prosperity, most American officials dismissed Honduran government charges of attempted communist infiltration into the country. Only Faust and Daniels cautioned that continued political suppression, poverty, and illiteracy provided the entrée for future penetration.

In 1945, when Carías indicated he would step down at the end of his term in 1949, the elite and representatives of the United and Standard Fruit companies became apprehensive because any change threatened their holdings and position. To these groups, Carías had provided effective leadership, a thought echoed by Ambassadors Erwin, Daniels, and Herbert Bursely, Consular Officer Faust, and State Department Desk Officer Gordon Reid. The fear of change, the Americans concluded, resulted in the uncontested electoral victory of Carías's handpicked successor, Juan Manuel Gálvez, in October 1948, who was expected to continue his mentor's ways. Ambassador Bursely's description of the warm reception given Carías at Gálvez's inauguration on January 1, 1949, verified what Military Attaché Thomas Burns observed in 1944 and what the diplomatic correspondence reported after that date. Specifically, Honduran politics was only a meaningless struggle among the various elites, with the "outs" wanting "in."

5

Nicaragua

IN many ways, Nicaragua paralleled its neighbors. The agriculturally based economy created a wide gap between rich and poor, and the government served the interests of the farmer. After 1936, dictator Anastasio Somoza ruled with an iron hand, firmly supported by the national guard. Opposition to him came from elite groups, no less authoritarian, but only anti-Somoza. In 1944 the idealistic middle sector, encouraged by the fall of Ubico and Hernández, demonstrated for constitutional reform, but thereafter made no political impact. Until 1949 Somoza remained in full control because of the guard's continued loyalty. When his handpicked successor, Leonardo Argüello, tried to wrest control of the guard from him in 1947, he was deposed and replaced by Somoza's uncle Victor Ramon y Reyes, who presided until his death in 1950. Throughout these years, the lower classes remained apolitical, and opposition came only from elite groups, most of which were in exile.

Coffee was Nicaragua's primary crop. Sesame, sugar, cereals, timber, and rubber were other important products. Since 1938 American capital had developed the gold mines, and in 1943 gold constituted the largest single export. The United States was the primary importer of Nicaraguan goods, accounting for 75 percent of the country's 1943 foreign trade. Industrial development was lacking, and a combination of poor banking policies and political influence resulted in a serious national financial condition. Inadequate communications also hampered growth. Economic activity was further stunted by Somoza, who had extensive interests in almost everything worthwhile: banana, coffee, and sugar plantations as well as banking and merchandising.[1]

The country's social structure retained its colonial characteristics: a small number of wealthy landed families at the top and a broad peasant class at the bottom. The agricultural economy contributed to the maintenance of this system, in which the landed few exercised paternalistic influence over the workers of the land. The upper class also included wealthy merchants and high government officials in the urban areas; the lower class, unskilled urban workers. A small middle sector had arisen, which consisted of small landowners, merchants, lesser government officials, and professionals. Movement from the lower to the middle sector was possible through acquisition of wealth or education, but the 70 percent illiteracy rate suggested limited mobility.[2]

Nicaragua's twentieth-century political history was characterized by almost continuous internal and external difficulties. Changes in administration, often brought about by revolution, were frequent. Almost all rulers governed arbitrarily and showed little regard for the spirit or letter of the constitution or law. After the overthrow of dictator José Santos Zelaya in 1909, politics became strongly influenced by the United States. Often the selection of presidents was made in accordance with the wishes of the State Department. Financial and economic guidance was given. Marines were stationed in the country to maintain order.

When the Good Neighbor Policy was inaugurated in 1933, U.S. forces were withdrawn. This left the government in the hands of Juan B. Sacasa, who governed until 1936, when overthrown by national guard General Anastasio Somoza. He was subsequently elected as president and inaugurated on January 1, 1937. The constitution presented a democratic framework, which provided for the nonreelection of an incumbent president and an elected two-house legislature. However, in practice Somoza dominated. His Liberal party controlled the bulk of the population. He changed Cabinet ministers at will. He appointed national guard commandants to the nation's fifteen departments, each of whom was responsible only to him. Civil liberties were suppressed. In effect, he governed the country arbitrarily and for the benefit of himself and his family.[3]

In December 1943 Somoza called for a Liberal party convention to convene in León on January 8, 1944, at which time he proclaimed that he had no intention of remaining in office beyond his legal term, ending on January 1, 1947, unless the majority of the people wished him to, and Congress amended the constitution to permit him to do so. "If you want me, very well," he told his audience after recanting the progress of his administration and denying stealing from the national treasury. Subsequently, the convention adopted the principles of the 1939 constitution as the party creed and called for women's suffrage; the right of minority parties to participate in government; and, in case of national emergency, the president's right to stand for reelection.

Amabassador to Nicaragua, John B. Stewart correctly interpreted the last proviso to be "window dressing" for congressional consideration of a reelection amendment to the constitution. Congress approved such legislation on April 27, 1944. Stewart, a career diplomat who enjoyed considerable Latin American experience, also noted that the Liberal party's dissident element, headed by Enoc Aguado, General Carlos Pasos, and Manuel Cordero Reyes, had not been brought back into the party's mainstream.[4]

Ambassador Stewart had sensed a split in its ranks for nearly a year. As the January 1944 convention approached, dissident leaders Manuel Cordero Reyes and General Carlos Pasos expected to lose their posts, or even be read out of the party. In his opening remarks, the convention president, Crisanto Sacasa, charged that some Liberals "had reached a point of infamy." The dissidents charged that Somoza had become a political and economic dictator and that the masses were suffering the consequences. Specifically, he was indicted for violating civil rights, usurping judicial power, accumulating private wealth, and excessive taxation—all of which made the nation impotent.

For Somoza to compare himself with U.S. President Franklin D. Roosevelt, Pasos charged, was a farce because the former did things for the people and was freely reelected to office. The dissidents, like Stewart, interpreted the León convention to mean that Somoza would seek reelection. They were determined to prevent his doing so through legal means. To be successful, however, Stewart believed the dissidents would need to join forces with the old-line Conservatives who supported former president Emiliano Chamorro, exiled in Mexico.[5]

The death of Reyes on January 12, 1944, temporarily set back the cause of the dissidents, also known as the Independent Liberals. Still, other sources of opposition to Somoza were evident. The fall of Maximiliano Hernández Martínez in Salvador and Jorge Ubico in Guatemala and pressure against Tiburcio Carías in Honduras caused repercussions in Nicaragua. Some believed that such pressures would bring Somoza down. The fall of Ubico created speculation that the national guard's loyalty to Somoza was suspect.

In May, Nicaraguan university students were arrested for staging a demonstration of sympathy for Salvadoran students. At the same time, several lawyers expressed opposition to the constitutional change permitting Somoza's possible reelection. In June, supreme court Vice-President Fernando Saballos spoke out against his anticipated reelection. Saballos charged that Somoza was surrounded by "yes men" who claimed that only he could maintain order and further contended that the president failed to realize his loss of popularity. In the late afternoon of June 27, students gathered at the Central University in Managua carrying banners constructed in the office of dissident leader Carlos Pasos. The crowd swelled to several hundred and heard speeches opposing Somoza's expected reelection and ridiculing the cost of maintaining the national guard. Wielding their banners debunking Somoza, the group set out to carry their demonstration before several foreign embassies, but were halted by the guard. Some 400 people were temporarily detained. The next day, June 28, some 3,000 women from all social classes paraded through downtown Managua protesting against Somoza. In response, the government organized two smaller pro-Somoza demonstrations, which were led by the president in cheers, laughter, and catcalls against the opposition. Stewart observed that, during the demonstrations, the people "had exhibited but little sullenness and, on the contrary, had shown good humor throughout."

Stewart may have misjudged the mood. The student demonstration on June 27 gave Somoza reason to close the Central University. On July 1 newspapers reminded the people that wartime martial law continued and that permits were needed in advance for political demonstrations. On July 2 the cathedral in Managua was closed by the national guard, and the Central Plaza was cleared of traffic to permit a demonstration by the

Conservatives. On July 3 round robins circulated among lawyers, doctors, and dentists urging them not to open their doors on July 5, but this had little effect. Managuan businessmen were warned that the opposition was preparing a sit-down strike in the near future. Although Somoza mingled freely among the people during the July 4 celebration, the presence of the cavalry prevented any anti-Somoza demonstration.[6] Both the government and the opposition were serious about their positions.

The opposition pressure bore fruit during a July 3 meeting of the Liberal party in Managua. Somoza agreed to veto the April constitutional amendment permitting his reelection. The veto satisfied approximately two-thirds of the party members, but not the dissidents following Carlos Pasos, who refused to sign a declaration adhering to party principles. Ambassador Stewart concluded that Somoza's action would do little to calm the tense political situation.[7]

Stewart believed that both Somoza and the opposition had gained victories during the events of June and early July. Somoza prevented bloodshed and a general strike, which had proved to be effective in ousting dictators in Salvador and Gautemala. The national guard remained loyal. The opposition's victories included the president's veto of the election reform bill and promises of a free press, government reform, and a halt to the export of staple foodstuffs. Labor gained a promise of social security legislation.

Somoza, however, was not secure with his victory. Not content with allowing dissident Liberal leaders to remain in the capital, he let it be known he was contemplating the exile of several persons to the Corn Islands. Pasos got the message. He and eleven other dissidents left for Salvador, and Carlos Montalban and five others departed for Costa Rica on July 14. Subsequently, another twenty-six dissidents were detained at Bluefields. These events led Stewart to conclude that Somoza had won the battle, which had begun with the student-initiated demonstrations, and that the opposition was now leaderless. Given Somoza's record, the concessions made on July 3 had little meaning. Stewart found no unusual anti-Somoza feeling among the people and believed that the maintenance of his approachable, jocular personality throughout the crisis had aided Somoza's popularity.[8]

Opposition to Somoza was not confined to within the country itself. In late May 1944 the *Unión Democrática Centroamericana,* an exile group based in Costa Rica, appealed to the diplomatic corps in Managua to intercede in preventing him from seeking reelection. Otherwise, the *Unión* promised that he would share the fate of deposed Salvadoran dictator Hernández. Similar threats came from Chamorro's conservative group in Mexico City. Somoza judged these threats to be meaningless because the exile groups were not linked to the June and July disturbances in Managua. An attempted invasion of Nicaragua from Costa Rica by forces under exiled Conservative Alfredo Noguero Gómez in October 1944 failed to ignite internal uprisings. The invasion's failure further solidified Somoza's position at home, but incensed the Nicaraguan exile camp in Mexico, where Gómez found sanctuary.[9]

Political calm greeted new Ambassador Fletcher Warren, who had previously served in Central America and had held key State Department positions, upon his arrival in the spring of 1945. He believed that the opposition to Somoza had climaxed in July 1944. Thereafter, the dissidents had left Nicaragua for Mexico, Guatemala, and Costa Rica, and, except for the ill-fated Noguera invasion, were unable to obtain support from abroad. For the most part, they were composed of industrialists and merchants, either dissident Liberals or Conservatives, who abhorred the philosophy of the Central American Unionists, which was linked to leftist Mexican labor leader Vicente Lombardo Toledano. Furthermore, the exiled political groups were factionalized. Not all Independent Liberals supported Carlos Pasos, and many Conservatives were disillusioned with the leadership of Emiliano Chamorro. Within Nicaragua, the opposition to Somoza dwindled, contributing to its air of hopelessness.

Chargé d'affaires Harold D. Finley, completing his fifteenth year of service in Central America, doubted that the dissident Independent Liberals and Conservatives could reach agreement on a candidate to challenge Somoza in the forthcoming presidential elections. Somoza sensed that the opposition's virility best served his interests, and it further contributed to his confidence in control over the political situation. Although adamantly vociferous against Somoza's potential reelection, the opposition, because of its disarray, was unable to find a compromise candidate to challenge the incumbent. Under such conditions, Warren concluded that no strong, personable, and able man was in sight and that, if Somoza chose not to run, he would be able to select a person to protect his interests.[10]

The Independent Liberal party, whose origins can be traced to Somoza's reelection bid in 1943 and 1944, did not have legal status because it had not participated in the last presidential election (1936). At Somoza's direction, the dissidents were expelled from the Liberal party on September 6, 1945. Although Ambassador Warren thought otherwise, the Independents remained committed to the ouster of Somoza. The Independent Liberals and traditional Conservatives were strange bedfellows, but the former recognized the necessity of an alliance with the latter.[11]

The Conservatives, Nicaragua's traditional second political party, were nominally headed by former President Emiliano Chamorro, exiled in Mexico. The party was split. Chamorro's followers remained committed to the demand that Somoza resign from the presidency or be overthrown by force. The second faction, also in Mexico, included Haracío Bolaños, Felipe Mantrea, Leónidas Abaunza, and Alfredo Sevilla. It shared the opinion of dissident Liberal Carlos Pasos that Somoza should be ousted by pacific means in order to save the country from bloodshed. This group was willing to accept a provisional president, including Somoza's brother-in-law Manuel Luis DeBayle, provided he not stand for election in 1947; that Somoza turn over leadership of the national guard to a U.S. military officer; and that a foreigner, preferably an American, supervise the presidential elections.

Warren learned that the Conservatives, in 1945, were only giving lip service to a political agreement with the Independent Liberals. The Conservatives intended to cooperate with all opposition forces until shortly before the scheduled February 1947 elections, when the party would demand support for its candidate, reportedly lawyer Maximo H. Zepeda. The Conservatives, at this point, rejected any pact that would support Enoc Aguado, whom Somoza was trying to win over with promises of a Cabinet post. In November 1945 Somoza rejected a Conservative party proposal that the government be placed in the hands of a triumvirate until elections were held. Ambassador Warren believed that the Conservative party was better organized and disciplined than the Independent Liberals and was therefore the stronger of the two opposition groups.[12]

Unable to negotiate a political agreement with the Conservatives, the Liberals pursued their own course in 1946. When their split from Somoza was confirmed at the party convention at León in January 1946, the Independent Liberals organized a mass demonstration against Somoza in Managua on January 27. The estimated 20,000 demonstrators were dispersed by the national guard. On March 6 the Independent Liberals convened at León to organize an executive committee and plan for a national convention and party platforms. The turnout for the party plebiscite on June 2 was poor. Despite inadequate preparation and the absence of strong organizational activity, government interference was given as the primary reason for the confusion and disappointing turnout. On June 1 the government issued a circular to all department *jefes políticos* stating that the Independent Liberals had no legal status under existing electoral laws and therefore could not hold party elections. Although Somoza rescinded the order that same evening, Warren concluded that he had successfully sabotaged the plebiscite, which denied the Independent Liberals a show of political strength. The delegates elected in June convened at León on September 2, 1946, and nominated Enoc Aguado for president.[13]

Aguado became the opposition candidate because the Independent Liberals united with the Conservatives following the return of Chamorro from Mexico on May 12, 1946. The seventy-five-year-old former president received a reception beyond all Conservative party expectations. An estimated 20,000 people, representing all social classes, gathered in Managua to greet Chamorro, who had been out of the country for ten years. Overwhelmed by the reception, he did not speak to the crowd, but issued a written statement calling for free elections after Somoza renounced his reelection bid and leadership of the national guard. Some Independent Liberals saw Chamorro as a political opportunist who would use the opposition schism to seek the presidency for himself.

These suspicions were put to rest on May 22, when he convinced the Conservative party national directorate to support the Independent Liberal candidate. The agreement, signed on August 17, pledged both parties to overthrow the dictatorship, guarantee civil liberties, initiate governmental and constitutional reforms, and establish a government that would provide minority representation. Although right-wing Conservatives favored Enrique Maria Sanchez, a wealthy landowner from León who had not previously been in politics, they accepted Aguado because of his broader appeal to the campesinos. The agreement also provided for a joint congressional ballot and participation in the Cabinet and other government posts. The joint platform called for tax and banking reform; reorganization of the national guard; increased foreign investment capital and expanded industrialization; the guarantee of civil liberties; and improved living, working, health, and educational conditions for the working masses.

Ambassador Warren viewed the platform as "a multitude of unattainable objectives designed to satisfy the largest number of interests." Although the agreement was considered to be the best possible, elements of both parties raised objections. Fernando Saballos headed a group of antipact Independent Liberals who believed they should pursue their own course. Felipe Argüello Bolaños was spokesman for the younger and "progressive" Conservatives, who contended that the pact had been dictated by the party's old guard.[14]

Before the agreement, Somoza had attempted to lure either the Independent Liberals or Conservatives into his camp to prevent their coming together. In early April 1946 he pleaded for party unity when he met with a delegation of Independent Liberals at the presidential palace. He proposed that each faction submit one name for a Liberal party presidential plebiscite and agree not to sponsor an official confirmed by the party's national convention. He promised not to interfere with the plebiscite nor to sponsor an official candidate. The Independent Liberals' counterproposal demanded the conversion of the national guard into a nonpolitical organization; the nonpoliticization of the national bank, railroad, communication services, and other institutions by the appointment of qualified managers and directors who previously had not been involved in politics; reorganization of the Liberal party; and immediate electoral reform.

If accepted, the agreement was to be witnessed by the diplomatic corps. The obvious objective was to eliminate Somoza from the political scene. A twenty-five-man commission, representing both factions, was appointed to conciliate the diametrically opposite proposals. Aguado correctly assumed that Somoza would not consider the Independent Liberal proposals, and he therefore suspended conciliation talks on May 2.

On May 27 the Independent Liberals made new proposals to Somoza that were designed to bring about a Liberal agreement upon a candidate before other issues were addressed. The intent was still the same: remove Somoza from politics. He was willing to agree to electoral reform and permit all political parties to have representatives at polling booths, but he was not willing to neutralize the national guard. Unofficially, he indicated he would not support an Independent Liberal presidential candidate. Ambassador Warren correctly judged that neither side would budge from its position. The Independent Liberals recognized the futility of their effort after meeting with Somoza at Corinto on June 15 and suspended further talks. Until he was willing to address the issue of democracy, the Independent Liberals believed that no grounds for discussion existed.[15]

Somoza also attempted to reach a compromise with the Conservatives. He unsuccessfully sought a meeting with Chamorro immediately upon his return from Mexico on May 12, 1946. Chamorro's position was accepted by the party directorate over the protest of a small group of wealthy landowners who believed that some understanding with Somoza was essential to protect their wealth. As part of the August pact, both Chamorro and Aguado pledged that their parties would not reach an agreement with Somoza before or after the 1947 presidential contest.[16]

Warren noted that the "striking feature of the political situation is the mutual distrust which pervades all sections of political life." Nobody trusted the president, who trusted no one but himself. The Independent Liberals were fearful that the Conservatives might strike a deal with Somoza, and the Conservatives looked with a jaundiced eye toward the Independent Liberals for possible double-dealing. Warren speculated that the opposition, if successful, would act no different from Somoza. Political repression would continue, and no improvement would occur in the country's economic conditions. "The opposition does not essentially hate authoritarian government . . . it merely hates General Somoza," Warren concluded. This was the only unifying force among the opposition.[17]

Somoza contributed to the confusion. After governing as a dictator since 1937, he announced in September 1944 that he would not be a candidate for reelection. Although some Americans believed that he had been a benevolent dictator, growing popular pressure forced him to renounce his intentions to seek reelection. He reiterated this position in August, October, and November 1945 as well as in January and August 1946. Few observers took him seriously. The popular view was best expressed by Aguado, who predicted that Somoza planned to play one opposition group off against the other; this would wear down his political opponents and enable him to remain in power. In May 1945 Ambassador Warren offered several reasons to explain why Somoza planned to remain on after 1947. Somoza sought the supreme court's opinion regarding his remaining in office by virtue of an "election" within the meaning of the constitution or by reason of "appointment" by a constituent assembly.

Somoza's private secretary, Manuel Zurita, made public statements claiming that the people wanted Somoza to remain in office, and on Army Day, May 27, the national guard distributed handbills advocating Somoza's retention. In July, undoubtedly with his knowledge, similar proclamations were issued in several towns across the country. These actions prompted Somoza to claim that he enjoyed popular support and that he was opposed only by a small minority. If his government was dictatorial, it certainly was a benevolent one, he asserted. His popularity was measured by the ability to walk among the people freely, all of whom had benefited from his administration. He claimed that the wealthy benefited from the national bank and his agricultural export policies, while the masses received housing and schools. He explained that the Labor Code was an effort to bring about harmony between capital and labor. Proud of his record, he was confident he could capture 60—65 percent of the votes in a national plebiscite. Such popularity, he argued, guaranteed him a future, unlike Jorge Ubico in Guatemala and Maximiliano Hernández Martínez in Salvador.[18]

Somoza often explained that, despite his desire to retire, he was forced to take the stance of an active candidate for several reasons. In August 1945 he explained to Ambassador Warren that he was "sick and worn out," but he permitted friends to advance his candidacy because they had learned that several national guard officers entertained presidential ambitions. He added that he "would not go through with the election when the time came." Nicaragua's ambassador to the United States, Guillermo Sevilla Sacasa, reiterated the same points to Warren in November and to Spruille Braden in December 1945. Sacasa added that Somoza was preventing political chaos by remaining an active candidate. Somoza, to Assistant Secretary of State Nelson Rockefeller in March 1944, and Sacasa, in his conversations with Warren and Braden, attempted to explain that Nicaragua was a country of low cultural achievement where political measures feasible in the United States and other countries were not suitable and where the people needed a strong governor.[19]

Whatever the interpretation of Somoza's contradictory statements, it seemed clear that, if he did not seek reelection, he would dictate the Liberal party candidate. Ambassador Stewart believed this was true, despite the party schism that occurred in 1944. In March 1945 Ambassador Warren reported that political observers in Managua were convinced that Somoza would dictate the selection of a friendly president and that he would remain as head of the national guard. This could be done constitutionally by his resigning from the presidency and appointing a favorite as president, who in turn would designate Somoza as head of the national guard, which could then supervise the 1947 election to ensure the victory of Somoza's "friend." A year later, Warren remained convinced that Somoza had sufficient power and support within the Liberal party to name its presidential candidate.[20]

Immediately following Somoza's retirement announcement in September 1944, speculation began as to who would be the chosen successor. Ambassador Stewart suggested that Somoza's brother-in-law, Colonel Luis Manuel DeBayle, was the most likely choice. DeBayle was optimistic about being selected, and his position was enhanced in February 1945 when Somoza explained that the party's official candidate needed broad-based support to ensure continued U.S. friendship. DeBayle was one of the few Liberals acceptable to Conservative landowners, thus satisfying Somoza's definition of popular support. In addition, Somoza's announced plans to visit the United States were interpreted as an effort to gain backing for DeBayle. Ambassador Warren concluded that these events pointed toward his candidacy. DeBayle, however, was not acceptable to the Independent Liberals, and in the political maneuvering during the early summer of 1946 he slipped from the prominent position. Furthermore, the fluid political situation and opposition pressure prevented Somoza from visiting the United States. Under such conditions and without Somoza's official blessing or an endorsement from Chamorro, DeBayle withdrew on July 15, 1946.

This left Lorenzo Guerrero and Alejandro Abaunza as the two leading candidates; the former was deemed to be the preferred and ultimate choice. The Liberal convention, in early August, remained deadlocked between the two. Somoza engineered another master stroke by arranging the nomination of seventy-one-year-old Leonardo Argüello, who combined the dual advantages of a "big name" Liberal likely to attract support from the Independent Liberals. His malleability, lack of vigor, and reported feeble health made Somoza's indirect *continuismo* probable.

According to Warren, Argüello's nomination contributed to the completion of the Conservative-Independent Liberal political agreement. Warren also believed that Argüello's brief campaign platform was more specific and realistic concerning the country's situation than that of the opposition. Included were calls for an attack on illiteracy, improved teacher's pay, modernization of agriculture to increase production, free distribution of untitled national land, and improved police standards.[21]

The political dynamics between 1944 and 1946 contributed to other problems: possible revolts, the status of the national guard, and possible intervention by the United States in Nicaragua's internal affairs. The only actual revolt during this period was that led by Alfredo Noguero Gómez in October 1944. Still, the threat of violence was constant. The Conservatives and dissident Liberals exiled in Mexico City were often linked to revolutionary plots. These industrialists and merchants found themselves allied with radicals, such as the *Democrática Centro-Americana,* whose philosophy was antithetical to their own. The Nicaraguans were not interested in imitating Mexico's one-party system or form of social democracy. Still, Emiliano Chamorro and Carlos Pasos drained their resources in the constant acquisition of Guatemalan and Cuban arms through Mexican intermediaries, but otherwise received no real moral or financial assistance abroad. On several occasions, Warren predicted that violence would erupt were Somoza to remain in office beyond 1947 because of the backlog of hatred against him.[22]

Somoza's major source of power had been the national guard, which he had headed since 1933. Throughout 1944, Ambassador Stewart believed that Somoza retained his sway over the guard and that its loyalty to the president was not in question despite rumors that it would engineer a coup and establish a triumvirate, as in Salvador and Guatemala. Ambassador Warren issued similar reports in 1945. During the political maneuvering of 1945 and 1946, Somoza clearly indicated that he would not give up control of the national guard, a stance interpreted by Warren to mean that he might relinquish the form (the presidency) but not the substance (the guard) of power. Warren was convinced that Somoza would never abandon his control of the guard, which he felt was essential for the protection of his family and its vast economic interests in the country.[23]

In 1945 the embassy reported a split in the guard between the younger officers who had graduated from the Military Academy and whose sense of obligation and patriotism was different from that of the *políticos,* who had been appointed to office under the patronage system. Holding higher ranks, the *políticos,* were convinced that "their salvation lies in support of the President for re-election." The *políticos* rallied behind Major Enrique

Gaitain; the *academicos* behind Colonel Hermogenes Prado. Somoza suggested that one of the reasons for his continued candidacy was the political ambitions of some guard officers. Still, the guard was clearly the most important element in Nicaraguan politics, Warren advised in March 1946. Both the Independent Liberals and Conservatives recognized its pro-Somoza stance. "In a word," Warren concluded, "the *Guardia* is feeling the same confusion that has affected the entire Nicaraguan people."

The opposition consistently feared that the guard would act against it, either on its own initiative or at Somoza's direction. American policymakers recognized this as a legitimate fear when, in the spring of 1945, the United States refused his request for 10,000 rifles to keep communism out of Nicaragua. Acting Secretary of State Joseph C. Grew explained that U.S. military supplies had been used previously to suppress the civilian population and that the postwar threat of communism was not a major issue in Central America.[24]

The American presence in Nicaragua is traceable to the Zelaya dictatorship in 1909. Following Somoza's ascendancy to power in 1937, the United States maintained correct and formal relations, but avoided giving the impression of supporting him. The Good Neighbor Policy precluded direct intervention in the country's internal affairs. On the other hand, Somoza seized every opportunity to point to the friendship between the two nations. His remark in February 1944 that the United States favored his *continuismo* exemplified his confidence in the Washington connection. The Nicaraguan ambassador to Washington, Guillermo Sevilla Sacasa, made similar statements.

Because of this attitude, Somoza understandably felt "let down" by the embassy's alleged unsympathetic attitude during the crisis of June 27 to July 5, 1944. Even permitting him to speak from the U.S. embassy balcony would have served his purpose. William P. Cochran, head of the Caribbean and Central American Affairs Division, denied there was any foundation for the Nicaraguans to believe the United States supported Somoza's *continuismo*. Cochran believed that the State Department was bending over backward to avoid giving that impression as well as any other manifestations of interference in the country's internal affairs. Secretary of State James F. Byrnes reaffirmed the nonintervention policy in November 1945. In a telegram to Warren, the secretary asserted that the United States did not approve of government by tyranny and that responsibility for change was a matter of local concern, not that of the United States.

When both Somoza and the opposition expressed interest in finding an acceptable compromise candidate in 1945, Warren suggested he be permitted to pursue the matter. Both Cochran and Braden refused inasmuch as such action was judged to be meddling in Nicaraguan domestic affairs. In the spring of 1946, when Somoza anticipated a trip to the United States, Cochran and the director of the Office of American Republics, Ellis O. Briggs, cautioned against any official contact with him because it would give the appearance of lending support to him and would undermine the department's hemispheric policies.[25]

The public pronouncements of noninvolvement did not prevent American officials from instructing Warren to deliver private messages to Somoza urging him to step aside and provide for a free election. Cochran advised Somoza in July 1945 that his reelection was not only illegal according to the Nicaraguan constitution, but was also not in the best interests of both his nation and the United States. Acting Secretary of State Joseph C. Grew, on August 8, 1945, suggested that Somoza be forced to understand that his reelection bid would result in a loss of American confidence. Secretary Byrnes pointed out on November 15, 1945, that the United States was friendlier toward and more desirous of cooperating with nations whose government rested upon the "freely expressed endorsement of the governed." Both Cochran and Braden were unsympathetic to Somoza's claim that his *continuismo* prevented the emergence of leftist or communist movements. On the contrary, they advised that only continued political, economic, and social repression spawned such activities. Despite these declarations, Somoza remained confident that the United States would back down before a fait accompli and therefore continued his political maneuvering.[26]

The Nicaraguan image of U.S. involvement in its domestic affairs brought pleas for election supervision. The opposition, believing in its own popularity and spurred by its disenchantment with Somoza, began the quest in 1944, and continued to election eve. Former presidents Emiliano Chamorro and Juan Bautista Sacasa, various delegates from the Conservatives and Independent Liberals, and exiles in Costa Rica and Mexico all paraded before the U.S. embassy in Managua, officials in the State Department, and U.S. missions in San José and Mexico City requesting American supervision of elections. Unless this occurred, the opposition charged that fraud would prevail and Somoza would retain power; under such conditions, violence was sure to follow. Disenchanted Liberal party members Geronimo Ramierez Brown and Luis Manuel DeBayle made similar pleas in 1946.

Somoza, confident of his popularity and of Liberal party success, often expressed a willingness to permit U.S. supervision of the presidential election. Until 1946, American officials refused the request. It was a no-win situation, Cochran observed on July 25, 1945. The United States was damned no matter what its position. Somoza wanted to demonstrate his friendship with the United States, a fact understood by the Conservatives. The Independent Liberals wanted to show that they had gained U.S. moral support regarding democracy, but were afraid that the Americans would not remember that democratic government in Nicaragua meant the "triumph of the Independent Liberal-Conservative opposition" faction.[27]

The United States appeared to move from its nonsupervision position in March 1946 when Cochran suggested to Chamorro that, if all parties requested a U.S. role, it would be received favorably in Washington. In June 1946 Braden added one other requirement: that the same request be approved by two to five other American republics before the United States would act. Such insurmountable requirements prevented U.S. election supervision in February 1947. Ambassador Warren concluded that Somoza's position was thus further strengthened because the national guard was left with the prime responsibility for this function.[28]

The presidential campaign was void of any real meaning. The Independent Liberals and Conservatives failed to cooperate in backing Aguado. The bellicose attitudes of Emiliano Chamorro and Carlos Pasos gave indications of a postelection revolution. In November 1946 Somoza retained complete control of the electoral machinery when he vetoed legislation providing for opposition representation on the electoral boards to assist with vote-counting. These factors pointed to an Argüello victory in February, but other events indicated he would act independently of Somoza.

Twice in January 1947 Somoza approached him about retaining control over the national guard and explained that he was the only one capable of controlling it. Argüello refused on the grounds that such actions opened charges of *continuismo*. Not satisfied with Argüello's promises of protection as a private citizen, Somoza sought, in vain, conciliation conferences with Chamorro and Aguado, both of whom could see no need to negotiate with the politically isolated dictator. On election eve, Warren expected an Argüello victory and felt that his defiance would free him from Somoza's shackles. For the same reasons, Warren did not expect any postelection turbulence. [29]

The February 23 elections were free of violence, but not government-inspired fraud, which enabled Argüello to win by 39,900 votes. The embassy staff shared the consensus of local opinion that the opposition won the election, probably by a considerable margin. The official count also gave the Liberal party control of the legislature and judiciary. Ambassador Warren did not think violence was in the offing despite Somoza's unhappiness over Argüello's obvious independent attitude following his election victory and his expressed intention to remove Somoza as head of the national guard. Warren reasoned that Somoza lacked sufficient control over the guard and that the opposition was satisfied with the election results. [30]

Direction of the guard emerged as the major political issue prior to Argüello's inaguration on May 1. Following a conversation with Somoza on March 6, Warren determined that Somoza saw his own future only in relationship to this factor. A month later, Somoza told Warren that "this man [Argüello] is so damn weak I feel that I must hold onto the strings for six months or possibly a year or else the government will be overthrown." Somoza concluded that he must remain as chief of the guard. Later that month, he reassigned department commanders to ensure that trusted officers were in key positions. [31]

Once inaugurated, Argüello took independent actions that served to increase the tension. Without Somoza's consent, on May 2 he removed Somoza's son "Tachito" from command of the presidential guard and exiled him to León as commanding officer. Argüello's May 6 Cabinet appointees were known for their opposition to Somoza, and his proposed reform measures included the cessation of military influence in government as well as bureaucratic graft and corruption. These actions brought support from the Independent Liberals and Conservatives, but angered *Somocistas*. [32]

Somoza reacted with a vengeance. A crisis was precipitated on May 23, when he ordered the guard to follow his orders only. In response, Argüello summoned Somoza to the presidential palace and ordered him to leave the country. Somoza refused and instead tried but failed to win the backing of Independent Liberal Carlos Pasos and Conservative Emiliano Chamorro. Isolated and fearing assassination, Somoza planned a coup, which was effected shortly after midnight on May 26. The next day, he forced congress to dismiss Argüello on charges of inept administration and compromising Nicaragua's internal tranquillity. Congress also accepted Somoza's suggestions for three presidential designates, including Benjamin Lucayo Sacasa, who was named as president. The Independent Liberals appeared willing to support Sacasa, if only to end the crisis. The Conservatives, whose main motivation was preserving their interests, also accepted him.

To Chargé d'affaires Maurice Bernbaum, the entire affair suggested that Nicaraguan politics was "based far more on convenience than on any considerations of democracy and principles which have hitherto constituted the basis of the anti-Somoza campaign." More succinctly, the politics constituted a struggle for power among elites only.[33] Bernbaum drew a parallel to the situation in Venezuela, where he had just completed his first foreign tour of duty.

Immediately all speculation centered upon the question of international recognition of the Sacasa administration. Somoza's belief that it would come quickly failed to materialize. State Department officers Ellis O. Briggs and Louis J. Halle recommended witholding recognition pending future events and consultation with other American republics. In the meantime, a replacement for Ambassador Warren, who had left Nicaragua ten days prior to the coup, was held up; the American military mission was withdrawn from the country; and Secretary of State George C. Marshall refused to see Ambassador Sevilla Sacasa officially or privately. These actions were received positively by the opposition within Nicaragua, but not by pro-Somoza elements, who claimed that American officials did not understand that Somoza was the only individual capable of maintaining order. This faction also charged that U.S. policy encouraged revolutionaries elsewhere in Latin America. Officially, the United States continued to express intentions of noninterference, but its decisions indicated the desire to restore constitutional government without Somoza.[34]

The opposition's future plans were based upon the elimination of Somoza as a result of the stiffening nonrecognition policy. Chargé d'affaires Bernbaum had no evidence, however, that either international disapproval or internal pressure would force Somoza out. In an effort to gain recognition, President Sacasa announced on June 10 that a constituent assembly would convene on August 29, following the election of delegates on August 3. The edict also granted juridical status to the Conservative party, and unnamed antidemocratic parties were outlawed. The assembly was charged with writing a new constitution, electing a new president and congress, and reorganizing the judiciary. Bernbaum correctly judged that the effort was designed to give the outside world the facade of a national solution and new legal order worthy of recognition. The opposition Independent Liberals recognized the need to remain united with the Conservatives, who refused Somoza's proferrings of a political agreement. Both parties continued to believe he would be forced out of the country.[35]

At the same time the government was attempting to establish its legal basis, its suppressed civil liberties. Opposition political meetings and demonstrations were denied, telephone service was cut off, newspapers closed, university student leaders arrested, and foreign journalists restricted in their reporting of events. Somoza's reported directive to the national guard to shoot anyone caught engaging in terrorist activities caused a national furor. The guard proceeded to the wanton search of cars, offices, and homes of opposition leaders. Throughout the countryside, key dissidents were arrested for allegedly planning guerilla warfare. Bernbaum suspected that the opposition often instigated the guard to demonstrate popular discontent with Somoza and forestall recognition.[36]

Amid widespread apathy, elections for the constituent assembly were held, as scheduled on August 3. Only Somoza's Liberal party ticket offered candidates. All other groups abstained. Reports from throughout the country indicated that voting was restricted to government workers and "poorly clad peons." The assembly quickly named Somoza's uncle, Victor Ramon y Reyes, as president and Mariano Argüello Vargas, another loyal *Somocista,* as vice-president. Despite the sham election and the new administration's *continuismo* character, Somoza believed that the government now had legal status and was worthy of recognition. Bernbaum thought otherwise and suggested that the de facto government was worse off than before and demonstrated that Somoza's power was "based on the *Guardia Nacional,* the largesse of a depleted Treasury and Government employees." Recognition was not forthcoming.[37]

Immediately after taking office, President Ramon y Reyes was rebuffed in his efforts to conciliate differences with the opposition. Although both the Independent Liberals and Conservatives continued their intraparty friction, both remained committed to the restoration of Leonardo Argüello as president. Bernbaum noted the existence of the continued widespread erroneous belief, particularly among the Conservatives, that the United States spoke the last word in Nicaraguan politics and that it still wished Somoza in power, either up front or behind the scenes. The opposition also maintained that U.S. assistance was necessary for the elimination of Somoza.[38]

To Bernbaum, battle lines were clearly drawn. Somoza refused to leave, controlling the country through the national guard. The nation's economic community was anti-Somoza for his looting of public funds and securing his personal wealth at the expense of the nation's welfare. Merchants and landowners lived in constant fear that their wealth would be lost. Somoza was in a weak position, kept in power only by armed force: the national guard. The majority of people in every walk of life were anti-Somoza, and the U.S. refusal to extend recognition to Ramon y Reyes helped to undermine the old idea that U.S. officials wanted Somoza to remain in power. Bernbaum concluded that all the elements of violence were present, forestalled only by the opposition's lack of unity and fear of the well-armed national military.[39]

Despite revolt rumors throughout September, Bernbaum noted that the opposition lacked arms or funds to acquire them. The ill-conceived attacks led by Conservative General Alejandro Cardenas at La India on September 7 and Muelle de los Bueyes on September 14 failed to cause a general uprising, but provided Somoza the opportunity to strengthen his hand by eliminating his opposition. The constituent assembly passed a law on September 17 "providing for military jurisdiction, trial and punishment in cases of revolutionary acts, banditry, terrorism or communism." In effect, martial law was established. National guard garrisons throughout the country were reinforced, and the air force patrolled the nation's highways, coastlines, and borders for arms shipments.

The government placed responsibility for the two uprisings on Emiliano Chamorro and forced him into exile in El Salvador. Somoza also wanted former President Argüello, who had been residing in the Mexican embassy since the May coup, out of the country. Bernbaum assisted in arranging for his safe-conduct emigration on November 30. From San

Salvador and Mexico City, Chamorro and Argüello, respectively, repeated pledges to overthrow Somoza by force.[40]

Somoza also used September's events to eliminate Nicaragua's Socialist party (PSN). It was composed of a small nucleus of labor leaders operating through the organized labor movement headed by the *Confederación de Trabajadores* (CTN), whose membership was unknown but estimated at 15,000. The union's strongest organized units covered the government-owned railway, mining, sugar, and dockworking industries. Socialist party membership was put at 1,200 and 500 of them were considered to be militant. The militants also occupied key labor posts and lost no opportunity to espouse propaganda calling for welfare legislation similar to that advocated by Mexican labor leader Vicente Lombardo Toledano.

Both Ambassador Stewart and the U.S. Federal Bureau of Investigation believed the evidence was insufficient to substantiate the charges that the PSN was communist-inspired and directed by the Soviet embassy in Mexico City and tied to Costa Rica's Vanguard labor movement. Significantly, PSN leader Armando Amador was a known communist. Others, including Juan Lorio, Carlos Perez Bermudez, and Manuel Perez Estrada, had worked closely with Guatemalan communists. The embassy staff was convinced that the PSN was a communist or quasi-communist organization but of local character only. Nicaragua had established diplomatic relations with the Soviet Union, but no exchange of diplomatic personnel had occurred. In 1946 relations between the two countries were considered "unimportant" by the State Department.

In its political maneuvering prior to the February 1947 presidential election, the PSN supported the candidacy of Independent Liberal Enoc Aguado because the social and economic provisions of his platform paralleled those of the Socialists. The government, concerned about PSN's potential voting impact, estimated that up to 75,000 people would follow the party's directives. Just before the election, the PSN directed its followers not to participate because Aguado and other opposition leaders were more concerned with their own political future than with the welfare of the people.

In the suppression of civil liberties following the overthrow of Argüello in May 1947, PSN leaders were interned on Ometepe Island, in Lake Nicaragua. They were released in mid-August by President Ramon y Reyes. On September 7 the party's central committee offered to support him provided it was permitted to organize and the government promised to enforce the dormant Labor Code. On the next day, the executive committee sought advice from Costa Rican Marxist Manuel Mora, who advised that PSN remain aloof from the political struggle until a revolution was well established. At that time, Mora suggested that the PSN cast its support to the victorious side on a quid pro quo basis.

The government was aware of PSN's contacts, and Bernbaum suspected that the September 17 law was deliberately written to include all possible groups, including the PSN. On January 18, 1948, twenty-six of its members, including Amador, were arrested in Managua, and two days later fourteen more were arrested in outlying districts for allegedly being connected with an unspecified oppositionist revolt.[41] The party was broken and Somoza had eliminated the remaining opposition leaders. On the surface, he appeared to be in firm control and could present a picture of domestic tranquillity.

The death of Leonardo Argüello in Mexico City on December 15, 1947, reopened the recognition question. His absence removed the last obstacle to the legitimacy of the Sacasa regime and provided the opportunity for lifting repressive measures. Under such conditions, the embassy's second secretary, Halleck L. Rose, speculated that recognition of the de facto regime could not long be delayed. Bernbaum encouraged continuation of nonrecognition as the best means of bringing about a negotiated settlement. Latin American resistance, however, had already weakened. Costa Rica was the first to grant recognition to Sacasa's government, on December 26, 1947. By the time of the Bogotá Conference, in March 1948, several other Latin American countries also extended recognition. The conference passed a resolution favoring recognition of de facto governments. Accordingly, the United States granted recognition on May 11, 1948.[42] The Americans had failed to dislodge Somoza by moral persuasion and diplomatic pressure.

For the next two years, the nation's politics repeated the past. Somoza remained in full control, bolstered by the national guard. The Independent Liberals and Conservatives failed to unite in their efforts to oust him, in part because each remained factionalized. In October 1949 Managuan political observers began to speculate about the next presidential election and whether or not Somoza could be prevented from becoming president. Calm prevailed over the political scene. American observers did not find the intense rivalry that had existed prior to 1948. Capus Waynick, a North Carolina journalist prior to his 1949 appointment as ambassador to Nicaragua, reported that Nicaragua was in a politically stable condition. Many people in the country, he wrote, "including Americans in business here, point to the pacification of the country as Somoza has kept the internal peace longer than any other man in the history of the country." This perception was not much different from that of Ambassador Fletcher Warren in 1945, who had noted that Somoza was "the most capable, the most intelligent and the most personable man in sight."

Such plaudits, however, did not endorse the dictatorship, but U.S. policy had gone adrift. In October 1949 Gordon Reid, desk officer in the Central America and Panama Affairs Division, who had been at that post since February 1947, described the change. In 1947, he observed, the policy had been toughness toward dictators and friendship toward nations demonstrating democratic tendencies. This was followed by a period of treating them both alike. In 1949 Reid was not "aware of our policy toward Somoza, our financial policy toward Somoza or our general attitudes towards the dictator."[43]

When Ramon y Reyes died in office in 1950, Somoza was appointed as acting president, and he was elected to a six-year term the following year. While campaigning for reelection in 1956, he was assassinated by a young political activist. His last presidential term was marked by increased civil and political restrictions and intensified friction with Costa Rica.

The presidency of Anastasio Somoza provided Nicaragua with a political tranquillity it had not known since the last quarter of the nineteenth century. At first his administration gave promise of bringing good government and stability to the country. Despite the appearance of constitutional procedure, he soon established an ironclad dictatorship. During his regime, a Labor Code was enacted, educational facilities expanded, health and sanitation programs introduced, and some low-cost housing constructed. But these benefits were diminished by political repression, lax administration, and poor financial planning. Poverty, illiteracy, and disease remained widespread.

Somoza's firm hand failed to stifle all opposition. The idealistic Allied goals of World War II and political events in Nicaragua during late 1943 and early 1944 raised the ire of its middle sector. The overthrow in 1944 of Maximiliano Hernández Martínez in Salvador and Jorge Ubico in

Guatemala instigated this group to demonstrate against Somoza and petition for his resignation. According to Ambassador John B. Stewart, this pressure resulted in Somoza's veto of a proposed constitutional amendment that paved the way for his reelection as well as his promises of expanded civil liberties and social reform. But he weathered the crisis and subsequently exiled opposition leaders. Political tension did not ease, because few people believed that he intended to step down after January 1, 1947. Ambassador Fletcher Warren noted that he behaved like a candidate from 1945 to early 1947, extolling the achievements of his administration and doing nothing to prevent support groups from doing the same. He chose not to run again. Instead, he engineered the Liberal party nomination of Leonardo Argüello, whose age and ill-health ensured Somoza's indirect *continuiso,* Warren concluded.

After the 1944 demonstrations, the opposition groups were fractured. Chargé d'affaires Harold Finley doubted that the Independent Liberals and Conservatives exiled in Mexico, Guatemala, and Costa Rica, could reach agreement on either a jointly sponsored revolution or presidential candidate. The opposition was united only in its hatred of Somoza, Warren observed, but not of authoritarian government. Despite the dissidents' agreement upon Enoc Aguado as a presidential candidate, Warren noted that mutual distrust continued.

Argüello captured the February 1947 presidential sweepstakes, a victory Warren believed rightfully belonged to Aguado. Despite old age and a lack of vigor, Argüello attempted to act independently of Somoza, which resulted in his overthrow on May 21, 1947. The immediate cause was Somoza's continued power over the national guard.

Since 1933, Somoza had been its commander, a post he kept after being elected as president in 1936. Throughout his tenure in office, the guard remained loyal to him, as was evident during the public demonstrations of June and July 1944. Ambassadors Stewart and Warren continually reported on this subject. When president-elect Argüello attempted to assert his control over the guard in 1947, Somoza deposed him. Opposition reaction was nil, probably attributable to fear of bloodshed and loss of property. Chargé d'affaires Maurice Bernbaum correctly observed that Argüello's downfall clearly demonstrated that national politics was a struggle among the elite only and Somoza controlled political events because he headed the national guard. Subsequent events verified this opinion. The congressional selection of Benjamin Lucayo

Sacasa as president in May 1947 and the "election" of Victor Ramon y Reyes were Somoza's master political strokes.

After the 1944 demonstrations, the middle sector was not heard from again. Somoza's promises of civil liberties went unfulfilled. The lower socioeconomic groups were apolitical. The government-initiated Labor Code was dormant. The *Confederación de Trabajadores* (CTN), sponsored by the Socialist party (PSN), was largely ineffective. Despite evidence of PSN's ties to Costa Rica's Vanguard party and the Soviet embassy in Mexico City, U.S. embassy officials were convinced that both the CTN and PSN were Marxist and only of a local character. Somoza did not share this opinion and smashed the PSN in January 1948.

During the five-year period 1944–49, Somoza remained in firm control. U.S. officials reported that he was able to resist the pressures for political change. Opposition from the elite was broken and its leadership exiled. The middle sector and lower socioeconomic groups remained outside the political apparatus. Propped by the national guard, Somoza continued to direct the course of the country's politics.

Conclusion

AS World War II drew to a close, forces of political change appeared in Central America. The four major components of the region's political structure were affected differently by these pressures in each country. U.S. officials throughout Central America and in the State Department recognized that the elite and the military, which had traditionally played a major role in the political dynamics, were being challenged by the emerging middle sector, which was demanding constitutional government, and the inarticulate masses, which sought economic and social improvements.

Throughout Central America the local elites were dominated by the landowners and the growing commercial sector. Until the 1930s, the elites played a major political role in all five nations as they fought to preserve their privileged status. During the 1930s, they lost their political dominance in four nations, according to U.S. diplomats. These groups remained outside the inner circles of Tiburcio Carías in Honduras, Jorge Ubico in Guatemala, Maximiliano Hernández Martínez in El Salvador, and Anastasio Somoza in Nicaragua. So long as their wealth and social position were not threatened, the elites were satisfied. Under such

153

circumstances, the Americans did not think they would challenge the political order. Only in Costa Rica did the landowning elite maintain its political prominence, which was camouflaged by free elections and the peaceful transfer of power.

The upper class did not participate in the political turbulence that erupted in the spring and summer of 1944 in El Salvador, Guatemala, Nicaragua, and Honduras. In the 1944 Costa Rican presidential campaign, the elite supported conservative candidate León Cortés in a vain attempt to retain control of the political apparatus. Thereafter, until 1949, the local elites throughout the region were on the political defensive except in Honduras and Nicaragua.

Although the Salvadoran "coffee aristocracy" played no role in the overthrow of Hernández, it supported the October 1944 coup of Colonel Osmín Aguirre y Salinas, who, according to Ambassador John. F. Simmons, promised to protect its interests. During the 1946 presidential campaign, Simmons noted that the landowners backed General Salvador Castaneda Castro over Arturo Romero because of the latter's appeal to the lower class and for the same reason opposed the 1945 constitutional revisions that potentially granted the government sweeping control over labor. Castaneda's administration was marred by vacillation, but so long as he did not raise taxes or improve the status of labor, Simmons, Ambassador Alfred Nufer, and Consul Overton G. Ellis concluded that the landowners would not engineer a coup. The elite was surprised by the December 1948 overthrow of Castaneda, according to consul Murat W. Williams and Office of American Republics Affairs Deputy Director Robert F. Woodward. Subsequently, the landowners opposed the 1950 presidential candidacy for Major Oscar Osorio because of his appeal to the middle sector and lower socioeconomic group, Ambassador George P. Shaw noted. The landowners were still maintaining their stance by 1949, but pressures for change were mounting.

Political activism by Guatemala's elite did not begin until late summer 1944, when Juan José Arévalo, whose "Spiritual Socialism" was anathema to the upper class, returned as expected from Argentina. Ambassador Boaz Long was not surprised that the elite sought, but failed to obtain, a compromise candidate to prevent Arévalo's election as president in 1945. During the next four years, the elite's status was threatened by several Arévalo-sponsored programs: a Labor Code, rent control, and social security. In response, the landowners formed the National Republican party in 1946, but, lacking organization and leadership and threatened with extinction by the government, it was ineffective. For this reason, State Department analysts Robert F. Woodward and William P. Cochran linked the landowners to a series of threatened revolts as they sought to maintain their privileges. Following the assassination of Colonel Francisco Araña, a moderate, in July 1949, Ambassador Richard C. Patterson and embassy secretary Ernest V. Siracusa believed that if the landowners did not soon risk their resources, they would have nothing to risk. The Americans perceived that their status was imperiled.

Costa Rican politics traditionally had been dominated by strong personalities from the upper class. Not so in 1944. National Republican party candidate Teodoro Picado aligned himself with local Marxist Manual Mora, and for the first time in the nation's history the competing parties were sharply divided over ideologies, Chargé d'affaires Edward G. Trueblood observed. Until 1948, however, Picado was unable to deliver on promised reforms for the lower socioeconomic groups because the unicameral legislature was controlled by elite factions: *Calderonistas* and *Cortesistas*. The opposition lukewarmly endorsed Otilio Ulate for the presidency in 1948, but Ambassador Hallet Johnson expected the more experienced Rafael Calderón Guardia to win the election. To everyone's surprise, Ulate won the election. This set in motion forces that resulted in a month-long civil war. To Ambassador Nathaniel P. Davis, it was caused by Calderón's insistence on the presidency, which was endorsed by Mora. The alliance, Davis believed, was responsible for the purge of *Calderonistas* from politics by the José Figueres junta in June 1948 following the civil war. The elite was no longer in a privileged position.

In Honduras, Ambassadors John Erwin and Herbert Bursely continually portrayed Carías in a favorable light. They believed that all social sectors were satisfied with his leadership, largely because of the nation's relative economic prosperity. His ability to mingle freely among the people demonstrated his popularity, Erwin concluded. The political opposition was disorganized, and exiled leaders like Angel Zuñiga Heute lacked adequate backing within the country. Such opposition, Central America and Panama Affairs Division analyst Robert Newbegin concluded, was typical of the traditional Central American pattern of the "outs" wanting "in." Political tranquillity prevailed in Honduras.

The Americans described Nicaraguan politics in similar fashion. Ambassadors John Stewart and Fletcher Warren as well as Consul Harold D.

Finley doubted that the opposition could unify against Somoza. In disarray at home and many of its leaders exiled in Mexico, Guatemala, and Costa Rica, it was only unified in its anti-Somoza attitude, as illustrated by its tenuous support of Enoc Aguado in the 1947 presidential campaign. The opposition was not antiauthoritarian. When President-elect Leonardo Argüello was deposed in May 1947 for attempting to act independently of Somoza, the landowners remained on the sidelines for fear of losing their wealth, Chargé d'affaires Maurice Bernbaum reported. Nicaraguan politics continued to be a struggle.

From 1944 to 1949, U.S. officials perceived that the favored position of the elites was under attack in Guatemala, El Salvador, and Costa Rica and that they remained outside the inner circles of government in Honduras and Nicaragua. Save in Costa Rica, the elites were disorganized and in disarray, unable to do much to preserve their positions.

Except in Costa Rica, the military in Central America traditionally had played a prominent role in national politics. The U.S. effort in 1923 to diminish that role failed. When the dictators emerged during the 1930s, the military became their chief prop. After 1944 its political role varied in each country.

In Costa Rica and Honduras, the military's position in politics was not evident, according to U.S. diplomatic reports from San José and Tegucigalpa, but for different reasons. Costa Rica abandoned large expenditures on the military in the 1920s, and by 1944 its size, ability, and prominence had been depleted. The army's ill-preparedness was evident in the 1948 civil war. The military remained loyal to Carías, as was evident in its suppression of isolated revolts from 1944 to 1948, but the lack of a major crisis in the country weakened its political prominence.

Nicaragua's national guard had been controlled by Somoza since 1933, and he continued to do so after he assumed the presidency four years later. In 1944 Ambassador John Stewart could find no reason to doubt the guard's loyalty to Somoza, as illustrated by its suppression of the June and July demonstrations against the dictator. Revolt rumors were rampant in 1945 and 1946, but Ambassador Fletcher Warren doubted any uprising could succeed because the guard remained committed to Somoza. The reported rift between younger and older officers was also dismissed by Warren, who believed that the reports reflected the popular confusion brought about by the possibility of Somoza remaining in office beyond 1947. Although handpicked by Somoza, President Leonardo Argüello insisted that Somoza relinquish command of the guard. The demand went unheeded and Argüello was overthrown in May 1947. The election of Ramon y Reyes in August that same year ensured Somoza's continued influence over the guard and indicated it would continue to occupy a prominent position in politics, Chargé d'affaires Maurice Bernbaum predicted.

In El Salvador and Guatemala, the military's presence was more pronounced. Backed by the military, Hernández was secure in his position in March 1944 when the Salvadoran congress extended his presidential term, Ambassador Walter Thurston concluded. The diplomat failed to perceive any split between older and younger officers a month later when thirteen military men were executed for their role in the unsuccessful uprising against Hernández, nor in May when he was toppled from power. New Ambassador John F. Simmons linked Colonel Osmín Aguirre y Salinas to the conservative landowners in the October 1944 coup, whose purpose was to stave off General Andrés Menéndez's connection with middle sector liberals. Aguirre's conservative military-landowner alliance was responsible for several Cabinet changes after General Salvador Castaneda's election in February 1945. Simmons's perception of the military also changed. He linked the younger officers to the Aguirre coup in 1944, but later identified the old line officers as those supporting Aguirre, upon whom Castaneda also eventually relied. Subsequently, Simmons pointed to Major Oscar Osorio as the leader of the younger officers. Osorio expressed the belief that the traditional landowner-military dictatorship could not endure. Simmons believed that the younger officers were linked to the numerous revolt plots in 1946 and 1947 because Castaneda's vacillation favored the elite. The younger military officers were responsible for the overthrow of Castaneda in December 1948, when he sought to extend his presidential turn. Osorio emerged as the leader of this military faction and was described by Ambassador Nufer as being neither political right nor left. The Salvadoran military was split on the issue of political reform.

American Republics Analysis and Liaison Division Assistant Chief Gerald Drew's perception of the Guatemalan military was similar to that of Ambassador Thurston in El Salvador. Drew expected that Ubico would be able to resist the pressure against him in June and July 1944 because of the military's continued loyalty. When Ubico was forced to resign in July 1944, Ambassador Boaz Long and Assistant Chief William P. Cochran of the Caribbean and Central American Affairs Division anticipated the army's continued political prominence, as evidenced by the opposition's acceptance of General Federico Ponce as provisional president. Only during the October 1944 coup, engineered by Major Francisco Javier Araña and Captain Jacobo Arbenz Guzman, did the Americans perceive any split within the military. Secretary of State Edward R. Stettinius, Jr., Ambassador Long, and Consul Affeld believed that the new military junta was leftist, but anti-Marxist, and therefore would be a moderating influence upon future politics. Division of Caribbean and Central American Affairs advisers Woodward and New-begin and embassy consular officer Andrew Donovan were more precise. The three concluded that the older officers remained tied to the land-owners. They were subsequently linked to several Cabinet changes and suspected coups d'etat between 1946 and 1948 because President Arévalo's policies threatened the elite's status. Ambassador Long detected a split between the Arbenz and Araña followers among the younger officers. Arbenz was portrayed as more ambitious and in agreement with Arévalo's philosophy and programs. Araña appeared interested in maintaining the country's newfound democracy. Tensions heightened in 1948 when he sensed that the nation was drifting leftward and expressed presidential ambitions, according to embassy secretary Milton Wells. Ambassador Patterson and Vice-consul Siracusa believed that Araña's assassination on July 18, 1949, was approved by both Arbenz and Arévalo and eliminated the final moderating influence from Guatemala's political scene.

The Costa Rican military was of no political importance, and the U.S. perception of this group in the other four countries differed. The Americans assumed its continued loyalty to Carías only because Honduras was unscathed by political turbulence. The Nicaraguan national guard's loyalty to Somoza was never questioned, and Argüello's effort to deny Somoza's control over it failed. The guard remained Somoza's major political prop. In El Salvador and Guatemala, U.S. officials found the military split between younger and older officers. The former favored political liberalism, and the latter remained committed to the upper class. In both countries, the younger officers themselves were fractured.

One element favored political liberalism only; the other, government-sponsored social reform. The latter won out.

As urban centers arose during the twentieth century throughout Central America, a middle sector became more identifiable. It included individuals possessing varying degrees of wealth: doctors, dentists, lawyers, small businessmen, white-collar middle management, university professors, students, and skilled labor. An amorphous group, they were unified only by their desire for political participation and an end to the oligarchical-based dictatorships that traditionally had dominated the politics of Central American nations. Influenced by the Allies' idealistic goals, the middle sector increased its expressed discontent with government by and for the elites. Beginning with the events in April 1944 in El Salvador and concluding with the end of Costa Rica's civil war in May 1948, the middle sector throughout Central America pressured for its objective and met varied success.

On March 1, 1944, Salvador's constituent assembly extended Hernández's presidential term for another four years. Editorializing in *La Prensa Gráfica,* José Quetglas pointed out that events in El Salvador bore no relationship to the practice of democratic ideals. Ambassador Thurston noted only that this opinion was a sincere representation of the opposition's liberal segment. The subsequent demonstrations and the general strike initiated by university students and backed by other middle sector elements were described without analysis by Thurston. Embassy consular officer Overton G. Ellis, however, estimated that virtually all the middle sector supported the movement to oust Hernández on May 11, 1944. Containing only one military officer, the new Cabinet formed by junta leader General Andrés Menéndez satisfied the middle sector. The rest were doctors. The junta also announced a program of civil liberties and promised free elections as well as constitutional government. The subsequent organization of several political parties in anticipation of elections was a natural phenomenon following thirteen years of dictatorial rule, Ambassador Simmons and Caribbean and Central American Affairs Division Assistant Chief Cochran pointed out. The hope for democracy was short-lived. The military's presence guaranteed the presidential election of General Castaneda in February 1945. Thereafter, American reports from San Salvador linked the middle sector to several revolt rumors, but otherwise it did not appear to be a significant factor on the nation's political scene.

U.S. officials failed to agree on the political importance of the middle sector. Consul Leslie Squires believed that, because of its ties to the upper class, it represented nothing more than another group of "outs" wanting "in." Central America and Panama Affairs Division political adviser Robert E. Wilson argued otherwise. He believed that the sector was the center of potential leadership, and, because it was more closely tied to the lower class, was a viable political element. Ambassador George Shaw reported that the middle sector supported PRUD when it was organized in 1949, and was therefore an important factor in Osorio's 1950 presidential election. U.S. officials lacked a clear perception of this emerging group.

Middle sector discontent with Guatemala's Ubico was first reported in 1941, when university students protested the national assembly's extension of the dictator's presidential term. In 1943 the Federal Bureau of Investigation (FBI) reported to the State Department that other members of the middle sector—notably professionals—were against Ubico. The fall of Hernández in El Salvador a year later caused repercussions in Guatemala. In June 1944 Ubico's threatened harsh response failed to stop a student strike for university reform. The movement soon included doctors, lawyers, and small businessmen, who demanded his resignation and the establishment of constitutional government. Ambassador Long observed that the middle sector lacked unity and leadership and therefore was forced to accept the military junta upon Ubico's resignation on July 1. The professionals and businessmen who had demanded the resignation formed the Social Democratic party, whose objective was the attainment of constitutional government. Because it lacked political experience and military support, Long and Cochran correctly predicted it would be ineffective. Initially, some middle sector members supported Arévalo on account of his political ideals, but were frightened away by his "Spiritual Socialism" and therefore supported the search for a compromise candidate prior to the February 1945 presidential election. Thereafter, embassy cables from Guatemala City did not portray the middle sector as a significant component in politics.

The Honduran middle sector, like other political elements, had exerted no influence since 1931 because Carías had suppressed all opposition. In July 1944 the FBI reported to the State Department that the intellectuals and professionals supported the more militant exile groups in Costa Rica, Guatemala, and Mexico and that propaganda from abroad was distributed by university students. At the same time, Military Attaché Thomas D. Burns and Chargé d'affaires John B. Faust noted that the middle sector lacked political punch because of its poor organization and leadership. For the same reasons, it was not capable of directing a general strike similar to those in El Salvador and Guatemala. When public protest erupted against Carías in July 1944, the crowds were small and ineffective. So, too, were the middle sector elements that demanded the resignation of Carías to save the country from bloodshed. Thereafter, the Americans in Tegucigalpa did not report middle sector political activity, but their sources of information were restricted.

A flurry of middle sector political activity occurred in Nicaragua during the spring and early summer of 1944. In May, Managuan university students were arrested for backing their counterparts in San Salvador. In June the students protested the constitutional proviso extending Somoza's presidential term beyond 1947. This protest drew support from other middle sector elements: doctors, dentists, lawyers, and small businessmen. Ambassador Stewart believed that this pressure was sufficient to cause Somoza's rejection of the proposed constitutional amendment. The middle sector's lack of organization and leadership, however, prevented it from making further immediate gains. In the political situation that followed, the middle sector did not take part, according to U.S. officials.

Costa Rica's middle sector was first recognized when the *Centro Para el Estudio de Problemas Nacionales* was formed in 1940. Five years later, it joined forces with *Acción Democrática,* the younger *Cortesista* element, to form the Social Democratic party. Both groups denounced the *personalismo* character of national politics and rejected communism as a means to solve the social and economic problems. Ambassador Johnson dismissed party leader José Figueres as an opportunist and potential revolutionary. Johnson did not view him or the Social Democrats, as serious alternatives to the political turbulence from 1944 through 1948. Figueres initiated the March 1948 civil war ostensibly to uphold Ulate's February election victory. The promise to put the country's political house in order contributed to the popular support given Figueres after the civil war. Ambassador Nathaniel Davis's observation that Figueres's social philosophy differed little from that of Mora went unnoticed by U.S. officials from July 1948, when Vanguard was legally dissolved, until Ulate's inauguration in November 1949. These officials were satisfied with the restoration of constitutional government.

According to the Americans, the middle sector in Central America achieved its greatest success in the spring and summer of 1944, when it played a significant part in the overthrow of Hernández and Ubico and forced Somoza to reject a constitutional amendment extending his presidential term. This sector was unsuccessful in Honduras in 1944. Furthermore, its deficiencies in leadership, organization, and allies in the region caused the Americans to discount it as a major political pressure group after 1944. In Costa Rica, where the middle sector was well led and organized, it was dismissed by U.S. officials as radical and opportunistic. In the region, they also overlooked the sector's socioeconomic philosophy, which appealed to the lower groups. The Americans failed to understand the potential significance of the middle sector in Central America's political dynamics.

The largest single element in the Central American political structure was the lower class. It included farm laborers, small farmers, and, in the urban areas, unskilled labor. During the twentieth century, the economic and social gap widened between this class and the middle and upper sectors. The dictators who emerged in the 1930s played upon the sympathies of the poor, but provided few practical benefits. The dictators, along with the elite, were determined not to permit this group to upset the region's socioeconomic-political status quo. During the period 1944–49, the communist issue surfaced in each of the five countries because of the alleged appeal to the poor of this doctrine.

Communism in Costa Rica could be traced to 1931, when Manuel Mora founded a local party that championed the cause of the lower class. It had grown in size and strength by 1943, and Mora reportedly was responsible for the Labor Code enacted in that year. His party's alliance with Teodoro Picado contributed to the latter's presidential election in 1944. The elite's congressional representatives, however, blocked reform proposals during this administration. Charges by the upper class that communism was threatening the nation were dismissed by U.S. officials. Ambassadors Fay Allen Des Portes and Hallet Johnson, Consul Alex A. Cohen, and Central America and Panama Affairs Division Assistant

Chief Murray A. Wise believed that the party was of local character only, that it had no direct ties to Moscow, and that its programs would be described as "liberal" in most countries. In 1947 and 1948 Vanguard became more isolated from the country's political apparatus. The party also became more militant. It remained, however, the only spokesman for the lower class.

The American perception of the party also changed. In October 1948 Ambassador Walter J. Donnelly and his staff concluded that communism was on the increase in Costa Rica, which potentially was important to Russia as a message and training center. Following Otilio Ulate's presidential election victory in February 1948, Ambassador Nathaniel Davis believed that Mora was struggling to save his party from extinction by maneuvering to have Rafael Angel Calderón seated in the presidential palace. The outlawing of the communists by junta leader José Figueres was compatible with his claim that the civil war saved the country from communism, but it was an explanation Davis found difficult to accept because the economic and social philosophies of Mora and Figueres were strikingly familiar.

State Department analyst Frederick B. Lyon concurred with the FBI in 1944 that communism had made no inroads in Guatemala despite the deep poverty of the Indians, who were tied to the nation's large landowners. In 1945 the new constitution banned political parties of international character. Following the fall of Jorge Ubico in 1944, five of the newly formed parties included in their platforms appeals to the lower class, but none of the five was connected to the landowners. Thus, from 1945 to 1949 the question of communism was connected with the administration of Juan José Arévalo. The elite charged that he was a Marxist and appointed communists to government positions. The Labor Code, rent law, and social security legislation he sponsored demonstrated his Marxist leanings, the elite charged.

Through 1948, U.S. opinion was divided. Assistant Secretary of State Spruille Braden was convinced that Arévalo was a communist and that he had a secret agreement with the movement. In 1945 and 1946 Ambassador Edwin Kyle dismissed the elite's charges against Arévalo as only an effort to discredit him. In 1947 Kyle wavered. He admitted that PAR's radical elements, some of whom demonstrated communist leanings, strongly influenced governmental policies. Consular officer Donovan doubted Arévalo's sincerity in denying communist infiltration into government. According to the consensus of embassy staff opinion in 1948, Arévalo himself was not a communist but the communists exerted a strong influence on his policies and had increased their hold on government posts. Robert Newbegin was surprised they had not made greater inroads in view of the administration's leftist sympathies since 1944. Ambassador Richard C. Patterson and Consul Siracusa warned that the nation would drift further left following Araña's assassination in 1949. In 1949 State's Office of Intelligence Research confirmed the 1948 embassy report regarding communist influence in government, but still could not confirm any Soviet role.

Communism had been outlawed in El Salvador since 1933. In 1944 the FBI concluded that, so long as Hernández continued to govern, communist infiltration was not to be feared. Immediately following the overthrow of Hernández in 1944, the communist issue emerged. Presidential candidate Arturo Romero was labeled as a communist by the elite during the 1944–45 campaign on account of his appeals to the lower socioeconomic group. The 1945 constitution, which gave the government potential sweeping power over labor, was disliked by the landowners. They labeled any legislation on behalf of labor as communist.

American officials lacked a good grasp of labor and communism in the country. In 1944 Consul Overton G. Ellis believed that the lower classes were politically apathetic. Consul Leslie A. Squires echoed that opinion in 1947. He explained that politics was a contest among the elite in which the masses of the people played no part. Coupled with the nation's rigid social and economic structures, Squires concluded that communism could make no inroads. Ambassadors Walter Thurston and John F. Simmons as well as Central America and Panama Affairs Division analyst Wilson disagreed. Thurston described Romero's reform proposals as a "merely Mexican" effort to solve legitimate problems. In 1945 Simmons believed that the laboring class was gaining a new consciousness regarding its deprived status. Wilson argued in 1947 that the nation's economic and social disparities made it a prey for communist infiltrators and that the personal nature of its politics would foster the communist ideology. Ambassador Nufer concurred with Wilson's assessment in 1948. Although Nufer saw evidence of a communist underground, he warned it would be naive to think that local Marxists were not receiving aid from abroad. He also believed they would be considered as liberals elsewhere.

Nicaragua's lower socioeconomic group remained outside the nation's political arena. Somoza's administration passed labor and housing legislation, but never carried out the programs. In 1945 the Socialist party was formed. Ambassador John Stewart and the FBI concluded that the evidence was insufficient to verify local allegations that the party was Marxist-oriented and linked to the Soviet embassy in Mexico City. The majority of the embassy staff disagreed, concluding that the party and its Marxism was only of a local character. The PSN was not active until 1947, when it made contact with Costa Rican communist Manuel Mora and offered to support President Reyes if he would enforce the dormant Labor Code. Chargé d'affaires Maurice Bernbaum concluded that this activity instigated a national law banning parties of international character. The law was used to break the party in January 1948.

In Honduras, American officials did not possess the means to measure the opinion of the lower socioeconomic group. The government often charged that Mexican labor leader Vicente Lombardo Toledano sent agitators into the country. A 1945 law provided that anyone found guilty of communist associations would be exiled. Despite such actions, Ambassador John Erwin observed no communist activity. He was convinced that the working man was happy with his rewards and that communism was not of any significant importance in the country. In 1948 Consul Faust and Ambassador Bursely illustrated the changing U.S. perceptions. Both cautioned that poverty and illiteracy provided a breeding ground for communism. Bursely noted the communist ideology in the platform of the newly formed Democratic party. Although he described it as "Mexican doubletalk" and insignificant, he suggested it was potentially appealing to the underprivileged.

Except in Costa Rica, the Americans were unable to judge the attitudes and opinions of the lower classes. In Costa Rica, where freedom of expression was greater, the laboring class was drawn to Manuel Mora's Vanguard party, and the perception of it by Americans paralleled their view of communism elsewhere in Central America. Consistently, U.S. officials understood that any appeal for social and economic reform was called communistic by the elites. The Americans described these demands as liberal, not radical. Until 1947 U.S. analysis clearly indicated that the communist movement in Central America was a "local show," not part of an international conspiracy. Any contact with the Soviet Union was indirect through its embassy in Mexico City. After 1947 U.S.

officials became more concerned. Costa Rica and Guatemala were considered to be potentially significant to the Soviet Union, and the Americans recognized that the deprivations of the lower classes made them a target for communist agitators.

Adhering to the nonintervention principles of the Good Neighbor Policy, the United States remained an observer of Central American politics from 1944 to 1949. Each of the nation's political mechanisms was viewed differently. In Costa Rica, the landowning elite and communists had been eliminated from the political scene by 1949, but the Americans failed to understand the economic and social goals of the middle sector. The landowners, old line military officers, and middle sector were no longer important to Guatemala's political maneuverings by 1949. In El Salvador, the movement was toward political liberalism and social reform that was championed by the middle sector and younger military officers, but the gains were negligible. In Nicaragua and Honduras, the traditional military-landowner clique remained in power, but for different reasons. Somoza imposed his will by force in Nicaragua. No visible opposition appeared against Carías in Honduras.

One U.S. perception common to all five countries involved communism. Since 1900 the United States had been concerned only with regional tranquillity. As the disparity between the elite and the laboring masses widened, the potential dangers were ignored. During the early cold war years, warnings from persons such as Costa Rican consular officer Edward G. Trueblood and State Department Desk Officer Robert E. Wilson that the wealth disparity was an explosive issue capable of being seized upon by the communists were ignored. Until 1947, U.S. officials viewed communism within the framework of local politics only: a threat to the established order. After 1947, there emerged a consensus of opinion, as expressed by Ambassadors Alfred Nufer, Nathaniel Davis, and Richard Patterson, that international communism was a potential danger. In either case, as a threat to the local order or as a global conspiracy, American officials failed to pursue a constructive policy toward the issue in Central America. Concerned with Europe and Asia, where communism, both local and international, caused havoc to the established order, the United States ignored Central America. There it continued to be only an observer of regional political dynamics.

Appendix

Biographical Sketches of U.S. Policymakers

William C. Affeld. Affeld joined the Foreign Service in 1931 following his graduation from the University of Minnesota. He served at Singapore, Kobe, and Hong Kong before being appointed as third secretary at Guatemala City in 1941. He remained there until 1945, when he became a political adviser to the Allied Expeditionary Force in Europe.

Norman Armour. After earning a Harvard law degree, Armour joined the Foreign Service in 1916. He served at several locations in Europe, the Far East, and Latin America until 1941, when he was designated as director of the Office of American Republics Affairs. In 1944 he was appointed as ambassador to Spain and later became a special assistant secretary of state.

William Tapley Bennett. Bennett was a native of Griffin, Georgia. He was employed as an economic analyst in the Foreign Service prior to military duty during World War II. Returning to the State Department in 1946, he served as a country and area specialist until he was named as acting assistant chief of the Division of Central America and Panama Affairs in 1949.

Barry T. Benson. Following World War I service with the navy, Benson worked as a salesman until he was appointed to the Federal Communications Commission in 1935. Two years later, he took a position with the Bureau of Foreign and Domestic Commerce, where he stayed until 1939. He was then assigned as consul at the U.S. mission in Calcutta, India. Prior to a similar appointment at Managua, in 1945– 47, he had also served at Bogotá and Pretoria.

Maurice M. Bernbaum. After graduating from Harvard in 1931, Bernbaum held various jobs in Washington, D.C., before joining the State Department in 1936. He served at Caracas prior to his 1945 appointment as vice-consul at Managua, where he stayed until December 1947.

Woodrow Borah. Borah was assigned to the Office of Strategic Services during World War II, before working for seven months in the State Department in 1945.

Spruille Braden. The son of an engineer, Braden pursued the same career in Latin America after graduating from Yale in 1914. During the years 1920– 38, he was a delegate to several Latin American conferences. From 1938 to 1942, he served as minister to Colombia and from 1942 to 1945 as minister to Cuba. In October 1945

167

he was confirmed as assistant secretary of state for American Republics Affairs, a post he held until he resigned in 1947.

Ellis O. Briggs. Subsequent to his graduation from Dartmouth, Briggs joined the Foreign Service in 1925. He served at Lima, Havana, and Santiago before becoming chief of the Caribbean and Central American Affairs Division in October 1945. A year later, he was designated as chief of the Office of American Republics.

Herbert S. Bursely. A former government clerk, Bursely worked as a Foreign Service officer in London, Dublin, Constantinople, Prague, Belgrade, and Mexico City before being appointed as assistant chief of the Office of American Republics in 1936. He was designated as ambassador to Honduras in December 1947, after a duty tour in Ankara.

James F. Byrnes. Although he was a self-educated individual, Byrnes was admitted to the South Carolina bar in 1903. In 1910 he was elected to the U.S. House of Representatives and in 1930 to the Senate. In 1941 he was named to the Supreme Court, only to resign in 1943 to direct the Office of War Mobilization. In July 1945 he was appointed as secretary of state, an office he held until January 1947.

John C. Cabot. Cabot joined the Foreign Service in 1926 following his education at Harvard and Oxford. He held several positions in Latin America and Europe prior to being posted to the State Department in 1941. He was assigned to the Caribbean and Central American Affairs Division in January 1944 and six months later became its chief.

Edward G. Cale. Winning a Ph.D. from the University of Virginia, Cale taught at Tulane University and the University of Richmond before joining the State Department in 1941. He held positions in the Commodities Division, Division of International Resources, and International Wheat Council.

John Willard Carrigan. In 1932, the year after his graduation from Harvard, Carrigan joined the Foreign Service. He served in Europe until he was appointed as vice-consul and third secretary at Managua in 1935. After a tour (1939–42) in Mexico City, he was assigned to State's Mexican Affairs Division in 1944. He was designated as first secretary and vice-consul at San José in 1946. The next year, he moved to Caracas.

William P. Cochran. In 1928, four years after graduating from the Naval Academy, Cochran joined the Foreign Service. He served at Auckland, Wellington, Lima, Managua, and Moscow before his appointment as assistant chief of the Caribbean and Central American Affairs Division in May 1944. A year later, he became its chief, a post he held until he was assigned to Berlin in August 1946.

Alex A. Cohen. Although Cohen was a native of the Netherlands, he served in the U.S. Army during World War I, prior to his emigration to the United States. After employment at the War Department, he became a clerk in the San José embassy in 1942 and was promoted to vice-consul in 1946.

Frank P. Corrigan. After receiving a degree in dentistry from Western Reserve University in 1906, Corrigan practiced his profession until 1932, when he was appointed as minister to El Salvador. Three years later, he was named to a similar position in Panama, where he remained until being assigned in the same capacity to Venezuela. In 1947 he became a political adviser to the U.S. Mission at the United Nations.

Paul C. Daniels. Following graduation from Yale in 1924, Daniels studied in France before joining the State Department in 1927. He served at La Paz, Managua, Rio de Janeiro, and Bogotá prior to his appointment as ambassador to Honduras in 1947.

Nathaniel P. Davis. After graduating from Princeton, Davis joined the State Department in 1919. He held several personnel positions through World War II. Just prior to his appointment as ambassador to Costa Rica, he served as a consular officer in Manila.

Allen Dawson. After leaving West Point in 1924, Dawson joined the Foreign Service. Throughout the 1920s and 1930s, he was posted to Rio de Janeiro, Panama, Mexico City, Bogotá, Managua, and La Paz until he was appointed as acting assistant chief of the Division of American Republics in 1943. After stints at Havana and Caracas, he was designated as chief of Brazilian Affairs in 1947. A year later, he was detailed to the National War College.

Fay Allen Des Portes. A native of South Carolina, Des Portes engaged in private business until he was elected to the state legislature in 1926. He was reelected until 1933, when he became minister to Bolivia. In 1936 he was appointed to the same position at Guatemala and in 1943 as ambassador to Costa Rica.

Juan de Zengotita. After graduating from Columbia University in 1938, Zengotita worked in private business until 1941, when he joined the Foreign Service. His assignments included Cuba, Colombia, Bolivia, and Mexico before he returned to the State Department for a year starting in 1948.

Walter J. Donnelly. In 1923, two years after graduating from Georgetown University's Foreign Service School, Donnelly joined the State Department's Bureau of Foreign and Domestic Commerce. Subsequently, he held posts in Rio de Janeiro, Panama, and Lima until he was appointed as ambassador to Costa Rica in April 1947.

Andrew E. Donovan. Donovan, a 1938 Harvard graduate, joined the diplomatic corps as a clerk at the Warsaw Embassy in 1939. From there, he went to Bogotá, Ciudad Trujillo, and La Paz before becoming the first secretary and consular officer at Guatemala City in December 1945. He was appointed to a similar position at San José in 1947.

Gerald Drew. After graduating from Harvard in 1929, Drew worked for the departments of Interior and Agriculture before joining the State Department in 1941 as a political analyst. He became assistant chief of the American Republics Analysis and Liaison Division in 1944, where he remained until 1946, when he was assigned to the Division of Special Inter-American Affairs.

Laurence Duggan. Duggan was a 1927 Harvard graduate. He first worked in publishing and the Institute of International Education before joining the State Department in 1930. He became chief of the American Republics Affairs Division and subsequently a political adviser to Secretary of State Cordell Hull.

Overton G. Ellis. Ellis joined the Foreign Service in 1932 following a business career abroad, mostly in Europe. He was assigned to San Salvador in August and remained there until June 1947.

John D. Erwin. A native of Meador, Kentucky, Erwin attended the Baylor Military Academy. From 1917 to 1937, he was a newspaper correspondent. In 1937 he was appointed as minister to Honduras and stayed there until 1947.

John B. Faust. Faust was born in Allendale, South Carolina. He joined the Foreign Service in 1926. He was posted at Asunción, Paris, Lisbon, and Santiago before being appointed as second secretary and consular officer at Tegucigalpa in July 1942, where he remained until May 1947.

Harold D. Finley. Following three years in the U.S. Army, 1917–20, Finley joined the Foreign Service. From 1920 until 1930, he was assigned to several European posts. His 1930 appointment to the San Salvador consulate initiated fifteen years of Central American and Caribbean duty, which ended in 1945 following a two-year appointment as first secretary and consular officer at Managua.

Gerhard Gade. Gade, a 1921 Harvard graduate, joined the State Department the next year. He served at Riga, Oslo, Montevideo, Athens, Rome, and Quito before being appointed as consular officer and second secretary at San Salvador in June 1940.

Raleigh A. Gibson. Immediately after graduating from the University of Illinois in 1917, Gibson joined the U.S. Army. He entered the Foreign Service in 1920 and served at Buenos Aires, Guadalajara, Tegucigalpa, and Mexico City prior to his appointment as first secretary and vice-consul at San José in 1943, where he remained until 1946. He was then reassigned to Salonika.

Joseph G. Grew. Following graduation from Harvard in 1902, Grew joined the Foreign Service. He served in Cairo, Vienna, and Berlin prior to his appointment as chief of the Western European Affairs Division in 1918. He became under secretary of state in 1924 and then ambassador to Turkey in 1927 and to Japan in 1931. After the outbreak of war in 1941, he returned to the department to head the Far Eastern Division. In January 1945 he again became under secretary of state, but resigned from government service at the war's end.

Louis J. Halle. Following graduation from Harvard in 1932, Halle worked in the private sector until 1941, when he joined the army. In 1943 he began his service with the State Department as a country specialist. In April 1945 he became assistant chief of the American Republics Analysis and Liaison Division. Subsequently, he became acting assistant chief of the Division of Special Inter-American Affairs and assistant to the director of Pan-American Cooperative Affairs.

Edward W. Holmes. After receiving a master's degree from the Fletcher School of Law and Diplomacy in 1946, Holmes joined the Foreign Service and was appointed as third secretary and vice-consul at Managua, where he remained until he moved to Caracas in 1947.

Cordell Hull. A native of Tennessee, Hull practiced law in that state until 1907, when he was elected to the U.S. House of Representatives. He was chairman of the Democratic National Committee in the 1920s and was elected to the U.S. Senate in 1930. He served as secretary of state from 1933 until 1944.

Lee M. Hunsaker. Hunsaker was born in Honeyville, Utah. He began his Foreign Service career in 1939 at Bogotá. He later served at Tegucigalpa prior to his vice-consul appointment at Puerto Cortés, Honduras, in 1943. A year later, he was assigned to Concepción.

Paul C. Hutton. Hutton, a 1926 West Point graduate, joined the diplomatic corps in 1930. He served in Panama, Bombay, Dublin, and Mexico before a four-year tour of duty (1941–45) in the State Department. He was then assigned as a consular officer in Guatemala, where he remained until 1947.

Hallet Johnson. Johnson, a Columbia University law graduate, was appointed as third secretary at the London embassy in 1912. Subsequently, he served at Stockholm, Santiago, Oslo, and Paris, and several administrative positions within the State Department prior to being appointed as ambassador to Costa Rica in December 1944.

Edwin Kyle. Kyle was a native of Texas. He earned a master's degree in agriculture from Cornell University in 1902. From 1920 to 1935, he was employed by Texas A&M University, eventually serving as dean of the School of Horticulture. He made several tours of Central and South America for the State Department prior to his appointment as ambassador to Guatemala in February 1945.

William S. Lester. After graduating from the University of Kentucky, Lester attended the Fletcher School of Law and Diplomacy from 1934 to 1936. He joined the State Department in 1941 as an analyst in the Office of the Coordinator of Inter-American Affairs. Subsequently, he was designated as research analyst and foreign specialist.

Boaz Long. Long was born in Warsaw, Indiana. He pursued private business interests in the United States and Mexico before his appointment as chief of the Latin American Affairs Division in 1914. He served as minister to Salvador, Cuba, Nicaragua, and Ecuador before his 1943 appointment to Guatemala.

Frederick B. Lyon. Lyon was a University of Michigan graduate. He served as a special representative for the State Department in Europe from 1923 to 1925 and was a commercial attaché at several European posts until 1933. After four years in private business, he rejoined the department and became assistant chief of the Foreign Activity Correlation Division in 1942 and chief in 1945.

George C. Marshall. A year after graduating from the Virginia Military Institute, Marshall joined the U.S. Army. He distinguished himself in many positions, including service during World War I and as chief of staff during World War II. After resigning from military service in 1946, he was sent to China by President Harry S. Truman in an effort to end the civil war. In January 1947 he became secretary of state, a post he held for two years.

Edward G. Miller. A former member of the law firm of Sullivan and Cromwell in New York, Miller was assigned to the U.S. embassy in Rio de Janeiro and later became an assistant on congressional affairs to Dean Acheson before Acheson was appointed as secretary of state. From 1949 until 1952, Miller was assistant secretary of state for the American Republics.

Harold E. Montamat. Montamat was born in Antwerp, Belgium. In 1931, two years after graduating from Dartmouth, he joined the Foreign Service. He was assigned to Havana, Nanking, Lima, La Paz, Panama, and Reykjavik before becoming second secretary and vice-consul at Tegucigalpa in 1949.

Robert Newbegin. Following his graduation from Yale, Newbegin attended Harvard Law School for two years prior to joining the Foreign Service in 1930. He served at Montevideo, Mexico City, Berlin, Ankara, and Ciudad Trujillo before his appointment as assistant chief of the Division of Caribbean and Central American Affairs in 1945. When the department was reorganized in 1946, he worked in the Central America and Panama Affairs Division until he was assigned to Bogotá in 1948.

Alfred Nufer. Nufer, a native of New York City, was educated in Geneva, Switzerland. From 1919 to 1928, he was in private business in Mexico. He became the U.S. commercial attaché at Mexico City in 1928. He also served in Havana prior to his appointment as ambassador to Salvador in April 1947.

Raymond K. Oakley. Following graduation from George Washington University, Oakley engaged in hotel work until 1933, when he joined the diplomatic service. He served at several Mexican posts—Bogotá, Cartablanca, and Buenos Aires—before returning to the department in July 1948.

Richard C. Patterson. Following World War I military service, Patterson was appointed an administrative officer to the U.S. Paris Peace Commission. After holding several positions in the private sector from 1921 to 1936, he served as assistant secretary of commerce and as a trustee of the Export-Import Bank. He later held the posts of ambassador to Yugoslavia (1944–47) and to Guatemala (1948).

Edward L. Reed. After graduating from Williams College in 1916, Reed served in the Marine Corps during World War I. His Foreign Service career began in 1920 as secretary in the U.S. embassy at Buenos Aires. After several subsequent appointments, mostly in Europe, he returned to the department's Latin American Affairs Division in 1933 and remained there through 1946.

Gordon Reid. After receiving a master's degree from Harvard in 1942, Reid became assistant to the director of the Institute of Inter-American Affairs. He was a country specialist from 1946 to 1948, when he was assigned to the Central America and Panama Affairs Division.

Nelson A. Rockefeller. The grandson of oil millionaire John D. Rockefeller and a 1930 Dartmouth College graduate, Nelson pursued a career in the family's business until 1940, when he was appointed as coordinator of the Office of Inter-American Affairs. He served as assistant secretary of state for Latin American Affairs from December 1944 to August 1945.

Halleck L. Rose. Rose attended Princeton University and Georgetown University's Foreign Service School before joining the diplomatic service in 1932. He served at Vera Cruz, Rotterdam, Warsaw, Berlin, Cuidad Trujillo, and Lisbon before being appointed as second secretary and vice-consul at Managua in April 1947.

George P. Shaw. Shaw, who was born in Pittsburg, Kansas, lacked any formal education beyond high school. He held a variety of jobs until appointed as vice-consul at Tampico in 1920. He served at Puerto Cortés, Tegucigalpa, San Luis Potosi, Cuidad Juarez, and Mexico City prior to becoming assistant chief of the Foreign Correlation Activity Division in 1943. He was appointed as Ambassador to Nicaragua in April 1948 and to a similar assignment in El Salvador in June 1949.

John F. Simmons. After graduating from Princeton in 1913, Simmons taught in Great Britain and Switzerland until 1916, when he was appointed as a clerk at the U.S. consulate in Vienna. Subsequent assignments included Paris, Mexico City, Cologne, Ottawa, and Rio de Janeiro. He was appointed as ambassador to Salvador in

September 1944, and stayed there until he accepted a similar position in Ecuador in 1947.

Ernest V. Siracusa. Siracusa, a 1940 Stanford University graduate, was assigned as a clerk at the American consulate at Mexico City in 1941. He also served at Tijuana and La Ceiba, Honduras, prior to his appointment as vice-consul and third secretary at Guatemala City, where he remained until returning to the State Department in 1949.

J. R. Solana. Solana graduated from Georgetown University's Foreign Service School in 1935 and joined the State Department a year later. After an eight-year assignment in Havana as vice-consul, he was assigned to Costa Rica in 1944 and remained there until 1947.

Leslie A. Squires. Following his 1936 graduation from Stanford, Squires pursued a journalism career until joining the State Department in 1942. He served in Cairo, Istanbul, Budapest, and with the Office of the Supreme Allied Command in the Mediterranean until his appointment as secretary and consul in San Salvador in November 1946. He was reassigned to Athens in August 1948.

Kennedon P. Steins. Following a stint in the U.S. Army during World War I, Steins held several jobs in private business until his appointment as assistant secretary of commerce in 1938 and as trustee of the Export-Import Bank. He returned to the private sector from 1939 until 1944, when he was appointed as ambassador to Yugoslavia, a post he held for three years. In 1948, he was appointed as vice-consul in Guatemala.

Edward R. Stettinius, Jr. After attending but not graduating from the University of Virginia, Stettinius worked for General Motors and U.S. Steel until 1938, when he was appointed as chairman of the War Resources Board. He became under secretary of state in 1943, secretary of state from December 1944 to June 1945, and ambassador to the United Nations from June 1945 to June 1946.

James B. Stewart. Stewart worked with the U.S. Geological Survey's Reclamation Service prior to joining the Foreign Service. He served at posts in Brazil, Cuba, and Mexico from 1915 to 1928, when he returned to the State Department for nine years prior to his 1942 appointment as minister to Nicaragua. He was named as ambassador there in 1943, when the consulate was raised to embassy status.

Walter Thurston. Thurston, a native of Denver, Colorado, worked for an American oil company in Mexico before joining the State Department in 1916. He served in various posts, including San José, Managua, and São Paulo, before his appointment as minister to San Salvador in 1942. A year later, the position was raised to the rank of ambassador.

J. D. Tomlinson. Tomlinson earned a B.A. at Northwestern in 1925, an M.A. at Columbia in 1927, and a doctorate at the University of Geneva in 1938. He worked in higher education from 1925 to 1942, when he joined the State Department. He became assistant chief of the Division of International Organization Affairs in 1946 and assistant chief of the Division of UN Economic and Social Affairs in 1948.

Edward G. Trueblood. Trueblood joined the State Department in 1928 and served as a consular officer in several Latin American locations before his San José assignment in June 1943, which lasted eighteen months. Following an assignment in Lima, Peru, he served in the Office of American Republics from August 1946 until January 1947.

Fletcher Warren. Appointed as vice-consul at Havana in 1921 immediately following graduation from the University of Texas, Warren served in Central America and Europe before becoming executive assistant to the assistant secretary of state in 1938. He subsequently served as assistant chief of the Foreign Activity Correlation Division and in Bogotá prior to appointment as ambassador to Nicaragua in 1945 and then to Paraguay in 1947.

S. Walter Washington. Washington joined the State Department in 1926 and served in several Latin American posts until he was appointed as first secretary and consular officer at the San José embassy in August 1944, a post he held for eleven months.

Livingston D. Watrous. Watrous joined the Foreign Service in 1940. He served for three years as third secretary and vice-consul at San José until he was reassigned to Buenos Aires in August 1945.

Capus M. Waynick. Following service with the U.S. Army during World War I, Waynick worked in North Carolina as a newspaper editor and publisher from 1919 until 1949, when he was appointed as ambassador to Nicaragua.

Milton K. Wells. Wells joined the State Department in 1931, a year following his graduation from George Washington University. After serving in the U.S. Army from 1942 to 1946, he returned to the department prior to his appointment as third secretary at Guatemala City in 1948.

Murat W. Williams. Williams was a University of Wisconsin graduate and Rhodes Scholar. He served in the U. S. Navy during World War II. In 1945 he was appointed as a country specialist in the State Department. In 1947 he was named as consul and second secretary at the embassy in San Salvador, where he remained until March 1949. At that time, he was reassigned to Bucharest.

Phillip P. Williams. After receiving a bachelor's degree from Stanford in 1934, Williams undertook graduate studies at Harvard prior to joining the State Department in 1936. He was posted at Ciudad Juarez, Rio de Janeiro, Buenos Aires, and Nassau before becoming second secretary and consul at Managua in September 1948.

Robert E. Wilson. Wilson, a native of Burlington, Iowa, joined the Foreign Service in 1936. He worked in Argentina and Bolivia before being appointed as vice-consul and third secretary at the embassy in San Salvador, where he remained until 1947. After two years in the State Department, he was reassigned in 1949 to Seville.

Murray A. Wise. Wise taught in Bogotá, Colombia, during the years 1932 – 39, before being inducted into the U.S. Army. He joined the State Department as assistant chief of the Central America and Panama Affairs Division in September 1946 and remained in that position until September 1948.

W. R. Wood. Wood attended the University of Texas from 1936 to 1940 prior to his appointment in November 1940 as vice-consul at Merida, Mexico, where he remained until he was appointed as an assistant to the executive officer of the American Republics Affairs Division in 1944.

Robert F. Woodward. Woodward, a graduate of the University of Minnesota, joined the Foreign Service in 1931. His posts included Buenos Aires, Rio de Janeiro, and La Paz before he was appointed as second secretary at Guatemala City in 1944. He was reassigned to Havana in 1945, and for a brief period the following year served in the Office of Caribbean and Central American Affairs. In 1947 he was appointed as deputy director of the Office of American Republics Affairs.

Notes

Introduction

1. For a fuller discussion of U.S. Caribbean policy, see Chester L. Jones, *The Caribbean Since 1900* (New York: Prentice Hall, 1936); Dana G. Munro, *The United States and the Caribbean Area* (Boston: World Peace Foundation, 1934); Dana G. Munro, *Intervention and Dollar Diplomacy in the Caribbean, 1900 – 1921* (Princeton: Princeton University Press, 1964); Dexter Perkins, *The United States and the Caribbean* (Cambridge: Harvard University Press, 1947); and Lester D. Langley, *The United States and the Caribbean 1900 – 1970* (Athens: University of Georgia Press, 1980).

2. Concerning Theodore Roosevelt's Caribbean policy, see H. K. Beale, *Theodore Roosevelt and the Rise of America to a World Power* (Baltimore: Johns Hopkins University Press, 1956); H. F. Pringle, *Theodore Roosevelt* (New York: Harcourt, Brace, 1956); H. C. Hill, *Roosevelt and the Caribbean* (Chicago: University of Chicago Press, 1927); and J. Fred Rippy, "Antecedents of the Roosevelt Corollary of the Monroe Doctrine," *Pacific Historical Review* 9(1940), 267 – 69. The most complete study of Taft is H. F. Pringle, *The Life and Times of William Howard Taft* (New York: Holt, Rinehart, 1939). Knox's career is surveyed in Samuel Flagg Bemis, ed., *The American Secretaries of State and Their Diplomacy,* Vol. IX (New York: Alfred H. Knopf, 1929). For a discussion of Dollar Diplomacy, see Dana G. Munro, *Intervention and Dollar Diplomacy,* 65 – 216. An analysis of Woodrow Wilson's policy can be found in George W. Baker, "The Caribbean Policy of Woodrow Wilson, 1913 – 1917" (Ph.D. dissertation, University of Colorado, 1961).

3. Wilfrid H. Callcott, *The Caribbean Policy of the United States 1890 – 1920* (Baltimore: Johns Hopkins University Press, 1942), 279 – 91; Dana G. Munro, *Intervention and Dollar Diplomacy in the Caribbean 1900 – 1921,* 65 – 216; U.S. Department of State, *Papers Relating to the Foreign Relations of the United States, 1907* (Washington, D.C., 1910), Part II, 601 – 728 (hereafter referred to as *FRUS*).

4. National Archives, Washington, D.C., General Records of the Department of State, RG 59, Decimal File 813.00 Tacoma/8, April 21, 1922, Dana G. Munro memorandum.

5. Tacoma/8, Munro memorandum, April 21, 1922; *FRUS*, 1911, 291 – 307. For a discussion of U.S. intervention in Nicaragua, see Langley, *Caribbean, 1900 – 1970,* 49 – 52; Harold Denny, *Dollars for Bullets: The Story of American Rule in Nicaragua*

(New York: Dial Press, 1929); U.S. Department of State, *The United States and Nicaragua: A Survey of Relations from 1909 to 1932* (Washington, D.C.: Government Printing Office, 1932); and *Complaint of the Republic of El Salvador before the Central American Court of Justice* (Washington, D.C.: Government Printing Office, 1916).

6. Tacoma/8, Munro memorandum, April 21, 1922.

7. For a discussion of the Washington Conference, see Thomas M. Leonard, *U.S. Policy and Arms Limitation in Central America: The Washington Conference of 1923* (Los Angeles: Occasional Paper Series, Center for the Study of Armament and Disarmament, California State University, 1982).

8. *Conference on Central American Affairs, Washington, December 4, 1922 – February 7, 1923,* Appendix: "Treaties, Conventions, and Protocols Approved and Adopted by the Conference on Central American Affairs" (Washington, D.C.: Government Printing Office, 1923); Library of Congress, Washington, D.C., Manuscript Division, Papers of Charles Evans Hughes, "Latin American Conferences, 1922– 1929."

9. For coverage of the Honduran crisis, see Raymond L. Buell, "The United States and Central American Stability," *Foreign Policy Papers* VII, 9(1931): 193– 97; Charles Hackett, "The Background of the Revolution in Honduras," *Review of Reviews* 69 (April 1924), 390– 96; Langley, *Caribbean 1900–1970,* 108– 10; Munro, *Caribbean Republics,* 132– 45, 290– 94; *FRUS,* 1924, Vol. II, 316– 24; and *FRUS,* 1925, Vol. II, 317– 25.

10. For a discussion of U.S. intervention in Nicaragua, see Langely, *Caribbean 1900–1970,* 116– 25; Munro, *Caribbean Republics,* 157– 256; William Kamman, *A Search for Stability: United States Diplomacy towards Nicaragua* (Notre Dame: University of Notre Dame Press, 1968); Henry L. Stimson, *American Policy in Nicaragua* (New York: Charles Scribner, 1927); Neill Macauley, *The Sandino Affair* (Chicago: Quadrangle Books, 1967); *FRUS,* 1926, Vol. II, 793– 820; *FRUS,* 1927, Vol. III, 317– 464; and *FRUS,* 1930, Vol. III, 418– 529.

11. The Guatemalan crisis is discussed in Buell, "Central American Stability," 200– 201; Kenneth J. Grieb, *Guatemalan Caudillo: The Regime of Jorge Ubico, Guatemala, 1931–1934* (Athens: University of Ohio Press, 1978), 1– 15; Kenneth J. Grieb, "American Involvement in the Rise of Jorge Ubico," *Caribbean Studies* 10(April 1970): 5– 21; *FRUS,* 1930, Vol. III, 172– 93; and *FRUS,* 1931, Vol. II, 393– 402.

12. The question of Salvadoran recognition is discussed in Munro, *Caribbean Republics,* 283– 90; L. H. Woosley, "Recognition of the Government of El Salvador," *American Journal of International Law* 28(1934): 325– 29; Kenneth Grieb, "The United States and the Rise of General Maximiliano Hernández," *Journal of Latin American Studies* 3(November 1971), 151– 72; Thomas P. Anderson, *Matanza: El Salvador's Communist Revolt of 1932* (Lincoln: University of Nebraska Press, 1971) 40– 63; *FRUS,* 1931, Vol. II, 169– 212; and *FRUS,* 1934, Vol. IV, 423– 56.

13. "American Policy and Problems in Central America," Stokely W. Morgan lecture to the Foreign Service School, Department of State, January 29, 1926, 810.00/24, June 2, 1926, enclosure 1; Franklin D. Roosevelt, "Our Foreign Policy: A Democratic View," *Foreign Affairs* 6(1928): 573– 86; National Archives, Washington, D.C., General Records of the Department of State, RG 59, Francis G. White Papers, "United States

and Latin America, 1927–1933"; Alexander DeConde, *Herbert Hoover's Latin American Policy* (Stanford: Stanford University Press, 1951). For a discussion of the Good Neighbor Policy, see Irwin F. Gellman, *Good Neighbor Diplomacy: United States Diplomacy in Latin America, 1933–1945* (Baltimore: Johns Hopkins University Press, 1979); Edward O. Guerrant, *Roosevelt's Good Neighbor Policy* (Albuquerque: University of New Mexico Press, 1950); and Brice Wood, *The Making of the Good Neighbor Policy* (New York: Columbia University Press, 1961).

14. For treatment of the banana industry, see Charles Kepner, *Social Aspects of the Banana Industry* (New York: Columbia University Press, 1936); Stacy May and Galo Plaza, *The United Fruit Company in Latin America* (Washington, D.C.: National Planning Association, 1958); Thomas P. McCann, *An American Company: The Tragedy of United Fruit* (New York: Crown Publishers, 1976); H. B. Arthur and G. L. Beckford, *Tropical Agribusiness: Structures and Adjustments—Bananas* (Boston: Division of Research, Graduate School of Business Administration, Harvard University, 1968); and Alfonso Bauer Paíz, *Cómo opera el yanqui capital en Central America: el coso de Guatemala* (Mexico: Editoria Ibero Mexicana, 1956).

15. For a discussion of the term "middle sector," see John J. Johnson, *Continuity and Change in Latin America* (Stanford: Stanford University Press, 1964).

16. General histories of Central America include: Thomas L. Karnes, *The Failure of Union: Central America 1824–1960* (Chapel Hill: University of North Carolina Press, 1961); William H. Koebel, *Central America: Guatemala, Nicaragua, Costa Rica, Honduras, Panama, and Salvador* (New York: Charles Scribners Sons, 1914); Dana G. Munro, *The Five Republics of Central America: Their Political and Economic Development and Their Relations with the United States* (New York: Oxford University Press, 1918); Frederick Palmer, *Central America and Its Problems* (New York: Moffat, Yard, and Company, 1910); Franklin D. Parker, *The Central American Republics* (New York: Oxford University Press, 1964); Mario Rodríguez, *Central America* (Englewood Cliffs, N.J.: Prentice Hall, 1965); and Ralph L. Woodward, *Central America: A Nation Divided* (New York: Oxford University Press, 1976).

17. For a discussion of the changing attitude of the United States toward the Soviet Union, see John Lewis Gaddis, *The United States and the Origin of the Cold War, 1941–1947* (New York: Columbia University Press, 1972). The global perception of communism is discussed by Thomas G. Paterson, *On Every Front: The Making of the Cold War* (New York: W. W. Norton, 1979). U.S. concern about hemispheric security is treated in J. Lloyd Mecham, *The United States and Inter-American Security, 1889–1960* (Austin: University of Texas Press, 1961), 246–317. For a discussion of post-World War II Caribbean policy, see Langley, *Caribbean, 1900–1970,* 187–210.

18. For Nelson A. Rockefeller's view of Latin America, see "Fruits of the Good Neighbor Policy," *New York Times Magazine,* May 14, 1944, 154; "Will We Remain Good Neighbors After the War?" *Saturday Evening Post,* November 6, 1943, 215:16–17; and "Portrait," *Time,* February 26, 1945, 45:22. On Spruille Braden, see Spruille Braden, *Diplomat and Demagogues: The Memoirs of Spruille Braden* (New Rochelle, N.Y.: Arlington House, 1971); "Democracy's Bull in the Latin American China Shop," *Time,* November 5, 1945, 46:42; T. M. Jones, "Good Neighbor, New Style," *Harper's,*

April 1946, 192:313 – 21; T. K. Jessup, "Our Battling Assistant Secretary of State," *Life* (March 25, 1946): 54 – 56+. On Edward G. Miller, see "Frankness of Friends," *Time,* February 19, 1951, 57:36; "Portrait," *New York Times Magazine,* January 8, 1950, 9; and Edward G. Miller, "Inter-American Relations in Perspective," *U. S. Department of State Bulletin,* 22 (April 3, 1950):521 – 23.

19. For a discussion of Edward R. Stettinius, Jr., see Richard L. Walker, "Edward R. Stettinius, Jr.," in *The American Secretaries of State and Their Diplomacy,* Vol. XIV (New York: Cooper Square Publishers, 1965); Walter Johnson, "Edward R. Stettinius," in Norman A. Graebner, ed., *An Uncertain Tradition: American Secretaries of State in the Twentieth Century* (New York: McGraw-Hill, 1961); and Thomas M. Campbell and George C. Herring, eds., *The Diaries of Edward R. Stettinius, Jr., 1943 – 1946* (New York: New Viewpoints Press, 1975). On James F. Byrnes, see George Curry, "James F. Byrnes," *The American Secretaries of State and Their Diplomacy,* Vol. XIV (New York: Cooper Square Publishers, 1965); and James F. Byrnes, *All in a Lifetime* (New York: Harper and Row, 1958). For the career of George C. Marshall, see Robert H. Ferrell, "George C. Marshall," *American Secretaries of State and Their Diplomacy* (New York: Cooper Square Publishers, 1966); and Robert Payne, *The Marshall Story: A Biography of General George C. Marshall* (New York: Prentice Hall, 1951).

Chapter 1

1. For a more complete discussion of Costa Rica's political history, see Chester L. Jones, *Costa Rica and Civilization in the Caribbean* (Madison: University of Wisconsin Press, 1935); James L. Busey, *Notes on Costa Rican Democracy* (Boulder: University of Colorado Press, 1967); Carlos Monge Alfaro, *Geografía social y humana de Costa Rica* (San José: Imprenta Universitaria, 1943); and Carlos Monge Alfaro, *Historia de Costa Rica* (San José: Tresjo Hnos., 1958).

2. Alex A. Cohen to State, March 19, 1948. The diplomatic correspondence used for this chapter is in the National Archives, Washington, D.C., Record Group 59, Department of State Decimal Files 818.00/*date;* 818.00B/*date,* and FW818.00/*date.*

3. Harry S. Truman Presidential Library, Independence, Missouri, Papers of Harry S. Truman, Confidential File, State Department memorandum, January 6, 1949 (hereafter referred to as Truman Papers).

4. Franklin D. Roosevelt Presidential Library, Hyde Park, New York, Harry Hopkins Papers, Federal Bureau of Investigation Reports, *Totalitarian Activities: Costa Rica Today, September 1943,* 12 – 24, 53 – 54 (hereafter referred to as Hopkins Papers, *Costa Rica Today*); C. C. Whitaker and A. R. Tennyson, *Economic and Commercial Conditions in Costa Rica* (London: His Majesty's Stationery Office, 1950); John P. Bell, *Crisis in Costa Rica* (Austin: University of Texas Press, 1971), 1 – 14.

5. Hopkins Papers, *Costa Rica Today,* 113 – 17; U.S. Department of State, Division of Research and Analysis, William S. Lester memorandum, January 13, 1947 (hereafter referred to as DRA); U.S. Department of State, Legal Division, unsigned letter, June 27, 1945 (hereafter referred to as Legal Division).

6. Hopkins Papers, *Costa Rica Today,* 113 – 17; Lester memorandum, January 13, 1947; Legal Division, unsigned letter, June 27, 1945.

7. Hopkins Papers, *Costa Rica Today,* 46 – 48; Fay Allen Des Portes to State, August 11, October 25, 1943; Edward G. Trueblood to State, October 5, 1943, January 3, 28, 1944. Calderón believed that acceptance of a compromise candidate was the best means of bringing the communist faction into the government and at the same time diluting its influence. Furthermore, a compromise candidate reduced the threat of a Cortés-initiated civil war were he to lose the 1944 presidential election. See A. A. Berle, Memorandum of a Conversation, October 15, 1943. For a discussion of the Calderón administration (1940 – 44) and the 1944 elections, see Oscar Aguilar Bulgarelli, *Costa Rica y sus hechos políticos de 1948* (San José: Editorial Costa Rica, 1970), 21 – 121.

8. Hopkins Papers, *Costa Rica Today,* 113 – 20; Des Portes to State, August 10, 11, 1943.

9. Hopkins Papers, *Costa Rica Today,* 47 – 48; U. S. Department of State, Division of American Republics, J. D. Tomlinson memorandum, October 11, 1943 (hereafter referred to as DAR); Des Portes to State, August 11, 1943; Trueblood to State, September 30, October 5, November 11, 1943, January 5, 28, 1944.

10. DRA, unsigned memorandum, November 13, 1943; DAR, Cochran memorandum, February 10, 1944; Des Portes to State, October 25, 1943; Trueblood to State, September 30, October 5, 1943, January 5, 20, 1944.

11. DRA, unsigned memorandum, November 13, 1943; DAR, Cochran memorandum, February 10, 1944; Des Portes to State, October 25, 1943; Trueblood to State, September 30, October 5, 1943, January 5, 20, 1944.

12. DAR, Tomlinson memorandum, October 11, 1943; DAR, Cochran memorandum February 5, 28, 1944; Des Portes to State, October 25, 1943, February 22, 1944; Trueblood to State, September 20, 1943, January 28, February 1, 1944; "Costa Rica Elects A President," *New York Times,* February 15, 1944, 10:3. In contrast, an unidentified American businessman returning to Managua, Nicaragua, from Costa Rica in January 1944 did not believe that the presidential campaign possessed the characteristics of a class struggle because rich and poor alike were evident in both the Picado and Cortés camps. President Franklin D. Roosevelt Personal Papers, PSF Diplomatic Collection, Box 40, Costa Rica.

13. Des Portes to State, February 16, March 22, 1944; Trueblood to State, February 7, 22, 1944; S. Walter Washington to State, October 2, November 2, 1944; Spruille Braden memorandum, November 23, 1944.

14. Office of Strategic Services, Research and Analysis Report 2503, "The First Months of the Teodoro Picado Administration in Costa Rica: August 1944" (hereafter referred to as OSS Report 2503); S. Walter Washington to State, October 2, November 2, 1944; Livingston D. Watrous Report, April 12, 1945; "Message of the President of Costa Rica," *Bulletin of the Pan American Union,* 79(August 1945):470 – 71. On the Picado administration, see Bulgarelli, *Costa Rica* 112 – 96.

15. Washington to State, October 2, November 2, December 25, 1944; Des Portes to State, February 16, 1944; Spruille Braden memorandum, December 29, 1945; "Costa Ricans in Protest," *New York Times,* July 20, 1945, 6:4.

16. OSS Report 2503; Des Portes to State, March 22, 1944; Washington to State, October 2, November 2, December 29, 1944; Watrous report, April 12, 1945.

17. Trueblood to State, February 1, 1944; Des Portes to State, March 22, 1944; Washington to State, October 2, 1944; Watrous to State, February 20, 1946; Hallet Johnson to State, February 27, July 29, 1945, May 22, 1946; DAR, Cochran memorandum, February 10, 1944; U.S. Department of State, Division of Caribbean and Central American Affairs, Murray Wise memorandums, December 10, 1945, July 15, 1946 (hereafter referred to as CCA).

18. Johnson to State, June 27, 1945, May 22, 1946; Legal Division, unsigned memorandum to the Secretary of State, June 27, 1945. The same disagreement was evident with *New York Times* reporters Milton Bracker and W. H. Lawrence. Bracker agreed with Johnson in his "President Picado Interview," September 1, 1946, 20:1. Lawrence shared the Legal Division's suspicions in his "Communism in Latin America," December 30, 1946, 5:7.

19. Clemson University Library, Clemson, South Carolina, James F. Byrnes Papers, *Policy and Information Statement: Costa Rica,* June 15, 1946; University of Virginia Library, Charlottesville, Virginia, Edward R. Stettinius, Jr., Papers, Box 280, "Mexico City Conference: Background Material" (hereafter referred to as Stettinius Papers).

20. Washington to State, December 29, 1944, February 9, 1945; Johnson to State, March 15, June 9, 25, July 9, 1945.

21. Washington to State, December 29, 1944, February 9, 1945; Johnson to State, March 15, 1945.

22. Washington to State, October 2, 1945; Johnson to State, February 27, March 15, 1945. For a discussion of the Social Democratic party, see Burt H. English, *Liberación in Costa Rica* (Gainesville: University of Florida Press, 1971), 1–65.

23. Johnson to State, March 15, 1945; U.S. Military Institute, Carlisle Barracks, Pennsylvania, Willis D. Crittenberger Papers, "Brief Survey of Costa Rica, April 1946" (hereafter referred to as Crittenberger Papers).

24. Watrous report, April 12, 1945; Watrous to State, February 20, 1946.

25. Johnson to State, December 10, 1945; Watrous to State, February 20, 1946; CCA, Wise memorandum, December 10, 1945.

26. Watrous to State, January 1, February 20, 1946; CCA, Wise memorandum, January 5, 1946; OSS Report 3565, "Current Policy Towards Costa Rica," February 1946.

27. Watrous to State, January 14, February 14, 20, 1946; CCA, Wise memorandums, January 5, February 25, 1946; OSS Report 3565, "Current Policy Towards Costa Rica Today"; "Costa Rica Has Close Elections," *New York Times,* February 12, 1946, 5:6.

28. Johnson to State, April 9, 17, May 4, 1946; Raleigh H. Gibson to State, April 27, May 14, June 10, 1946; CCA, Wise memorandum, April 9, 1946.

29. Watrous to State, January 14, 1946; Johnson to State, April 9, May 4, 13, June 10, 11, 16, December 3, 1946; Gibson to State, May 14, June 10, 1946; CCA, Wise memorandums, December 10, 1945, February 25, May 15, 1946.

30. Gibson to State, August 7, 1946.

31. Johnson personal letter to Secretary of State James F. Byrnes, October 1, 1946; Johnson to State, December 3, 1946; Gibson to State, October 18, 1946; CCA, J.R. Solana memorandum, October 31, 1946.

32. Johnson personal letter to Spruille Braden, January 9, 1947; Johnson to State, January 3, 28, February 4, 1947; Johnson memorandum, January 9, 1947; CCA, Tapley W. Bennett memorandum, January 9, 1947.

33. Johnson to State, January 28, February 4, 1947.

34. Johnson to State, February 14, 1947; "Costa Rican Convention," *New York Times,* February 13, 1947, 18:1; "Opposition Picks Candidate," *New York Times,* February 14, 1947, 4:4.

35. Johnson to State, January 28, February 4, 14, March 27, 1947; "Calderon Guardia Enters Race," *New York Times,* February 19, 1947, 28:5; "Nominated in Costa Rica," *New York Times,* March 24, 1947.

36. John W. Carrigan to State, June 20, July 10, 1947; Cohen to State, August 22, 1947.

37. Carrigan to State, June 20, July 10, 1947; Cohen to State, August 22, November 7, 1947.

38. Central America and Panama Affairs Division, Bennett memorandum, October 9, 1947 (hereafter referred to as CPA); Crittenberger Papers, "Diary," July 23, 1947; Carrigan to State, August 1, 4, 8, 1947; Cohen to State, August 22, 1947.

39. Carrigan to State, June 30, July 10, August 1, 4, 8, 1947, January 8, 1948; Cohen to State, August 22, November 7, 14, December 18, 1947, February 6, 1948.

40. Carrigan to State, June 20, July 10, August 4, 1947; Cohen to State, August 22, 1947.

41. DRA, Lester memorandum, May 22, 1947. The memorandum reflected the collective thinking of Woodrow Borah, B. S. Guynn, and William Lester.

42. Carrigan to State, June 20, 1947.

43. Donnelly to State, October 9, 1947; Carrigan to State, October 30, 1947; CPA, Bennett memorandum, October 16, 1948; Crittenberger Papers, "Notes," August 6, 1947. Subsequently, the *New York Times* linked Vanguard's platform to the "party line." See "Communist Pattern Seen," *New York Times,* November 10, 1947, 10:4.

44. Cohen to State, November 7, December 18, 1947, January 12, 23, February 6, 1948.

45. Cohen to State, November 11, 1947, February 6, 1948.

46. Cohen to State, February 13, 1948; CPA, Bennett memorandum, February 12, 1948.

47. Cohen to State, February 13, 19, 1948; Nathaniel P. Davis to State, February 27, 1948; "Uncounted Votes Burn in Costa Rica," *New York Times,* February 11, 1948, 18:6.

48. Cohen to State, February 19, March 5, 1948.

49. Cohen to State, March 1, 1948; "Costa Rican Vote Clouded by Fraud," *New York Times,* February 10, 1948, 17:2; "Ulate is Costa Rican Victor," *New York Times,* February 29, 1948, 9:1.

50. Cohen to State, March 5, 1948; "Costa Rica Annuls Presidential Election," *New York Times,* March 2, 1948, 15:3.

51. Davis to State, March 22, 1948.

52. Davis to State, March 19, April 2, 1948.

53. Davis to State, March 19, 22, April 21, 1948; Cohen to State, April 1, 4, 16, 23, 1948; Maurice M. Bernbaum to State, March 18, 1948; "Costa Rica Seats Acting President," *New York Times,* April 23, 1948, 10:3; "Ex-President Praises Foe," *New York Times,* April 23, 1948, 10:3.

54. Davis to State, March 19, 1948; Cohen to State, April 1, 16, 1948.

55. The truce negotiations are treated in *FRUS,* 1948, 488–524. For a discussion of the civil war, see Bulgarelli, *Costa Rica,* 197–397; and Miguel Acuna, *El 48* (San José: Tresjo Hnos., 1974).

56. Davis to State, April 12, 26, 1948.

57. Davis to State, March 19, 1948; Cohen to State, April 1, 1948.

58. Cohen to State, April 1, 1948; Davis to State, April 21, 1948.

59. Davis to State, March 19, 1948; Cohen to State, April 1, 6, 1948; "Costa Rica Seats Acting President," *New York Times,* April 21, 1948, 18:3; "President Will Quit Costa Rican Post," *New York Times,* May 2, 1948, 54:6; "Costa Rica Has New Rule," *New York Times,* May 9, 1948, 28:1; "Rivals Bow to Ulate, But Junta Will Rule," *New York Times,* May 3, 1948, 6:4.

60. Davis to State, June 7, 1948.

61. Cohen to State, April 16, 1948.

62. Cohen to State, June 10, July 10, 22, 1948; John N. Speaks memorandum, June 28, 1948; "Rights Curbed, Reds Seized in Costa Rica," *New York Times,* June 20, 1948, 24:5.

63. Cohen to State, September 9, 1948; Davis to State, November 5, 1948.

64. Cohen to State, October 4, 27, December 19, 1948, January 4, 1949; Davis to State, October 4, December 9, 1948.

65. Davis to State, December 9, 1948; Cohen to State, December 10, 1948, January 4, 1949; "Ulate Party Tops Costa Rican Poll," *New York Times,* December 9, 1948, 25:2; "Costa Rican Election Returns," *New York Times,* December 11, 1948, 23:3.

66. Cohen to State, January 4, March 31, April 21, 1949; Davis to State, March 17, April 4, 1949; CPA, Monthly Political Summary: Costa Rica, February 1949; "Costa Rican Junta Stays On," *New York Times,* February 5, 1949, 5:2.

67. Cohen to State, April 21, July 21, August 24, 1949. On the 1949 constitution, see Marco Tulio Zeledon, *Historia constituciónal de Costa Rica en el hienio 1948–1949* (San José: F. Aguilar, 1950); and República de Costa Rica, Ministerio de Gobernación, *Constitución política de Costa Rica, 7 noviembre de 1945* (San José: Imprinta Nacional, 1955).

68. Cohen to State, July 21, 1949; Joseph N. Flack to State, September 9, 1949.

69. Cohen to State, March 3, July 28, August 18, 24, 1949; "Costa Rica Bars Party," *New York Times,* August 18, 1949, 12:7; CPA, Monthly Political Summary: Costa Rica, August 1949.

70. Andrew E. Donovan to State, October 5, 1949; "Costa Ricans Go to Polls," *New York Times,* October 3, 1949, 2:5; "Ulate Wins in Costa Rica," *New York Times,* October 4, 1949, 13:1; "Costa Rica Inducts New Top Executive," *New York Times,*

November 9, 1949, 19:3; J. E. Webb, "U.S. Expresses Gratification with New Costa Rican Government," *U.S. Department of State Bulletin,* November 28, 1949, 21:833.

71. OSS Report 4780, "Political Development and Trends in the Other American Republics of the 20th Century: Costa Rica," October 1, 1949.

72. Ibid.

73. Truman Library, Oral History Collection, José Figueres Interview, July 8, 1970, Transcript 33; Charles D. Ameringer, *Don Pepé: A Political Biography of José A. Figueres of Costa Rica* (Albuquerque: University of New Mexico Press, 1978). For a more complete bibliography of Figueres, see Harry Kantor, *Bibliography of José Figueres* (Tempe: Arizona State University Press, 1972).

74. Samuel Guy Inman, "Democracy Returns to Costa Rica," *World Interpreter,* 1:4, December 23, 1949, located in the Edward G. Miller Papers, Truman Library; John D. Martz, *Central America: The Crisis and the Challenge* (Chapel Hill: University of North Carolina Press, 1959), 210–32; Acuna, *El 48.*

75. Cohen to State, March 17, 1948.

76. Bell, *Crisis in Costa Rica,* 41–61.

77. Truman Library, Truman Papers, Confidential File, State Department memorandum, January 6, 1949, 3.

Chapter 2

1. Byrnes Papers, *Policy and Information Statement: El Salvador,* 1–3 (hereafter referred to as *Policy Statement: Salvador*); Hopkins Papers, Federal Bureau of Investigation, *Totalitarian Activities: El Salvador Today 1943,* 5–12 (hereafter referred to as *El Salvador Today*); R. H. Tottenham Smith, *Economic and Commercial Conditions in El Salvador* (London: His Majesty's Stationery Office, 1948, 1951).

2. Alfred Nufer to State, September 9, 1947. The diplomatic correspondence used for this chapter is in the National Archives, Record Group 59, Department of State Decimal Files 816.00/*date,* 816.00B/*date,* and FW816.00/*date.* Works on Salvadoran political history include: Francisco Gavidia, *Historia moderna de El Salvador* (San Salvador: Ministerior de Cultura Hispánica, 1950); Alberto de Mestas, *El Salvador* (Madrid: Ediciones Cultura Hispánica, 1950); and Alastair White, *El Salvador* (New York: Praeger Publishers, 1973).

3. Hopkins Papers, *El Salvador Today,* 28–34.

4. J. Edgar Hoover, director of the FBI, to Adolf A. Berle, assistant secretary of state, October 13, 1943. Hernández's elimination of the communists is treated in Anderson, *Matanza.*

5. Walter Thurston to State, February 24, March 1, 1944; "El Salvador Re-elects President," *New York Times,* March 1, 1944, 6:4.

6. CCA, Cochran memorandum, April 10, 1944, Thurston to State, April 11, 1944; "Salvador Lists Toll in Revolt," *New York Times,* April 16, 1944, 28:4. Nothing in the State Department files substantiates Thurston's subsequent statement that the coup

leaders expected the diplomatic corps to intervene on their behalf in urging Hernández not to resist. See White, *El Salvador,* 115–16, footnote 60.

7. CCA, Cochran memorandum, April 10, 1944; Thurston to State, April 30, 1944; Overton G. Ellis to State, April 22, 1944; Franklin D. Roosevelt Library, Frank P. Carrigan Personal Papers, William P. Cochran to Carrigan, undated.

8. CCA, John C. Cabot memorandum, April 24, 1944; Federal Bureau of Investigation, "Revolutionary Activities in El Salvador," May 21, 1944.

9. FBI, "Revolutionary Activities in El Salvador," May 21, 1944; Thurston to State, May 6, 1944; Cordell Hull to Thurston, May 6, 1944.

10. FBI, "Revolutionary Activities in El Salvador," May 21, 1944.

11. Ibid.; Thurston to State, May 6, 1944.

12. Hull to Thurston, May 6, 1944.

13. FBI, "Revolutionary Activities in El Salvador," May 21, 1944; Thurston to State, May 9, 18, 20, 1944; Hull to Salvadoran Foreign Minister Julio Avila, May 15, 1944.

14. FBI, "Revolutionary Activities in El Salvador," May 21, 1944; Thurston to State, May 9, 18, 20, 1944; Hull to Salvadoran Foreign Minister Julio Avila, May 15, 1944; "Salvadoran Cabinet Named," *New York Times,* May 11, 1944, 2:6; "El Salvador Elated as Ex-Ruler Leaves," *New York Times,* May 12, 1944, 3:4.

15. FBI, "Revolutionary Activities in El Salvador," May 21, 1944; Thurston to State, May 11, 12, 18, 20, June 23, 1944.

16. CCA, Cochran memorandums, June 1, 16, 28, 1944; DAR, Analysis and Liaison Division, G. M. Bauer memorandum, June 20, 1944; Thurston to State, May 26, 31, June 6, 21, 1944; Gerhard Gade to State, July 15, 1944.

17. CCA, Cochran memorandum, September 11, 1944; Thurston to State, May 31, June 6, August 26, September 22, 1944; "El Salvador Still Torn," *New York Times,* May 17, 1944, 3:5.

18. CCA, Cochran memorandums, September 5, 11, 1944; Thurston to State, September 17, 1944.

19. John F. Simmons to State, October 26, November 1, 1944; Ellis to State, October 24, 1944; "Revolt Casts Out Salvador Regime," *New York Times,* October 22, 1944, 30:3.

20. Simmons to State, October 26, 1944; CCA, Cochran memorandum, November 9, 1944; Franklin D. Roosevelt Papers, President's Secretary's File, Box 95, "Edward R. Stettinius, Jr., June–November, 1944," October 31, November 7, 14, 1944.

21. Simmons to State, November 10, 21, December 7, 23, 1944; CCA, Cochran memorandum, January 10, 1945.

22. Simmons to State, December 26, 1944, January 5, 9, 11, 16, 19, 23, 1945; Stettinius Papers, Box 227, "Daily Developments, Summary of," February 20, 24, 1945; Box 235, "Minutes, Secretary's Staff Committee," February 9, 1945; Box 280, "Mexico City Conference—Background Material: Salvador"; *FRUS, 1945,* Vol. IX, 1065–74; "Aguirre Plans Election," *New York Times,* December 4, 1944, 12:7; "Salvadoran Nominee Unopposed," *New York Times,* January 12, 1945, 12:4; "Salvadoran President Named," *New York Times,* January 18, 1945, 3:1; "Amnesty in El Salvador," *New York Times,* March 3, 1945, 7:1; "Salvador Opens Borders," *New York Times,* March 10, 1945, 18:3.

23. Simmons to State, January 8, 16, 1945.

24. Simmons to State, March 7, May 22, 1945; Stettinius Papers, Box 227, "Daily Developments, Summary of," January 19, 1945; Franklin D. Roosevelt Papers, President's Secretary's File, Box 91, "State Department—Special Information Folder 1945," January 20, 1945.

25. Simmons to State, January 9, April 27, 1945, February 5, 1946.

26. Simmons to State, March 21, June 13, 15, 28, July 24, 1945; CCA, Cochran memorandum, August 8, 1945.

27. Simmons to State, March 21, April 27, May 22, June 1, 15, 20, 1945, August 8, 1946.

28. Simmons to State, May 22, December 26, 1945; Gade to State, November 3, 1945.

29. Simmons to State, June 13, 28, July 10, September 10, 1945, April 10, July 26, 1946; "Ex-Dictator Leader of Salvadoran Revolt," *New York Times,* June 13, 1945, 4:2; "Salvadoran Rebels Go to Mexico," *New York Times,* July 9, 1945, 14:2.

30. Simmons to State, July 26, August 13, 15, 16, 21, 23, 28, September 9, 23, 1946; "El Salvador Ousts 3 Cabinet Ministers," *New York Times,* September 23, 1946, 5:3.

31. Simmons to State, September 23, 27, October 11, 17, November 27, December 12, 1946; CCA, Murat W. Williams memorandums (2) September 26, 1946; "New Salvador Cabinet," *New York Times,* October 16, 1946, 16:3; Byrnes Papers, *Policy Statement: Salvador,* 6.

32. Simmons to State, August 8, December 26, 1945, April 10, 1946; Byrnes Papers, *Policy Statement: Salvador,* 6–7.

33. Simmons to State, January 23, 1945.

34. Gade to State, December 20, 1945; Simmons to State, December 27, 1946. For coverage of Salvador's constitutional history, see Ricardo Gallardo, *Las constituciones de El Salvador,* 2 vols. (Madrid: Ediciones Cultura Hispánica, 1961).

35. Gade to State, December 20, 1945; Simmons to State, December 27, 1946; Gallardo, *Las constituciones,* Vol. II.

36. Simmons to State, January 29, February 5, 1946.

37. Simmons to State, January 17, April 18, June 27, 1947; Robert E. Wilson to State, July 18, 30, 1947; Albert F. Nufer to State, August 19, 27, September 2, 5, October 24, 1947.

38. Simmons to State, June 6, 1947; Nufer to State, August 19, September 5, October 13, 1947.

39. Simmons to State, January 15, June 27, 1947; CCA, Williams memorandum, January 24, 1947.

40. Simmons to State, February 6, June 27, 1947; Nufer to State, September 5, 1947.

41. Nufer to State, September 5, October 24, 1947; Williams to State, November 7, 1947.

42. Leslie A. Squires to State, November 28, 1947.

43. Nufer to State, November 30, 1948.

44. Nufer to State, September 5, October 10, 1947.

45. Squires to State, November 28, 1947; CPA, Robert E. Wilson memorandum, December 17, 1947.

46. CPA, Wilson memorandum, December 17, 1947.

47. Nufer to State, April 30, 1948.

48. Simmons to State, January 15, 1947; Nufer to State, October 24, 1947, March 18, May 18, 27, November 12, 1948.

49. Simmons to State, January 15, 1947; Ellis to State, February 10, 1947; Nufer to State, September 2, 1947, April 12, May 18, 27, 1948; Williams to State, November 28, 1947, March 11, August 16, 1948; CPA, Williams memorandum, February 14, 1948.

50. Simmons to State, June 27, 1947; Wilson to State, July 30, 1947; Nufer to State, May 18, 20, 27, 1948.

51. Nufer to State, March 18, December 3, 1948.

52. Nufer to State, May 27, October 21, November 12, 1948; CPA, Monthly Political Summary: El Salvador, October 1948.

53. Williams to State, December 5, 1947, January 15, 1948; Nufer to State, July 8, August 13, 19, October 21, 1948.

54. Nufer to State, August 13, December 3, 1948; Williams to State, December 16, 1948; CPA, Robert F. Woodward memorandum, December 21, 1948; CPA, Monthly Political Summary: El Salvador, December 1948.

55. Nufer to State, August 13, December 3, 1948; Williams to State, December 16, 1948; CPA, Woodward memorandum, December 21, 1948; Williams to State, December 17, 1948; CPA, J. de Zengotita memorandums (2) December 15, 1948; "Junta Takes Over in San Salvador," *New York Times,* December 18, 1948, 6:7; "Salvador Junta Gets Backing," *New York Times,* December 16, 1948, 15:2; "El Salvador Pledges Democracy, Free Vote, and a New Constitution," *New York Times,* December 27, 1948, 13:2.

56. Nufer to State, December 22, 1948.

57. Nufer to State, January 4, 6, 14, February 4, March 31, April 2, 1949; Williams to State, March 11, 1949; CPA, Monthly Political Summary: El Salvador, January, February, March 1949; "Osorio Now Heads El Salvador Junta," *New York Times,* January 7, 1949, 15:7. Córdova was permitted to leave the country. He took up residence in Tegucigalpa, Honduras.

58. Nufer to State, March 31, April 2, 12, July 8, 1949.

59. Nufer to State, January 4, 21, 28, February 2, March 25, April 7, July 15, 1949; George P. Shaw to State, September 2, 1949; unsigned telegram, State Department to Nufer, January 26, 1949.

60. Shaw to State, October 14, 1949; CPA, Monthly Political Summary, October 1949.

61. Shaw to State, October 28, November 1, 1949.

62. Robert Wieland to State, December 30, 1949; CPA, Monthly Political Summary: El Salvador, December 1949.

63. OSS Report 4780, "Political Development and Trends in Other American Republics in the 20th Century: El Salvador," October 1, 1949.

Chapter 3

1. Hopkins Papers, Federal Bureau of Investigation Reports, *Totalitarian Activities: Guatemala, July 1944,* 10–14 (hereafter referred to as Hopkins Papers, *Guatemala Today*); OSS Report 5123, "Guatemala: Communist Influence," October 25, 1950.

2. OSS Report 988, "Survey of Guatemala, 1943," 1–4. For a fuller treatment of Guatemalan political history, see Amy Elizabeth Jensen, *Guatemala: A Historical Survey* (New York: Exposition Press, 1955); Chester Lloyd Jones, *Guatemala: Past and Present* (Minneapolis: University of Minnesota Press, 1939); and Nathan L. Whetten, *Guatemala: The Land and the People* (New Haven: Yale University Press, 1961). The Ubico regime is analyzed in Grieb, *Guatemalan Caudillo.*

3. Hopkins Papers, *Guatemala Today,* 40–46.

4. Ibid., 47–50; Gerald Drew memorandums, February 9, 23, 1943. The diplomatic correspondence used for this chapter is in the National Archives, Record Group 59, Department of State Decimal Files 814.00/*date,* 814.00B./*date,* and FW814.00/*date.*

5. Long to State, April 21, 1944, June 21, 22, 23, 1944; DAR, William P. Cochran memorandum, April 28, 1944. For a discussion of the 1944 Salvadoran revolt against Hernández, see chapter 2.

6. Long to State, June 22, 23, 1944; "Guatemala Students Out," *New York Times,* June 24, 1944, 36:5.

7. Long to State, June 23, 1944; DAR, Cochran memorandum, June 23, 1944. DAR Chief Laurence Duggan doubted that the Indians were important because they were considered "phlegmatic and ask only to be left alone," DAR, Duggan memorandum, June 26, 1944; "Guatemala in Grip of Rising Tension," *New York Times,* June 27, 1944, 36:5.

8. Long to State, June 23, 1944.

9. DAR, Cochran memorandum, June 29, 1944; Long to State, July 3, 1944, enclosure "Ubico Manifesto"; "Guatemala Under Military Junta as Unrest Forces President Out," *New York Times,* July 2, 1944, 7:2; "Junta in Guatemala Promises Election," *New York Times,* July 3, 1944, 7:1.

10. Long to State, June 30, July 1, 4, 1944. Kenneth J. Grieb, downplaying the selection of the triumvirate, stated that they were the only officers "available" at the moment. This account was based upon an interview with Ernesto Rivas. See Grieb, *Guatemalan Caudillo,* 273–75.

11. Long to State, July 4, 5, 7, 14, 1944; DAR, Cochran memorandum, July 7, 1944.

12. Long to State, July 14, 21, September 2, 12, 1944; DAR, Cochran memorandum, July 27, 1944.

13. Long to State, August 29, September 12, 1944.

14. Long to State, September 1, 1944; DAR, Cochran memorandum, July 27, 1944.

15. Long to State, July 27, September 1, 1940; DAR, Duggan memorandum, October 23, 1943.

16. Long to State, September 1, 1944.

17. Ibid.

18. Long to State, July 27, September 1, 22, 26, 29, October 6, 1944; Norman Armour to Long, September 26, 1944; CCA, Cochran memorandum, October 11, 1944.

19. Long to State, September 22, 29, October 3, 13, 1944; Affeld to State, October 17, 1944.

20. Long to State, September 29, October 13, 1944.

21. Affeld to State, October 24, 26, 1944; "Guatemala Ousts Regime in Revolt," *New York Times,* October 21, 1944, 5:1.

22. Affeld to State, October 24, 26, 1944; Long to State, October 31, November 3, 1944; Franklin D. Roosevelt Papers, PSF Files, Box 95, Edward R. Stettinius, Jr., Folder, "Special Information for the President," October 24, 31, 1944; "Guatemala Tense under Rebel Rule," *New York Times,* October 24, 1944, 12:3. Affeld was unable to determine the role of General Miguel Ydígoras Feuntes, who appeared at the embassy on October 16, prior to the revolt, apparently as a representative of the younger officers. His name was mentioned on October 19 as a member of the junta that intended to succeed Ponce. Following the revolt, Feuntes milled around the U.S. embassy as if ready to seek asylum were things not to go his way. Eventually, he was deported to Mexico with Ponce.

23. Long to State, October 31, 1944, January 4, 1945; OSS Report 2791, "The First Two Months of the New Guatemalan Government (November– December, 1944)." Arévalo's Argentine experience is discussed in Edward L. Reed to State, January 8, 1945.

24. Long to State, November 3, 7, 1944, January 5, 1945.

25. Long to State, November 17, 24, December 7, 1944; Affeld memorandum November 27, 1944; Robert F. Woodward memorandum, December 16, 1944.

26. Long to State, November 7, 24, 1944.

27. Long to State, December 7, 11, 1944, January 3, March 19, 1945; Affeld to State, December 21, 1944; Woodward memorandum, December 16, 1944; Stettinius Papers, Box 280, Folder "Mexico City Conference—Background Materials, Guatemala"; "New Guatemala Charter," *New York Times,* March 14, 1945, 5:2.

28. Long to State, January 8, 18, February 9, 1945; Woodward to State, October 1, 1945.

29. Woodward to State, April 24, 1945; Kyle to State, October 1, 1945; CCA, Cochran memorandum, May 1, 1945; FBI report, "Communism in Guatemala," August 23, 1945; CCA, Robert Newbegin memorandum, October 15, 1945; Embassy staff report to State, May 6, 1948. For a fuller account of Arévalo's life and philosophy, see Juan José Arévalo, *Anti-Kommunism in Latin America: An X-Ray of the Process Leading to New Colonialism,* translated from the Spanish by Carlton Beals (New York: L. Stuart Co., 1963); Juan José Arévalo, *La Argentina que yo viví, 1927 – 1944* (Mexico City: Costa Amic, 1974); Juan José Arévalo, *Carta política al gobierno de Guatemala con motivo de laber acceptado la candidatura presidencial* (Mexico City: Costa Amic, 1963); Juan José Arévalo, *Discursos en la presidencia* (Guatemala City: n.p., 1947); Juan José

Arévalo, *Guatemala, la democracia y el imperio* (Mexico City: Editorial Americana Nueva, 1954); Juan José Arévalo, *The Shark and the Sardines,* translated from the Spanish by Jane Cobb and Raul Osequeda (New York: L. Stuart Co., 1961); Marie Berthe Dion, *Las ideas sociales y políticas de Arévalo* (Mexico City: Editorial Americana Nueva, 1958); and Clemente Marroquín Rojas, *La carta política del ciudadano Juan José Arévalo* (Guatemala City: Escribe Canato Ocara, 1965).

30. Embassy staff report to State, May 6, 1948; Donovan to State, January 21, April 16, May 2, June 25, 1946, June 17, 1947; Kyle to State, January 2, 1947; CPA, Murray W. Williams memorandum, January 10, 1947.

31. Embassy staff report to State, May 6, 1948; Donovan to State, January 25, February 11, 1946; FBI reports, "Jose Manuel Fortuny," May 28, 1946, "Alfred Pellecer Vidas," June 11, 1946; Wells to State, March 10, 31, 1949.

32. Embassy staff report to State, May 6, 1948; Butler Library, Columbia University, New York City, Oral History Project, Spruille Braden, Transcript 991 (hereafter referred to as Oral History, Braden).

33. Embassy staff report to State, May 6, 1948; Wells to State, March 19, 1948; CPA, Robert E. Wilson memorandum, May 6, 1948.

34. Embassy staff report to State, May 6, 1948; Wells to State, November 7, 1947, September 22, 1948; CPA, Williams memorandum, May 22, 1947.

35. Kyle to State, January 2, 3, 1947; Wells to State, January 20, 1948; CPA, Williams memorandum, January 10, 1947.

36. Embassy staff report to State, May 6, 1948; CPA, Robert E. Wilson memorandum, May 6, 1948; Donovan to State, January 25, 1948.

37. Wells to State, July 21, 1948, March 24, 1949; Richard C. Patterson to State, April 28, 1949.

38. Wells to State, July 1, 23, August 10, 1948.

39. Kyle to State, October 1, 1946, January 31, 1947; Kyle memorandum on Guatemala, September 1, 1948; Donovan to State, June 3, 1947; Wells to State, November 7, 1947; CPA, Robert Newbegin memorandum, March 12, 1948; Embassy staff Report to State, May 6, 1948; Byrnes Papers, *Policy and Information Statement: Guatemala,* June 15, 1946; Crittenberger "Diary," August 7, 1947; Oral History, Braden, 1807. Ambassador Kyle was well received by the Arévalo administration. See John M. Olin Library, Cornell University, Ithaca, New York, Edwin J. Kyle Papers, "Words of Undersecretary of Agriculture at Dinner given Ambassador Kyle by the Ministry of Agriculture at National Fair of Guatemala, Guatemala City, August 16, 1946"; press statement, "President of the Republic of Guatemala," October 29, 1946; Francisco Valdes Calderón to Kyle, July 19, 1948; Juan José Arévalo to Kyle, August 21, 1948.

40. Raymond K. Oakley memorandum, November 3, 1949; Edward G. Cale memorandum, December 8, 1949.

41. OSS Report 5123, "Guatemala: Communist Influence," October 23, 1950. Another brief study, attributed to W. Tapley Bennett, March 23, 1950, is in the Truman Library, Papers of Richard C. Patterson, Jr. (hereafter referred to as Patterson Papers). A discussion of the growth of communist influence in Guatemala, based

largely upon Guatemalan sources, is in Donald M. Schneider, *Communism in Guatemala: 1944 – 1954* (New York: Frederick A. Praeger, 1958). A justification for 1954 intervention by the United States because of communist influence in Guatemala is presented in U.S. State Department, *A Case History of Communist Penetration* (Washington, D.C.: Government Printing Office, 1957).

42. Patterson Papers, Bennett memorandum, "Some Aspects of Communist Penetration in Guatemala," March 23, 1950.

43. Woodward to State, April 24, July 13, September 1, 1945; Kyle to State, October 1, 1945; Donovan to State, January 9, 21, February 28, April 10, 1946; CCA, Cochran memorandums, April 24, July 19, 1945; CCA, Newbegin memorandum, October 15, 1945; "Guatemalan Removal," *New York Times,* January 12, 1946, 9:7.

44. Woodward to State, April 24, June 5, 8, July 13, 1945; Donovan to State, July 26, 1946; Kyle to State, January 2, 1947; "Guatemalan Unrest Seen," *New York Times,* January 9, 1945, 6:4.

45. Woodward to State, July 13, August 17, 1945; Donovan to State, February 12, 28, May 22, June 25, 1946; CCA, Cochran memorandum, May 1, 1945; CCA, Williams memorandum, July 26, 1946.

46. Paul Hutton to State, October 8, 11, 1946; CPA, Williams memorandum, October 17, 1946; "Guatemalan Favors Accord," *New York Times,* October 7, 1946, 10:4.

47. Kyle to State, January 21, 29, 31, 1947; Donovan to State, January 2, March 18, 19, 25, 1947; "Guatemalan Voting Opens," *New York Times,* January 25, 1947, 4:3.

48. Siracusa to State, May 20, 1948; Wells to State, June 22, 1948; CPA, Wilson memorandum, June 22, 1948.

49. Donovan to State, February 13, June 3, 6, 13, 1947; Kyle to State, February 21, 1947; Wells to State, November 7, 1947; CPA, Williams memorandums, February 18, June 13, 1947; Steins memorandum, June 22, 1948.

50. Kyle to State, March 1, 1948; Wells to State, March 19, 1948.

51. Wells to State, October 5, 12, 1948; CPA, Monthly Political Summary, October and November 1948.

52. Wells to State, August 24, 1948.

53. Wells to State, December 16, 1948, January 18, 31, 1949; Patterson to State, January 31, 1949.

54. Woodward to State, June 6, 1945; Byrnes to Kyle, August 30, 1945; CCA, Cochran memorandum, July 19, 1945.

55. Long to State, February 9, April 9, 1945; Woodward to State, May 21, October 1, 9, 25, 1945; CCA, Cochran memorandum, May 1, 1945; Stettinius Papers, Box 280, "Summary of Daily Developments," February 20, 1945; "Guatemala Erases Liberties for Month," *New York Times,* October 3, 1945, 8:8; "60 Arrested in Guatemala," *New York Times,* October 4, 1945, 8:5; "Guatemala Traitors Sentenced," *New York Times,* October 28, 1945, 31:6; "Guatemala Dooms Three," *New York Times,* October 29, 1945, 9:3.

56. Donovan to State, April 8, 16, May 2, June 25, 1946; Kyle to State, September 16, 18, 1947.

57. Donovan to State, September 24, 26, 1947; Wells to State, October 31, 1947; CPA, Wilson memorandums, October 2, 6, 1947.

58. Wells to State, March 19, June 22, July 29, 1948; CPA, Wilson memorandum, June 22, 1948; CPA, Juan de Zengotita memorandum, February 3, 1949; CPA, Monthly Political Summary, March 1948; "Guatemala Offers Amnesty," *New York Times,* March 5, 1948, 3:5.

59. Long to State, November 17, 1944, January 3, February 9, March 9, 1945; Woodward to State, December 16, 1944, August 18, September 1, 1946; Donovan to State, January 21, April 29, May 2, July 8, 1946; Kyle to State, January 21, 29, 1947; Wells to State, January 26, July 29, 1948; Zengotita to State, February 3, 1949; CPA, Wilson memorandum, December 4, 1947.

60. Woodward to State, April 24, 1945; Kyle to State, January 2, 1947, and memorandum, September 1, 1948; Wells to State, November 12, 1948, June 3, 1949; CCA, Cochran memorandum, May 1, 1945; CPA, Williams memorandum, January 10, 1947.

61. Wells to State, June 3, 1949.

62. Wells to State, July 18, September 29, November 7, 1949; Patterson to State, July 22, 25, 27, 1949; Steins to State, July 25, December 9, 1949; CPA, Siracusa memorandum, July 29, 1949; CPA, Monthly Political Summary, July 1949; "Revolt Breaks Out in Guatemala after Shooting of Army's Leader," *New York Times,* July 19, 1949, 1:2; "Guatemala Calls on Reserves Help," *New York Times,* July 20, 1949, 14:3.

63. Patterson to State, July 22, 1949; Siracusa memorandum, July 22, 29, 1949; CPA, Wise memorandum, July 29, 1949; Truman Library, Patterson Papers, Patterson to Cornelius Mara, August 17, 1949. Subsequently, the government arrested thirty-three persons in connection with Araña's death, twenty-one of whom were described by the embassy staff as "small fish." Fourteen were eventually found guilty of sedition and rebellion. Wells to State, September 29, November 7, 1949; Steins to State, December 9, 1949; "21 arrested in Guatemala," *New York Times,* November 2, 1949, 6:4; "Guatemala Banishes Eight," *New York Times,* November 5, 1949, 6:8.

64. Patterson to State, May 11, Wells to State, June 3, 15, November 16, 18, 1949.

65. For a discussion of the Arbenz regime, see Schneider, *Communism in Guatemala;* and Richard B. Chardkoff, "Communist Toehold in the Americas" (Ph. D. dissertation, Florida State University, 1967). For the 1954 U.S.-sponsored intervention, see Department of State, *Case History of Communist Penetration;* Charles G. Fenwick, "Jurisdictional Questions Involved in the Guatemalan Intervention," *American Journal of International Law* 48:4 (1954): 597–602; Max Gordon, "A Case History of U.S. Subversion: Guatemala, 1954," *Science and Society* 35:2 (1971): 129–55; Richard Immerman, *CIA in Guatemala* (Austin: University of Texas Press, 1982); Phillip B. Taylor, Jr., "The Guatemalan Affair: A Critique of United States Foreign Policy," *American Political Science Review* 50:3 (1956): 787–807; and Guillermo Toiello, *La batalla de Guatemala* (Mexico City: Caudernos Americanos, 1955).

66. OSS Report 4780, "Political Development and Trends in Other American Republics in the 20th Century: Guatemala," October 1, 1949.

67. Patterson Papers, Bennett memorandum, "Some Aspects of Communist Penetration in Guatemala," March 23, 1950.

Chapter 4

1. Richard D. Adams, *Cultural Surveys of Panama, Nicaragua, Guatemala, El Salvador, Honduras* (Washington, D.C.: Pan American Sanitary Bureau, 1957).

2. Byrnes Papers, *Policy and Information Statement, June 15, 1946: Honduras* (hereafter referred to as Byrnes Papers, *Policy Statement: Honduras*); G. E. Stockley, *Economic and Commercial Conditions in Honduras* (London: His Majesty's Stationery Office, 1949); G. E. Stockley, *Economic and Commercial Conditions in Honduras* (London: His Majesty's Stationary Office, 1951).

3. OSS Report 4780, "Political Development and Trends in Other American Republics in the 20th Century: Honduras," October 1, 1949; J. Edgar Hoover, director of the Federal Bureau of Investigation, to Adolf A. Berle, assistant secretary of state, "Revolutionary Tendencies in Honduras," July 6, 1944; Stettinius Papers, Box 280, Folder, "Mexico City Conference—Background Material: Honduras." For a fuller discussion of Honduran political history, see William S. Stokes, *Honduras: An Area Study in Government* (Madison: University of Wisconsin Press, 1950); José Francisco Martínez, *Honduras histórica* (Tegucigalpa: [S.N.], 1974); Victor Carceres Lana, *Feches de la historia Honduras* (Tegucigalpa: [S.N.], 1964); Medaro Mejía, *Historia de Honduras* (Tegucigalpa: Editorial Andrade, 1969); and Lucas Paredes, *Dramapolítico de Honduras* (Mexico: Editoria Latina Americana, 1958). Constitutional histories of Honduras include: Luis Mariñas Ofero, comp., *Las constituciónes de honduras* (Madrid: Ediciones Cultura Hispania, 1962); and Universidad Nacional Autónoma de Honduras, *Recopilación de las constituciónes de Honduras, 1825–1965* (Tegucigalpa: La Universidad, 1977).

4. Byrnes Papers, *Policy Statement: Honduras*. The State Department Decimal Files for Honduran political affairs are 815.00/*date*, 815.00B/*date*, and FW815.00/*date*. Gordon S. Reid memorandum, October 14, 1949; Milton Bracker, "Good Neighbor: Measures of U.S. Millions Found Remote to Millions of Latins," *New York Times,* September 2, 1945, 4:5.

5. Erwin to State, November 2, 1944, March 3, July 23, 1945, January 16, February 1, 1946, February 18, 1947. Erwin believed there were only six millionaire families in Honduras, but none had two million. Erwin to State, February 18, 1947.

6. Daniels to State, July 18, 1947; Faust to State, April 3, 1946.

7. Erwin to State, February 18, 1947; Faust to State, April 3, 1946; Daniels to State, July 18, 1948; Dawson memorandum, January 21, 1947.

8. FBI, "Revolutionary Tendencies in Honduras," July 6, 1944; Military Intelligence Division, Report No. 760, "Political Situation in Honduras," January 21, 1944 (hereafter referred to as MID, "Political Situation in Honduras").

9. FBI, "Revolutionary Tendencies in Honduras," July 6, 1944; MID, "Political Situation in Honduras," January 21, 1944.

10. FBI, "Revolutionary Tendencies in Honduras," July 6, 1944; MID, "Political Situation in Honduras," January 21, 1944; Faust to State, January 21, 1944. From abroad, Liberal party leader Zuñiga Heute wrote several works critical of Carías, including: *Carta bierta a Tiburcio Carías Andino, dictador de la república de Honduras*

(Mexico City: n.p., 1943); *Cartas: una actitud y una senda, veleidades de una veleta* (Kingston, Jamaica: Times Publishing Co., 1937); and *Un gobierno de facto: ¿Por qué es inconstitucional el régimen que preside Tiburcio Carías Andino, dictador de Honduras?* (Mexico City: n.p., 1943).

11. FBI, "Revolutionary Tendencies in Honduras," July 6, 1944; Faust to State, May 12, 1944; Raleigh Gibson to State, June 6, 1944; Lee Hunsaker to State, August 8, 1944; CCA, William P. Cochran memorandums, May 19, June 13, 28, July 29, 1944; DAR, Lawrence Duggan memorandum, June 27, 1944.

12. FBI, "Revolutionary Tendencies in Honduras," July 6, 1944; Erwin to State, May 31 (2) July 7, 1944; Hunsaker to State, August 8, 1944; Walter Thurston to State, July 27, 1944; CCA, Cochran memorandum, June 9, 1944; "Honduras Reported under Martial Law," *New York Times,* June 4, 1944, 26:7; "Carias Still in Office," *New York Times,* July 6, 1944, 5:5.

13. FBI, "Revolutionary Movement in Honduras," July 28, 1944; Hunsaker to State, August 8, 1944; Erwin to State, November 3, 1944; CCA, Cochran memorandum, July 19, 1944; "Honduras, Nicaragua Report More Tension," *New York Times,* July 10, 1944, 5:5; "Nicaraguan Exiles to Keep Up Fight," *New York Times,* July 16, 1944, 5:6; "Honduran Finds U.S. Will Not Oust Carias," *New York Times,* July 27, 1944, 6:7.

14. FBI, "Revolutionary Movement in Honduras," July 28, 1944; Hunsaker to State, August 8, 1944.

15. FBI, "Revolutionary Movement in Honduras," July 28, 1944; FBI, "Revolutionary Movement in Honduras," August 24, 1944; Thurston to State, August 17, 1944; Erwin to State, September 29, 1944; CCA, W. H. Wood memorandum, October 6, 1944; CCA, Cochran memorandum, October 13, 1944.

16. Erwin to State, November 2, 3, December 18, 1944; "Rebels Cross Honduran Border," *New York Times,* October 17, 1944, 12:6; "Honduran Rebels Routed," *New York Times,* October 18, 1944, 13:1; "Honduras Revolt Grows," *New York Times,* October 19, 1944, 6:2; "Honduras Battles Reported," *New York Times,* October 24, 1944, 12:3; "Bandit Rises in Honduras," *New York Times,* November 20, 1944, 6:4; "Honduran Rebels Liquidated," *New York Times,* November 20, 1944, 6:1.

17. Erwin to State, March 6, 1945.

18. Erwin to State, April 17, 1945; "Insurgent Hondurans Defeated," *New York Times,* April 21, 1945, 8:4; "Wider Honduran Revolt Is Seen," *New York Times,* April 23, 1945, 4:7; "Honduran Revolt Reported Over," *New York Times,* April 24, 1945, 8:4.

19. Overton G. Ellis to State, June 26, 1946.

20. FBI, "Revolutionary Activity in Honduras," August 14, 1946; FBI, "Revolutionary Activities—Honduras," September 13, 1946; Erwin to State, October 1, 1946.

21. Harold E. Montamat to State, January 2, 1948; Foreign Activity Correlation Division, J. W. Amshey memorandum, December 16, 1947.

22. Erwin to State, May 31, 1944; V. Mejía Colindres to Spruille Braden, October 4, 1945; CCA, Cochran memorandum, June 9, 1944; CPA, Woodward memorandums, December 9, 12, 1947; DAR, Newbegin memorandum, December 9, 1947; Foreign Activity Correlation Division, Amshey memorandum, December 16, 1947. The treaties referred to by Mejía Colindres were signed in Washington in 1923 but abrogated at

the 1933 Central American Conference, held in Guatemala. See Leonard, *U.S. Policy and Arms Limitation in Central America.*

23. Erwin to State, August 11, 1944, February 8, 19, 1945; Faust to State, March 14, August 14, 1946; CCA, Cochran memorandums, June 13, 28, 1944; DAR, Duggan memorandum, June 27, 1944; OSS Report 4780, "Political Development Honduras"; Foreign Activity Correlation Division, Amshey memorandum, December 16, 1947; "Honduras Lifts State of Seige," *New York Times,* January 22, 1946, 4:7.

24. Erwin to State, August 11, 1944, March 21, 1945; Faust to State, August 14, 1946; Daniels to State, September 2, 1947.

25. Faust to State, August 30, 1945, April 22, 1946; Erwin to State, May 7, June 28, 1945, January 16, August 23, 1946.

26. MID, "Political Situation in Honduras," January 21, 1944.

27. Erwin to State, April 9, 1947; Daniels to State, July 18, August 1, 1947; Montamat to State, October 2, 17, 1947; CCA, Reid memorandum, April 23, 1947; "Honduras Trouble Reported," *New York Times,* March 8, 1947, 8:8; "Tensions Grow in Honduras," *New York Times,* March 31, 1947, 11:3; "Honduran Quits Command," *New York Times,* April 16, 1947, 17:4.

28. Erwin to State, April 9, 1947; Daniels to State, August 14, 1947; Montamat to State, October 2, 17, December 4, 1947, January 2, March 12, 1948; CCA, Reid memorandum, April 23, 1947; "Galvez Nominated in Honduras," *New York Times,* February 23, 1948, 4:2.

29. MID, "Political Situation in Honduras," January 21, 1944; Daniels to State, July 28, 1947; Montamat to State, December 4, 1947.

30. Daniels to State, August 14, 1947; DAR, Newbegin memorandums, December 9, 19, 1947.

31. Montamat to State, April 23, 1948.

32. Montamat to State, April 1, 1948; Herbert S. Bursely to State, May 21, 1948; "Zuniga Huete Is Nominated," *New York Times,* May 18, 1948, 5:2.

33. Bursely to State, June 16, 1948; Lt. Col. H. S. Isaacson, "Report on Visit to North Coast," June 26, 1948 (hereafter referred to as Isaacson Report).

34. Bursely to State, June 16, 1948; Isaacson Report.

35. Bursely to State, June 16, July 2, August 8, 13, 27, 1948. For an analysis of the Guatemalan-Honduran boundary dispute, see *Guatemala-Honduras Special Boundary Tribunal: Opinion and Award* (Washington, D.C.: Government Printing Office, 1933).

36. Bursely to State, July 30, August 1, September 24, 1948.

37. Bursely to State, August 27, September 24, 1948.

38. Montamat to State, September 10, 1948; Bursely to State, September 24, 29, 1948; "Liberals Shun Honduran Vote," *New York Times,* September 27, 1948, 3:5; "Hondurans Elect Galvez," *New York Times,* October 11, 1948, 9:7; "Galvez Big Victor in Honduran Voting," *New York Times,* October 12, 1948, 12:7.

39. Bursely to State, October 11, 20, 1948; "Honduran Cabinet Named," *New York Times,* January 3, 1949, 13:2; "Honduran Cabinet Named, *New York Times,* January 6, 1949, 18:7.

40. Bursely to State, January 1, 1949.

41. Bursely to State, January 10, 28, 1949; Montamat to State, March 20, June 29, 1949; CPA, Monthly Political Summary, January 1949; "Honduran Cabinet Named," *New York Times,* January 3, 1949, 13:2; "Honduran Cabinet Named," *New York Times,* January 6, 1949, 18:7.

42. Bursely to State, April 1, August 26, December 8, 1949; CPA, Monthly Political Summaries, February, March, May, July, August, and October 1949.

43. Bursely to State, December 8, 1949.

Chapter 5

1. Byrnes Papers, *Policy and Information Statement: Nicaragua,* 1– 2 (hereafter referred to as Hopkins Papers, *Policy Statement: Nicaragua*); FBI, *Axis Activities in Nicaragua,* April 3, 1942, 2– 3 (hereafter referred to as FBI, *Axis Activities: Nicaragua*); N. O. W. Steward, *Economic and Commercial Conditions in Nicaragua, 1950* (London: His Majesty's Stationery Office, 1951).

2. Hopkins Papers, *Policy Statement: Nicaragua,* 3; FBI, *Axis Activities: Nicaragua,* 2– 3; John M. Ryan et al., *Area Handbook for Nicaragua* (Washington, D.C.: Government Printing Office, 1970), 75– 84.

3. Histories of Nicaragua include: Floyd Cramer, *Our Neighbor Nicaragua* (New York: Frederick A. Stokes Publishing Co., 1929); Chester Zeleya Goodman, *Nicaragua en la independencia* (San José: Editorial Universitaria Central Americana, 1971); William Kamman, *A Search for Stability: United States Diplomacy toward Nicaragua, 1925– 1933* (Notre Dame: University of Notre Dame Press, 1968); and Neill Macaulay, *The Sandino Affair* (Chicago: Quadrangle Books, 1967). Works emphasizing the years since 1937 include: Gustavo Alemán-Bolaños, *Un lombrosiano Somoza, 1937– 1944* (Guatemala City: Editorial Hispania, 1945); Alberto Bayo, *Tempestadin el Caribe* (Mexico City: n.p., 1950); Manuel Cordero Reyes, *Nicaragua bayo el régimen de Somoza a los gobiernos y pueblos de América* (San Salvador: Imprenta Fuenes, 1944); Eduardo Crawley, *Dictators Never Die: A Portrait of Nicaragua and the Somoza Dynasty* (New York: St. Martin's Press, 1979); and Richard Millett, *Guardians of the Dynasty* (New York: Orbis Books, 1977).

4. James B. Stewart to State, January 11, 17, 1944; "Somoza Reveals Plans," *New York Times,* January 9, 1944, 35:1; "Nicaragua Liberals Act," *New York Times,* January 11, 1944, 5:5; "Nicaragua Alters Constitution," *New York Times,* April 25, 1945, 6:4. The State Department Decimal Files for Nicaraguan political affairs are 817.00/*date,* 817.00B/*date,* and FW817.00/*date.* For an analytical history of Nicaragua's constitutions, see Emilio Alvarez Lejurza, *Las constituciónes de nicaragua: exposición crítica y textos* (Madrid: Ediciones Cultura Hispania, 1958).

5. Stewart to State, January 11, 17, 1944.

6. Stewart to State, July 3, 5, 10, October 27, 1944; "Nicaraguans Fight Somoza Re-Election," *New York Times,* May 22, 1944, 9:3; "Managua Strife Reported," *New York Times,* June 22, 1944, 6:6; "Nicaraguan Youths Held," *New York Times,* June 30, 1944, 4:7.

7. Stewart to State, July 5, 10, 1944; "Somoza Refuses to Run," *New York Times,* July 6, 1944, 5:5.

8. Stewart to State, July 5, 10, 14, August 17, 1944; "Honduras, Nicaragua Report More Tension," *New York Times,* July 16, 1944, 5:5.

9. Stewart to State, June 20, October 17, 1944; "Nicaragua Amnesty Voted," *New York Times,* August 6, 1944, 21:3; "Somoza Says He'll Stay," *New York Times,* August 9, 1944, 7:1; "Costa Rica Holds Exiles," *New York Times,* October 2, 1944, 13:6; "New Clash in Costa Rica," *New York Times,* October 4, 1944, 13:6; "Nicaraguan Rebel Killed," *New York Times,* October 10, 1944, 5:2; "Nicaraguans Fought Rebels," *New York Times,* October 11, 1944, 10:7; "Somoza Invites Exiles Home," *New York Times,* November 1, 1944, 13:2; "7 Exiles Reach Mexico," *New York Times,* November 11, 1944, 4:7.

10. Harold D. Finley to State, March 27, 1945; Fletcher Warren to State, July 26, September 25, November 28, 1945.

11. Warren to State, July 26, September 25, 1946.

12. Stewart to State, November 11, 1944; Warren to State, July 26, October 26, November 11, 1945, March 13, 19, 1946.

13. Warren to State, January 25, March 13, June 6, September 3, 1945; "Nicaraguans Nominate Aguado," *New York Times,* September 3, 1946, 7:1.

14. Warren to State, May 7, 18, August 20, 30, September 13, October 1, 4, 1946; CCA, Newbegin memorandum, August 22, 1946; "Chamorro to End Exile," *New York Times,* May 18, 1946, 5:1.

15. Warren to State, April 16, May 7, June 27, 1946; Barry T. Benson to State, April 16, 1946.

16. Warren to State, May 18, August 8, September 3, 1946.

17. Warren to State, May 7, 1946.

18. Stewart to State, October 27, 1944; Warren to State, July 24, 31, August 4, 8, 29, October 25, November 28, 1945, January 14, 16, 1946; CCA, Cochran memorandums June 27, 28, 1946; Stettinius Papers, Box 280, Folder, "Mexico City Conference—Background Materials: Nicaragua"; FBI, *Axis Activities: Nicaragua,* 2.

19. Warren to State, August 8, 1945; Warren personal letters to William P. Cochran, November 12, 15, 1945; CCA, Cochran memorandum, December 12, 1945; "Rockefeller in Managua," *New York Times,* March 16, 1944, 11:4; "Rockefeller Pleases," *New York Times,* March 17, 1944, 5:1; "Rockefeller Departs," March 18, 1944, 4:5.

20. Stewart to State, July 5, 1944; Finley to State, March 27, 1945; Warren to State, January 14, 1946; James F. Byrnes to Warren, February 21, 1946.

21. Stewart to State, September 27, October 1, 1944; Warren to State, January 14, March 19, July 15, August 8, October 4, 1946; CCA, Cochran memorandum, October 13, 1944; Milton Bracker, "Somoza Said to Net $80,000 on U.S. Deal," *New York Times,* August 26, 1946, 10:2.

22. Stewart to Senate, October 17, 27, 1944; Warren to State, July 24, 31, September 9, November 11, 1945, September 18, December 2, 1946; Warren personal letter to Cochran, November 15, 1945.

23. Stewart to State, February 8, July 10, October 27, 1944; Finley to State, March

27, 1945; Warren to State, September 13, 25, October 26, 1945, January 16, March 19, June 27, 1946; CCA, Cochran memorandum, October 3, 1945.

24. Warren to State, August 8, November 5, 1945, March 19, May 7, 1946; two unsigned telegrams from the U.S. embassy in Managua to Assistant Secretary of State Spruille Braden, dated May 1, 1946; Franklin D. Roosevelt Papers, Confidential File, Folder 76 – 20, "CF Justice, Lend-Lease and State."

25. Stewart to State, July 10, 1944; Cochran to Finley, March 29, 1945; Warren to State, May 29, September 26, October 25, November 28, 1945, April 24, 1946; Byrnes to Warren, November 15, 1945; CCA, Cochran memorandums, December 12, 1945, April 23, 1946; DAR, Ellis O. Briggs memorandum, April 10, 1946; Spruille Braden Papers, John W. Cabot to Braden, September 21, 1945; Hopkins Papers, *Policy Statement: Nicaragua,* 1.

26. Warren to State, August 18, 1945; Joseph C. Grew to Warren, August 7, 1945; Byrnes to Warren, November 15, 1945; CCA, Cochran memorandums, July 25, December 17, 1945.

27. Stewart to State, June 20, July 19, November 10, 1944; Warren to State, August 18, September 5, November 5, 1945, January 14, March 19, 29, May 27, June 27, 1946; Cochran personal letter to Warren, November 12, 1945; Byrnes to Warren, February 21, 1946; CCA, John M. Cabot memorandum, May 10, 1944; CCA, Cochran memorandum, July 25, 1945; CCA, Newbegin memorandums, January 11, 14, October 23, November 8, 1946; DAR, Philip Bonsal memorandum, March 17, 1944; DAR, Laurence Duggan memorandum, May 20, 1944.

28. Warren to State, July 28, 1946; CCA, Cochran memorandums, March 21, 22, June 27, 28, 1946; CCA, Newbegin memorandum, June 3, 1947.

29. Warren to State, November 27, December 2, 27, 1946, January 22, 23, 28, 1946; CPA, Newbegin memorandum, January 30, 1947.

30. Warren to State, February 13, 26, 1946; Warren personal letter to Braden, March 3, 1947; Franklin D. Roosevelt Library, Papers of Adolfe A. Berle, Warren to Berle, March 19, 1946 (hereafter referred to as Berle Papers); CPA, Gordon Reid memorandum, February 5, 1947; Milton Bracker, "Nicaragua to Vote Under Guns Today," *New York Times,* February 2, 1947, 16:3; Bracker, "Nicaraguan Voting Free, Orderly, Violence Flares after Polls Close," *New York Times,* February 3, 1947, 1:2; "Nicaraguan Election Proclaimed," *New York Times,* February 24, 1947, 11:4.

31. Warren to State, March 6, April 2, 1947; Maurice Bernbaum to State, May 7, 1947; CPA, Reid memorandum, March 6, 1947; Berle Papers, Warren to Berle, March 19, 1947; "Somoza Keeps Army Command," *New York Times,* March 10, 1947, 13:3.

32. Bernbaum to State, May 26, June 6, 1947. U.S. disapproval of Argüello's fraudulent election victory was evident in its refusal to send a special mission to his inauguration. See Truman Library, Truman Papers, Official File, Dean Acheson memorandum to the president, April 3, 1947.

33. Bernbaum to State, May 27, 28, 31, June 6, 1947; "Somoza Resumes Rule in Nicaragua," *New York Times,* May 27, 1947, 1:4; "Nicaragua Names Sacasa President," *New York Times,* May 28, 1947, 11:1; "Somoza in Cabinet, Heads All Forces," *New York Times,* May 29, 1947, 7:2, 3.

34. Bernbaum to State, June 30, July 3, 31, 1947; George C. Marshall to Bernbaum, June 2, 1947; CPA, Newbegin memorandum, June 29, 1947; CPA, Reid memorandum, July 27, 1947; DAR, Briggs memorandum, May 27, 1947; DAR, Louis J. Halle memorandum, June 6, 1947; "Somoza Says Coup will be Approved," *New York Times,* May 30, 1947, 9:3. Subsequently, Spruille Braden claimed sole responsibility for the U.S. decision not to recognize the Sacasa regime. "I just took a stand that, as a matter of fact . . . I would not recognize the Nicaraguan regime under Somoza taking over in a revolutionary way." Spruille Braden Papers, Oral History, Spruille Braden, 1396.

35. Bernbaum to State, June 11, July 3, 31, 1947; CPA, Reid memorandum, June 6, 1947.

36. Bernbaum to State, June 23, July 1, 14, 25, 1947.

37. Bernbaum to State, August 4, 6, 15, 19, 1947; "Nicaragua Elects 49," *New York Times,* August 4, 1947, 3:8; "New Nicaraguan President, *New York Times,* August 15, 1947, 7:3.

38. Bernbaum to State, August 13, 17, 19, 1947.

39. Bernbaum to State, August 13, 17, 19, 1947.

40. Bernbaum to State, September 4, 18, 23, 29, October 2, 1947; "3 Slain in Nicaragua," *New York Times,* September 10, 1947, 4:5; "Nicaragua Rebels Routed," *New York Times,* September 12, 1947, 4:7; "Nicaraguan is Exiled," *New York Times,* September 28, 1947, 4:7; "Nicaragua Curbs Arguello," *New York Times,* October 15, 1947, 9:7; "Arguello Off for Mexico," *New York Times,* November 30, 1947, 29:5.

41. Stewart to State, November 24, 30, 1944; Warren to State, October 3, 1946; Benson to State, October 31, 1946; E. W. Holmes to State, January 29, 1947; Bernbaum to State, September 22, October 16, 1947; H. L. Rose to State, January 5, 16, 1948; FBI, "Report on Amando Flores Amador," November 6, 1946; FBI, "Report on Communist Activities in Nicaragua," November 22, 1945; FBI, "Report on the Socialist Party in Nicaragua," December 4, 1946; FBI, "Report on the Socialist Party in Nicaragua," February 6, 1947; FBI, *Axis Activities: Nicaragua,* 5; W. H. Lawrence, "Brazilian Reds Get 10% of Votes: Expect to Get 16%, Survey Shows," *New York Times,* December 30, 1946; 5:8; "26 Seized in Managua Raid," *New York Times,* January 30, 1948, 10:5; "Managua Holds 14 More as Reds," *New York Times,* January 23, 1948, 12:5.

42. Bernbaum to State, October 3, December 16, 18, 1947, January 20, 1948; CPA, Reid memorandum, December 10, 1947; "Costa Rica Recognizes Reyes," *New York Times,* December 27, 1947, 7:6. For a discussion of U.S. policy concerning recognition of the Ramon y Reyes administration, see Department of State Decimal File 817.01/ May 1947 to May 1948.

43. Warren to State, September 25, 1945; Bernbaum to State, January 20, February 5, 27, March 21, May 22, 1948; George P. Shaw to State, October 30, 1948, February 1, 12, May 18, 1949; Philip P. Williams to State, June 8, 28, 1949; Capus M. Waynick to State, August 3, October 4, November 11, December 31, 1949; Milton K. Wells to State, March 8, 1949; CPA, Reid memorandums, December 19, 1948, October 14, 1949; CPA, Monthly Political Summary, October 1948, January, February, March, May, July, August, October, and December 1949; OSS Report 4780, "Political Development and Trends in the Twentieth Century: Nicaragua," October 1, 1949.

Bibliography

Unpublished Documents

The primary documents utilized in the research for this book were the State Department Decimal Files, which are located in Record Group (RG) 59, Diplomatic Branch, National Archives. Two groups, 8——.00/*date* and FW 8——.00/*date*, contain materials relating to national politics in Central America. The third, 8——.00B/*date*, covers communism within each country. Other government agencies and units—the Federal Bureau of Investigation, Central Intelligence Agency, and Army and Navy intelligence groups—forwarded various materials on these subjects to the State Department. When these materials were not filed, they were often cross-referenced back to the originating agency.

Costa Rica
    818.00/*date*
    FW818.00/*date*
    818.00B/*date*
El Salvador
    816.00/*date*
    FW816.00/*date*
    816.00B/*date*
Guatemala
    814.00/*date*
    FW814.00/*date*
    814.00B/*date*
Honduras
    815.00/*date*
    FW815.00/*date*
    815.00B/*date*
Nicaragua
    817.00/*date*
    FW817.00/*date*
    817.00B/*date*
Department of State Lot Files: OSS Research and Analysis Reports

Personal Papers

Butler Library, Columbia University, New York City.
Spruille Braden
Clemson University Library, Clemson, South Carolina.
James F. Byrnes
George C. Marshall Research Foundation, Lexington, Virginia.
George C. Marshall
John M. Olin Library, Cornell University, Ithaca, New York.
Edwin J. Kyle
Franklin D. Roosevelt Library, Hyde Park, New York.
Adolf A. Berle
Frank P. Corrigan
Harry Hopkins
Franklin D. Roosevelt
Charles W. Taussig
John C. Wiley
Harry S. Truman Library, Independence, Missouri.
Merwin L. Bohan
Nathaniel P. Davis
Edward G. Miller
Richard C. Patterson, Jr.
Harry S. Truman
University of Virginia Library, Charlottesville, Virginia.
Edward R. Stettinius, Jr.
United States Army Military History Institute, Carlisle Barracks, Pennsylvania.
Willis D. Crittenberger

Oral Histories

Butler Library, Columbia University, New York City.
Spruille Braden
Harry S. Truman Library, Independence, Missouri.
J. Wesley Adams
Merwin L. Bohan
George M. Elsey
José Figueres
Kenneth F. Hertford
William Sanders

Guides and Reference Works

Bayitch, S. A. *Latin America and the Caribbean: A Bibliographical Guide to Works in English*. 2 vols. Coral Gables, Florida: University of Miami Press, 1967.

Burns, Richard Dean, ed. *Guide to American Foreign Relations since 1700*. Santa Barbara, California: ABC-CLIO, 1983.

Central America: A Bibliography. Los Angeles: California State University, Latin American Studies Center, 1970.

Deal, C. W., ed. *Latin America and the Caribbean: A Dissertation Bibliography*. Ann Arbor, Michigan: University Micro Films, 1978.

Kantor, Henry. *Bibliography of José Figueres*. Tempe, Arizona: Arizona State University Press, 1972.

New York Times Index. New York: Times Publishing Company, 1944 – 49.

Purport Lists for the Department of State Decimal File, 1910 – 1944. Washington, D.C.: National Archives and Records Service, 1976.

Reader's Guide to Periodical Literature. New York: Wilson, 1944 – 49.

Published Documents

Complaint of Costa Rica before the Central American Court of Justice. Washington, D.C.: Government Printing Office, 1916.

Complaint of the Republic of El Salvador before the Central American Court of Justice. Washington, D.C.: Government Printing Office, 1917.

Conference on Central American Affairs, Washington, December 4, 1922 – February 7, 1923. Washington, D.C.: Government Printing Office, 1923.

Guatemala-Honduras Special Boundary Tribunal: Opinion and Award. Washington, D.C.: Government Printing Office, 1933.

República de Costa Rica, Ministerio de Gobernación. *Constitución política de Costa Rica, 7 noviembre de 1945*. San José, Costa Rica: Imprenta Nacional, 1955.

Steward, N. O. W. *Economic and Commercial Conditions in Nicaragua, 1950*. London, England: His Majesty's Stationery Office, 1951.

Stockley, G. E. *Economic and Commercial Conditions in Honduras*. London, England: His Majesty's Stationery Office, 1949.

———. *Economic and Commercial Conditions in Honduras*. London, England: His Majesty's Stationery Office, 1951.

Tottenham-Smith, R. H. *Economic and Commercial Conditions in El Salvador*. London, England: His Majesty's Stationery Office, 1948 and 1951.

United States Department of State. *A Case History of Communist Penetration*. Washington, D.C.: Government Printing Office, 1957.

———. *Papers Relating to the Foreign Relations of the United States*. Washington, D.C.: Government Printing Office. Selected volumes: 1907 – Vol. II (1910); 1911 (1918); 1924 – Vol. II (1939); 1926 – Vol. II (1941); 1927 – Vol. III (1942); 1930 – Vol. III (1945); 1931 – Vol. II (1946); 1934 – Vol. IV (1951); 1948 – Vol. IX (1972).

———. *The United States and Nicaragua: A Survey of Relations from 1909 to 1932*. Washington, D.C.: Government Printing Office, 1932.

Whitaker, C. C., and Tennyson, A. R. *Economic and Commercial Conditions in Costa Rica*. London, England: His Majesty's Stationery Office, 1950.

Biographies and Related Materials

Alemán-Bolaños, Gustavo. *Un lombrosiano: Somoza, 1937 – 1944*. Guatemala City, Guatemala: Editorial Hispania, 1944.

Ameringer, Charles D. *Don Pepé: A Political Biography of José A. Figueres*. Albuquerque: University of New Mexico Press, 1978.

Arévalo, Juan José. *Anti-Kommunism in Latin America: An X-Ray of the Process Leading to New Colonialism*. Translated from the Spanish by Carlton Beals. New York: L. Stuart, 1963.

––––––. *La Argentina que yo viví, 1927 – 1944*. Mexico City, Mexico: Costa Amic, 1974.

––––––. *Carta política al gobierno de Guatemala con motivo de laber acceptado la candidatura presidencial*. Mexico City, Mexico: Costa Amic, 1963.

––––––. *Discursos en la presidencia, 1945 – 1947*. Guatemala City, Guatemala: n.p., 1947.

––––––. *Guatemala, la democracia y el imperio*. Mexico City, Mexico: Editorial Americana Nueva, 1954.

––––––. *The Shark and the Sardines*. Translated from the Spanish by Jane Cobb and Raul Osequeda. New York: L. Stuart, 1961.

Bayo, Alberto. *Tempestadin el Caribe*. Mexico City, Mexico: n.p., 1950.

Beale, H. K. *Theodore Roosevelt and the Rise of America to a World Power*. Baltimore: Johns Hopkins University Press, 1956.

Bemis, Samuel Flagg, ed. *The American Secretaries of State and Their Diplomacy*. Vol. 10. New York: Alfred A. Knopf, 1929.

Braden, Spruille. *Diplomat and Demagogues: The Memoirs of Spruille Braden*. New Rochelle, N.Y.: Arlington House, 1971.

Byrnes, James F. *All in a Lifetime*. New York: Harper and Row, 1958.

Campbell, Thomas M., and Herring, George, eds. *The Diaries of Edward R. Stettinius, Jr., 1943 – 1946*. New York: New Viewpoints Press, 1975.

Crawley, Eduardo. *Dictators Never Die: A Portrait of the Somoza Dynasty*. New York: St. Martin's Press, 1979.

Curry, George, and Ferrell, Robert H., eds. *The American Secretaries of State and Their Diplomacy*. Vol. 14. New York: Cooper Square Publishers, 1965.

DeConde, Alexander. *Herbert Hoover's Latin American Policy*. Stanford, California: Stanford University Press, 1951.

Dion, Marie Berthe. *Las ideas sociales y políticas de Arévalo*. Mexico City, Mexico: Editorial Americana Nueva, 1958.

Ferrell, Robert H., ed. *The American Secretaries of State and Their Diplomacy*. Vol. 15. New York: Cooper Square Publishers, 1965.

Grieb, Kenneth J. *The Guatemalan Caudillo: The Regime of Jorge Ubico, Guatemala, 1931 – 1934*. Athens, Ohio: University of Ohio Press, 1978.

Hill, H. C. *Roosevelt and the Caribbean*. Chicago: University of Chicago Press, 1927.

Johnson, Walter. "Edward R. Stettinius." In *An Uncertain Tradition: American Secretaries of State in the Twentieth Century*, edited by Norman A. Graebner. New York: McGraw-Hill, 1961.

Marroquin Rojas, Clemente. *La carta política del ciudadano Juan José Arévalo*. Guatemala City, Guatemala: Escribe Canato Ocara, 1965.

Payne, Robert. *The Marshall Story: A Biography of General George C. Marshall*. New York: Prentice Hall, 1951.

Pringle, H. F. *The Life and Times of William Howard Taft*. 2 vols. New York: Holt, Rinehart, 1939.

——. *Theodore Roosevelt*. New York: Harcourt Brace, 1956.

Reyes, Manuel Cordero. *Nicaragua bayo el régimen de Somoza a los gobiernos y pueblos de América*. San Salvador, El Salvador: Imprenta Fuenes, 1944.

Stimson, Henry L. *American Policy in Nicaragua*. New York: Charles Scribner, 1927.

Walker, Richard L. "Edward R. Stettinius, Jr." In *The American Secretaries of State and Their Diplomacy*, vol. 14, edited by Samuel Flagg Bemis and Robert H. Ferrell. New York: Cooper Square Publishers, 1965.

Zuñiga Heute, Angel. *Carta bierta a Tiburcio Carías Andino, dictador de la república de Honduras*. Mexico City, Mexico: n.p., 1943.

——. *Cartas: una actitud y una senda, veleidades de una veleta*. Kingston, Jamaica: Times Publishing Company, 1937.

——. *Un gobierno de facto ¿por ques es inconstitucional el régimen que preside Tiburcio Carías Andino, dictador de Honduras?* Mexico City, Mexico: n.p., 1943.

Secondary Works

Acuna, Miguel. *El 48*. San José: Tresjo Hnos., 1974.

Adams, Richard. *Cultural Surveys of Panama, Nicaragua, Guatemala, El Salvador, Honduras*. Washington D.C.: Pan American Sanitary Bureau, 1957.

Alvarez Lejurza, Emiliano. *Las constituciónes de Nicaragua: exposición crítica y textos*. Madrid, Spain: Ediciones Cultura Hispania, 1950.

Anderson, Thomas P. *Matanza: El Salvador's Communist Revolt of 1932*. Lincoln, Nebraska: University of Nebraska Press, 1971.

Arthur, H. B.; Beckford, G. L.; and Houck, James P. *Tropical Agribusiness: Structures and Adjustments—Bananas*. Boston: Division of Research, Graduate School of Business Administration, Harvard University, 1968.

Baker, George W. "The Caribbean Policy of Woodrow Wilson, 1913–1917." Ph.D. dissertation, University of Colorado, 1961.

Bell, John P. *Crisis in Costa Rica*. Austin, Texas: University of Texas Press, 1971.

Bulgarelli, Aguilar. *Costa Rica y sus hechos políticos de 1948*. San José, Costa Rica: Editorial Costa Rica, 1970.

Busey, James L. *Notes on Costa Rican Democracy*. Boulder, Colorado: University of Colorado Press, 1967.

Callcott, Wilfrid H. *The Caribbean Policy of the United States, 1890–1920*. Baltimore: Johns Hopkins University Press, 1942.

Carceres Lana, Victor. *Fechas de la historia Honduras*. Tegucigalpa, Honduras: Editorial Andrade, 1969.

Chardkoff, Richard B. "Communist Toehold in the Americas." Ph.D. dissertation, Florida State University, 1967.

Cramer, Floyd. *Our Neighbor Nicaragua*. New York: Frederick A. Stokes, 1929.

de Mestas, Alberto. *El Salvador*. Madrid, Spain: Ediciones Cultura Hispanica, 1950.

Denny, Harold. *Dollars for Bullets: The Story of American Rule in Nicaragua*. New York: Dial Press, 1929.

English, Burt H. *Liberación in Costa Rica*. Gainesville, Florida: University of Florida Press, 1971.

Gaddis, John Lewis. *The United States and the Origins of the Cold War, 1941–1947*. New York: Columbia University Press, 1972.

Gallardo, Ricardo. *Las Constituciónes de El Salvador*. 2 vols. Madrid, Spain: Ediciones Cultura Hispanica, 1961.

Gavidia, Francisco. *Historia moderna de El Salvador*. San Salvador, El Salvador: Ministerior de Cultura Hispanica, 1950.

Gellman, Irwin. *Good Neighbor Diplomacy: The United States in Latin America 1933–1945*. Baltimore: Johns Hopkins University Press, 1979.

Guerrant, Edward O. *Roosevelt's Good Neighbor Policy*. Albuquerque: University of New Mexico Press, 1950.

Immerman, Richard. *The CIA in Guatemala: The Foreign Policy of Intervention*. Austin: University of Texas Press, 1982.

Jensen, Amy Elizabeth. *Guatemala: A Historical Survey*. New York: Exposition Press, 1955.

Johnson, John J. *Continuity and Change in Latin America*. Stanford, California: Stanford University Press, 1964.

Jones, Chester L. *The Caribbean since 1900*. New York: Prentice Hall, 1936.

———. *Costa Rica and Civilization in the Caribbean*. Madison, Wisconsin: University of Wisconsin Press, 1935.

———. *Guatemala: Past and Present*. Minneapolis: University of Minnesota Press, 1939.

Kamman, William. *A Search for Stability: United States Diplomacy Towards Nicaragua*. Notre Dame, Indiana: University of Notre Dame Press, 1968.

Karnes, Thomas L. *The Failure of Union: Central America, 1824–1960*. Chapel Hill, North Carolina: University of North Carolina Press, 1961.

Kepner, Charles. *Social Aspects of the Banana Industry*. New York: Columbia University Press, 1936.

Koebel, William. *Central America: Guatemala, Nicaragua, Costa Rica, Honduras, Panama, and Salvador*. New York: C. Scribner's Sons, 1914.

Langley, Lester D. *The United States and the Caribbean, 1900–1970*. Athens, Georgia: University of Georgia Press, 1980.

Leonard, Thomas M. *U.S. Policy and Arms Limitation in Central America: The Washington Conference of 1923*. Occasional Paper Series, Center for the Study of Disarmament, California State University-Los Angeles, 1982.

Macauley, Neill. *The Sandino Affair*. Chicago: Quadrangle Books, 1967.

McCann, Thomas P. *An American Company: The Tragedy of United Fruit*. New York: Crown Publishers, 1976.

Mariñas Ofero, Luis, comp. *Las constituciónes de Honduras*. Madrid, Spain: Ediciones Cultura Hispanica, 1962.

Martínez, José Francisco. *Honduras histórica*. Tegucigalpa, Honduras: S.N., 1974.

Martz, John D. *Central America: The Crisis and the Challenge*. Chapel Hill, North Carolina: University of North Carolina Press, 1959.

May, Stacy, and Plaza, Galo. *The United Fruit Company in Latin America*. Washington, D.C.: National Planning Association, 1958.

Mecham, J. Lloyd. *The United States and Inter-American Security, 1889–1960*. Austin, Texas: University of Texas Press, 1961.

Mejia, Medaro. *Historia de Honduras*. Tegucigalpa, Honduras: Editorial Andrade, 1969.

Millett, Ricard. *Guardians of the Dynasty*. New York: Orbis Books, 1977.

Monge Alfaro, Carlos. *Geografía social y humana de Costa Rica*. San José, Costa Rica: Imprenta Universitaria, 1943.

———. *Historia de Costa Rica*. San José, Costa Rica: Tresjo Hnos., 1958.

Munro, Dana G. *The Five Republics of Central America: The Political and Economic Development and Their Relationship with the United States*. New York: Oxford University Press, 1918.

———. *Intervention and Dollar Diplomacy in the Caribbean, 1900–1921*. Princeton, New Jersey: Princeton University Press, 1964.

———. *The United States and the Caribbean Area*. Boston: World Peace Foundation, 1934.

Paíz, Alfonso Bauer. *Cómo opera el yanqui capital en Central America: el coso de Guatemala*. Mexico City, Mexico: Editoria Ibero Mexicana, 1956.

Paredes, Lucas. *Drama político de Honduras*. Mexico City, Mexico: Editoria Latina Américano, 1958.

Paterson, Thomas G. *On Every Front: The Making of the Cold War*. New York: W. W. Norton & Company, 1979.

Palmer, Frederick D. *Central America and Its Problems*. New York: Moffet, Yard, and Company, 1910.

Parker, Franklin D. *The Central American Republics*. New York: Oxford University Press, 1964.

Rodríquez, Mario. *Central America*. Englewood Cliffs, New Jersey: Prentice Hall, 1965.

Ryan, John M., et al. *Area Handbook for Nicaragua*. Washington, D.C.: Government Printing Office, 1970.

Schneider, Donald M. *Communism in Guatemala, 1944–1954*. New York: Frederick A. Praeger, 1958.

Stokes, William S. *Honduras: An Area Study in Government*. Madison, Wisconsin: University of Wisconsin Press, 1950.

Toiello, Guillermo. *La batalla de Guatemala*. Mexico City, Mexico: Cuadernos Américanos, 1955.

Universidad Nacional Autónoma de Honduras. *Recopilación de las constituciónes de Honduras*. Tegucigalpa, Honduras: La Universidad, 1977.

Whetten, Nathan L. *Guatemala: The Land and the People*. New Haven, Connecticut: Yale University Press, 1961.

White, Alastair. *El Salvador*. New York: Praeger Publishers, 1973.

Wood, Brice. *The Making of the Good Neighbor Policy*. New York: Columbia University Press, 1961.

Woodward, Ralph Lee. *Central America: A Nation Divided*. New York: Oxford University Press, 1976.

Zeledon, Marco Tulio. *Historia constituciónal de Costa Rica en el hienio 1948 – 1949*. San José, Costa Rica: F. Aguilar, 1950.

Zeleya Goodman, Chester. *Nicaragua en la independencia*. San José, Costa Rica: Editorial Universitaria Central Americana, 1971.

Journals and Magazines

Buell, Raymond L. "The United States and Central American Stability." *Foreign Policy Papers, VII* 9(1931): 193 – 97.

"Democracy's Bull in the Latin American China Shop." *Newsweek* 46(November 5, 1945): 42.

Fenwick, Charles G. "Jurisdictional Questions Involved in the Guatemalan Intervention." *American Journal of International Law* 48(1954): 4.

"Frankness of Friends." *Time* 57(February 19, 1951): 36.

"Fruits of the Good Neighbor." *New York Times Magazine* (May 14, 1944): 154.

Gordon, Max. "A Case History of U.S. Subversion: Guatemala, 1954." *Science and Society* 35(1971): 129 – 55.

Grieb, Kenneth J. "American Involvement in the Rise of Jorge Ubico." *Caribbean Studies* 10(April 1970): 5 – 21.

———. "The United States and the Rise of General Maximiliano Hernández." *Journal of Latin American Studies* 3(November 1971): 151 – 72.

Hackett, Charles. "The Background of the Revolution in Honduras." *Review of Reviews* 69(April 1924): 390 – 96.

Jessup, T. K. "Our Battling Assistant Secretary of State." *Life* 20(March 1946): 54 – 55+.

Jones, T. M. "Good Neighbor, New Style." *Harper's* 192(April 1946): 313 – 21.

Miller, Edward G. "Inter-American Relations in Perspective." *U.S. Department of State Bulletin* 22(April 3, 1950): 521 – 23.

"Portrait." *New York Times Magazine* 9(January 8, 1950): 9.

"Portrait." *Time* 44(February 26, 1945): 22.

Rippy, J. Fred. "Antecedents of the Roosevelt Corollary of the Monroe Doctrine." *Pacific Historical Review* 9(1940): 267 – 69.

Roosevelt, Franklin D. "Our Foreign Policy: A Democratic View." *Foreign Affairs* 6(1928): 573 – 86.

Taylor, Philip B., Jr. "The Guatemalan Affair: A Critique of United States Foreign Policy." *American Political Science Review* 50(1956): 787 – 807.

Webb, J. E. "U.S. Expresses Gratification with New Costa Rican Government." *U. S. Department of State Bulletin* 21(November 1949): 833.

"Will We Remain Good Neighbors After the War?" *Saturday Evening Post* 215(November 6, 1943): 16 – 17.

Woosley, L. H. "Recognition of the Government of El Salvador." *American Journal of International Law* 28(1934): 325 – 29.

Newspapers

New York Times, 1944 – 49.

Index